C000109396

CARING FOR BODY AND SOUL

PENNSYLVANIA STATE UNIVERSITY PRESS
UNIVERSITY PARK · PENNSYLVANIA

Caring for Body and Soul

BURIAL and the AFTERLIFE
in the Merovingian World

Bonnie Effros

Title page illustration of the seventh-century Wittislingen brooch reproduced
with permission of the Prähistoriche Staatssammlung,
Museum für Vor-und Frühgeschichte (Munich).

Library of Congress Cataloging-in-Publication Data

Effros, Bonnie, 1965–
Caring for body and soul : burial and the afterlife in the Merovingian world /
Bonnie Effros.
p.   cm.
Includes bibliographical references and index.
ISBN 0-271-02196-9 (alk. paper)
1. Funeral rites and ceremonies—Gaul—History. 2. Merovingians—Funeral
customs and rites. 3. Merovingians—History. 4. Merovingians—Antiquities. 5. France—
History—To 987. 6. Gaul—Antiquities. I. Title.

GT3170 .E34 2002
393'.09364—dc21
2001056016

Copyright © 2002 *The Pennsylvania State University*
All rights reserved
Printed in the United States of America
Published by The Pennsylvania State University Press
University Park, Pa. 16802-1003

It is the policy of The Pennsylvania State University Press to use acid-free paper
for the first printing of all clothbound books. Publications on uncoated stock satisfy the minimum
requirements of American National Standard for Information Sciences—Permanence of
Paper for Printed Library Materials, ANSI Z39.48–1992.

In fond memory of my grandparents,

Max Hochman and Dorothy Katel Hochman
and
Milton Effros and Davida Gage Effros

Obsecro, nulla manus violet pia iura sepulcri,
Personet angelica donec ab arce tuba:
"Qui iaces in tumulo, terrae de pulvere surge,
Magnus adest iudex milibus innumeris."

—ALCUIN, Carmina 123

CONTENTS

ABBREVIATIONS

AB	*Analecta bollandiana*
AHM	*Archives historiques du Maine*
AK	*Archäologisches Korrespondenzblatt*
AM	*Archéologie médiévale*
Annales ESC	*Annales: Économies, sociétés, civilisations*
BAR	British Archaeological Reports
BM	*Bulletin monumental*
CA	*Cahiers archéologiques*
CBA	Council for British Archaeology
CCM	*Cahiers de civilisation médiévale*
CCSL	*Corpus christianorum series latina*
CESCM	Centre d'études supérieures de civilisation médiévale
ChLA	*Chartae latinae antiquiores*
CIFM	*Corpus des inscriptions de la France médiévale*
CNRS	*Centre national de la recherche scientifique*
CSEL	*Corpus scriptorum ecclesiasticorum latinorum*
EME	*Early Medieval Europe*
Études mérovingiennes	*Études mérovingiennes: Actes des journées de Poitiers 1er–3 mai 1952* (Paris: Éditions A. et J. Picard, 1953)
FS	*Frühmittelalterliche Studien*
ILCV	*Inscriptiones latinae christianae veteres*

L'inhumation privilégiée	Yvette Duval and Jean-Charles Picard, eds., *L'inhumation privilégiée du IVe au VIIIe siècle en Occident: Actes du colloque tenu à Créteil les 16–18 mars 1984* (Paris: De Boccard, 1986)
JRS	*Journal of Roman Studies*
JTS	*Journal of Theological Studies*
MGH	*Monumenta Germaniae historica*
MMS	Münstersche Mittelalter-Schriften
Nouveau recueil	*Nouveau recueil des inscriptions chrétiennes de la Gaule antérieures au VIIIe siècle*
PL	*Patrologia latina*
Poetae	*Poetae latini aevi carolini*
RA	*Revue archéologique*
RICG	*Recueil des inscriptions chrétiennes de la Gaule antérieures à la Renaissance carolingienne*
RSR	*Revue des sciences religieuses*
RV	*Rheinische Vierteljahrsblätter*
SC	*Sources chrétiennes*
SRG	*Scriptores rerum Germanicarum in usum scholarum*
SRM	*Scriptores rerum Merovingicarum*
TRW	Transformation of the Roman World
Zum Grabfrevel	Herbert Jankuhn, Hermann Nehlsen, and Helmut Roth, eds., *Zum Grabfrevel in vor- und frühgeschichtlicher Zeit: Untersuchungen zu Grabraub und "Haugbrot" in Mittel- und Nordeuropa,* Abhandlungen der Akademie der Wissenschaften in Göttingen, philologisch-historische Klasse, 3d ser., no. 113 (Göttingen: Vandenhoeck & Ruprecht, 1978)

ACKNOWLEDGMENTS

IN THE DECADE since beginning this project, I have incurred many debts to family, friends, and colleagues who patiently guided and encouraged me on the long path to completion of this book. I owe great thanks foremost to the enthusiasm and flexibility of Richard H. Rouse, who taught me to recognize the personal bonds between early medieval communities as attested by the physical traces they left behind. In the early stages of research, the input of Alain Dierkens and Friedrich Prinz also proved instrumental to my understanding of the very disparate sources at my disposal. Comments and bibliography from Frederick Paxton, Peter Brown, and Bailey Young likewise helped to steer my reading. I am especially grateful to lengthy discussions with Patrick Geary in the course of my work at UCLA as well as afterward. His thoughtful critique served both to contextualize and to broaden this analysis.

In recent years, I have had assistance from a number of friends and colleagues. Isabel Moreira has been extremely generous with her time in discussing visionary material and Merovingian society in general. Richard Gerberding, Guy Halsall, and Jörg Jarnut read the manuscript in its entirety and with their judicious comments contributed greatly to its improvement. The input of Mark Handley and Jean Michaud played an important role in my revisions of the epigraphy chapter, and Falko Daim and Franz Siegmeth made possible the production of professional-quality maps. Patrick Périn and Chantal Dulos kindly offered assistance with photographs and unpublished materials from French archaeological sites. Walter Pohl helped me to strengthen some of the historical discussions, while Cécile Treffort, Frans Theuws, and Max Diesenberger supplied insight into the varied sources. Peter Potter and Keith Monley gave much guidance and encouragement in the final stages of manuscript revision and production. All shortcomings that remain, however, are of my own doing.

Financial support for this project has included a Deutsche Akademisches Austauschdienst Stipendium (1991–92), a UCLA History Departmental Fellowship (1992–93), and an Edward A. Dickson Fellowship (1993–94). During these years, I made extensive use of the collections of the Monumenta Germaniae historica, Bayerische Staatsbibliothek, Bibliothèque nationale, and the University of California, Berkeley. Revisions continued during my tenure of an Izaak Walton Killam Memorial Postdoctoral Fellowship in the Department of History and Classics at the University of Alberta (July 1994–December 1995). A Bernadotte E. Schmitt grant (1995) supported the purchase of some of the photographs appearing in this work. One semester's stay at the Camargo Foundation in Cassis, France (fall 1997), and a Berkshire Summer Fellowship at the Mary Ingraham Bunting Institute at Radcliffe College (summer 1998) were also instrumental to improvements in the monograph. Four Summer Research Fellowships (1996–98, 2000) and one unit of Assigned Time for Research (2001) from Southern Illinois University at Edwardsville permitted me to travel repeatedly to European libraries and Harvard University to make necessary additions and updates. Along the road to completion of this work, Nicole Bériou made available affordable housing in Paris; Lyn O'Connor of the Bunting Institute provided a spare office during a second summer in Cambridge.

At SIUE, David Steinberg, Steve Hansen, Wayne Santoni, and Ellen Nore were particularly supportive and flexible in adjusting my time for research and teaching. At SUNY, Binghamton, Donald Quataert, Richard Trexler, and Leslie Levene have made my transition to a new department in the final stages of production as smooth as possible, as have Peter Barnet, Melanie Holcomb, and Charles Little at The Metropolitan Museum of Art during my tenure of a Sylvan C. Coleman and Pamela Coleman Memorial Fund Fellowship (2001–2).

On a personal note, I wish to thank my parents, Richard and Gail Effros, for their constant support throughout this process. Michelle Effros, Jim Effros, Ed and Rita Effros, Joseph (ז״ל) and Bea Katel, Nina Caputo and Mitch Hart, Wulf Kansteiner and Sonja Wolf, Lori Weintrob, Dorothea and Roland Stevens, Dianne Golden, Grace Benveniste, Roberta Shapiro, Barbara Goldoftas, Carole Frick, Anne Valk, Eric Ruckh, Sara Wolper and Jake Viebrock, Jonathan Blitz, Beth Rabin and Steve Finkel, Monika Kraft, Martin Taylor, and George and Debbie Hensley have extended their friendship, hospitality, and good humor to this lengthy undertaking. I dedicate this book to the memory of my grandparents, Max and Dorothy Hochman, and Milton and Davida Effros, who did not live to see this project to completion but whose belief in the value of education made this accomplishment possible in the first place.

⇥ • ⇤

Introduction

Recent studies have highlighted the dynamism of late antiquity and the early Middle Ages, a period during which centers of power shifted northward from the Mediterranean under new leadership.[1] From the fifth century onward, what we now define as medieval culture began to emerge in western Europe; it incorporated a blend of Roman and Germanic customs. In this milieu, the relationship between the living and the dead was especially significant in defining pagan and Christian communities and shaping conceptions of the afterlife.[2] Funerals and cemeteries, some of them at ancient sacred sites or the shrines of saints, acted as arenas in which the identity and status of ruling families and the members of monastic houses were established and contested. Burial rites provided families with an opportunity to display not only their religious devotion but also their wealth. Funerary rituals thus enabled them to express

1. Traditionally, this period had been neglected by American scholars in favor of the High Middle Ages. Gabrielle M. Spiegel, "In the Mirror's Eye: The Writing of Medieval History in America," in *Imagined Histories: American Historians Interpret the Past,* ed. Anthony Molho and Gordon S. Wood (Princeton: Princeton University Press, 1998), 238–62; Charles Homer Haskins, *The Renaissance of the Twelfth Century* (Cambridge: Harvard University Press, 1927).
2. Peter Brown, *The Cult of Saints: Its Rise and Function in Latin Christianity* (Chicago: University of Chicago Press, 1981); Patrick J. Geary, *Living with the Dead in the Middle Ages* (Ithaca: Cornell University Press, 1994); Caroline Walker Bynum, *The Resurrection of the Body in Western Christianity, 200–1336* (New York: Columbia University Press, 1995).

rivalry, since this form of nonproductive expenditure often obligated contemporaries to try to outdo them.[3]

Written sources from the fifth through eighth centuries in Gaul and surrounding territories devote much attention to the interment rites and places of saints and powerful leaders in their representation of power and belief in early medieval society. The archaeological evidence stemming from burial rituals is also prolific, since the vast majority of sites that have been excavated in Merovingian Gaul and outlying regions are cemeteries rather than settlements. Insufficient attention, however, has been given to coordinating these materials in an interdisciplinary fashion in the interpretation of burial custom by archaeologists and historians. Beyond the significant number of early medieval written sources, such as hagiographical works, concentrating on events related to the interment of the saints, proceedings of church councils, epitaphs and inscribed objects, wills, penitentials, law codes, historical works, monastic Rules, and sacramentaries assist in interpreting the significance of early medieval burial rites among a larger portion of the population. Holy sepulchers, though they provided a ritual focal point for Christian communities, were thus not the only grave sites that reflected and sustained powerful networks of elites in early medieval kingdoms in western Europe.

The material derived by historians and archaeologists from normative written sources related to burial sites, however, frequently reveals conflicting attitudes and practices. In Merovingian Gaul, for instance, practices documented in the written record composed by clerical leaders often contradict the activities performed by the general lay population as attested in the archaeological record.[4] Some of the discrepancies result

3. Georges Bataille, "The Notion of Expenditure," in *Visions of Excess: Selected Writings, 1927–1939*, Theory and History of Literature 14, ed. and trans. Allan Stoekl (Minneapolis: University of Minnesota Press, 1985), 116–23. This sort of rivalry, however, is far more evident in fifth-century graves than those of later generations, when burial deposits became increasingly modest.

4. The term "Merovingian" in this text refers not only to members of the Frankish royal dynasty but also to their subjects from the late fifth to the early eighth century. Despite the shortcoming of

from historical and geographical developments: namely, the fact that much of the extant written record was composed in the late Roman cosmopolitan centers to the south of the Loire. By contrast, the bulk of the archaeological evidence has been retrieved from cemeteries north of the Loire, where the presence of the Franks was stronger.[5] Archaeological artifacts, moreover, are more abundant in graves from the north of Gaul than the south. Demographic shifts in the population's composition do not suffice, however, to articulate distinctions between written and archaeological narratives of burial in fifth- to eighth-century Gaul. The situation is undoubtedly far more complex, since it is impossible on the basis of either human remains or material evidence to distinguish between individual Franks and Gallo-Romans, or clerics and laypersons.[6] Similarly, burials in the south of Gaul were often made in stone sarcophagi, which were frequently reused and likewise more vulnerable to pillage by eighteenth- and nineteenth-century antiquaries than graves of plain earth predominant further north.

Legislation read in isolation also creates a misleading image of Merovingian burial mores, since these measures enjoyed varying degrees of success in their application. For instance, although the penalties promulgated in secular law codes for grave robbery included capital punishment, they do not seem to have been effective in quelling this widespread practice. Archaeological finds reveal that inhabitants engaged in the illicit

---

this usage, since the name did not serve this function in the early Middle Ages, this terminology offers the benefit of not distinguishing sharply between contemporary ethnic populations. As is discussed below, the determination of the ethnicity of the dead from written and archaeological evidence is often a treacherous undertaking.

5. For a detailed description of the archaeological evidence and its varying interpretations, see Bonnie Effros, *Merovingian Mortuary Archaeology and the Making of the Early Middle Ages* (Berkeley and Los Angeles: University of California Press, forthcoming).

6. Otto Gerhard Oexle, "Die Gegenwart der Toten," in *Death in the Middle Ages*, Mediaevalia Louvaniensia ser. 1, studia 9, ed. Hermann Braet and Werner Verbeke (Louvain: Leuven University Press, 1983), 57ff.; Patrick J. Geary, "The Uses of Archaeological Sources for Religious and Cultural History," in *Living with the Dead in the Middle Ages*, 30–38.

activity on a regular basis.[7] The juxtaposition and contrast of physical evidence with traditional written sources are therefore central to the construction of a more critical *histoire des mentalités*.[8]

One of the main obstacles to achieving a better understanding of early medieval funerary custom lies in the probability that burial constituted a familial responsibility and, moreover, a rite in which close members of the deceased's kin group represented the main actors. As a consequence, contemporary documents written by the clerical elite reveal little about customs practiced by the vast majority of the laity. From the dearth of evidence, it seems probable that the clergy played a minor role, if any, in this rite for all but elites and those in religious orders.[9] The few surviving liturgical sources in pre-Carolingian Gaul only reveal clerics' attempts and not their ability to lay claim to greater influence over the liturgical aspects of burial from the sixth century onward. They thereby sought to establish control over the symbolic delineation of membership in the community of the elect. Because the laity originally effected their relationship with the dead without the spiritual intervention of clerical representatives, the clergy's role as intermediaries was at first tentative. Centuries passed before their influence became exclusive.[10] The practical implications of such liturgical developments are difficult to ascertain through archaeological sources. On the whole, however, extant physical evidence makes it apparent that clerical descriptions of and prescriptions for Christian

7. Helmut Roth, "Archäologische Beobachtungen zum Grabfrevel im Merowingerreich," in *Zum Grabfrevel,* 60–65.

8. Roger Chartier, "Intellectual History and the History of *Mentalités:* A Dual Re-evaluation," in *Cultural History: Between Practices and Representations,* trans. Lydia G. Cochrane (Cambridge: Polity Press, 1988), 25–39.

9. But Frederick Paxton posits greater correspondence between Christian texts and burial activity in Merovingian Gaul. Frederick S. Paxton, *Christianizing Death: The Creation of a Ritual Process in Early Medieval Europe* (Ithaca: Cornell University Press, 1990), 47–91.

10. Patrick J. Geary, "Exchange and Interaction Between the Living and the Dead in Early Medieval Society," in *Living with the Dead in the Middle Ages,* 89–91; Bonnie Effros, "Beyond

mortuary rites in Merovingian Gaul must have differed significantly from day-to-day practices.[11]

My main objective in this study is therefore to examine burial custom primarily through written sources of the Merovingian period, whether their authors described the deposition of personal possessions in graves, prescribed funerary activities through legislation, or commemorated the dead through epigraphical markers and liturgical rites. In some cases, it will also be possible to test this information against archaeological evidence. Despite long-held hypotheses positing an alleged transition from "pagan" practice to a more "spiritualized" Christian liturgical commemoration of the dead, early medieval sources do not support these interpretations. This transition resulted not from inhabitants in Gaul becoming "better" Christians but from the clergy's successful promotion of new and powerful means for families to express their status and identity through funerary rituals. It is therefore necessary to move beyond anachronistic valuations of what are today considered normative Christian rites and recognize the shortcomings of such theories. Although there is no way to ascertain the extent to which modern perceptions of Merovingian funerary rites have been distorted by the survival of only some sorts of documents and archaeological material and not others, this discussion is meant to increase recognition of the many types of rituals that helped to create and reinforce an idealized vision of a community's divine and human hierarchies. From the fifth to the eighth century, funerary traditions evolved for many reasons but did not change dramatically in response to the spread of Christianity to rural populations.

Cemetery Walls: Early Medieval Funerary Topography and Christian Salvation," *EME* 6 (1997): 1–23. But for a proposal of a process of "clericalization" dating to late antiquity, see Megan McLaughlin, *Consorting with Saints: Prayer for the Dead in Early Medieval France* (Ithaca: Cornell University Press, 1994), 28–30.

11. Yvette Duval, *Auprès des saints corps et âme: L'inhumation "ad sanctos" dans la chrétienté d'Orient et d'Occident du IIIe au VIIe siècle* (Paris: Études augustiniennes, 1988), 46 ff.

Burial ritual throughout the Merovingian period served to commemorate the deceased and establish their places in relation to the living and the dead. Whereas grave goods and epitaphs seem to have been the most visible ingredients of funerals from the fifth through the seventh century, church burial and commemorative Masses were likely the most notable investments made at least by elite families from the eighth century onward. This study thus underlines the significant adaptability and flexibility of Western Christianity through the lens of burial ritual from the fifth to the eighth century. Not only did clerics effectively insinuate themselves into funerary practices, but they also developed new rites that met the needs of the Christian population.

With the acknowledgment that all aspects of burial practice were closely intertwined, I have taken the practical step of arranging the chapters in this book topically by the sorts of surviving evidence for rites employed by early medieval families. In Chapter 1, I address written sources describing the clothing, personal possessions, and vessels that constituted the majority of goods deposited with the dead in the fifth, sixth, and seventh centuries. Although most early medieval authors wrote about the use of such objects among the living rather than for the dead, their comments help to explain the potential ideological functions of clothing and other sorts of bodily adornment in Merovingian society. Their symbolic value often played a role just as important as their material worth. In addition to conveying information regarding a person's identity, the vocabulary of corporal adornment reflected competition over the commodities involved in funerary display.[12] Restricted access to luxury objects reinforced such mores and influenced other forms of exchange.[13] Yet, the specific signifi-

---

12. Ellen-Jane Pader, *Symbolism, Social Relations, and the Interpretation of Mortuary Remains,* BAR International Series 130 (Oxford: BAR, 1982), 18 ff.

13. Arjun Appadurai, "Introduction: Commodities and the Politics of Value," in *The Social Life of Things: Commodities in Cultural Perspective,* ed. Arjun Appadurai (Cambridge: Cambridge University Press, 1986), 38–40.

cance of particular pieces of clothing, weaponry, and personal adornment is seldom directly accessible. Reading ethnicity and religious belief from grave objects, for instance, is a highly inaccurate process.[14] Garments and other grave goods, such as weaponry, often had a long history[15] and therefore could fulfill a variety of amuletic, magical, and votive functions.[16] These observations highlight the limitations of heuristic analyses of grave goods, since everyday objects often acquired new symbolism in a funerary context.

Not only did written sources hint at the symbolism of objects so important to burial custom, but legislation also regulated their use. As discussed in Chapter II, secular law codes monitored the transmission of moveable property from one generation to the next and gave particular attention to protecting human remains, sepulchers, and the possessions of the deceased. Because burial rites involving the deposition of grave goods rendered them physically inaccessible to the living after the funerary ceremony came to a close,[17] survivors wanted to assure themselves that those objects would not be stolen by contemporaries.[18] Judging from the regularity with which sepulchers were violated in the Merovingian kingdoms, however, these laws were not enforced effectively. Clearly, valuable votive objects remained far too attractive to be easily forgotten, and were

14. Walter Pohl, "Telling the Difference: Signs of Ethnic Identity," in *Strategies of Distinction: The Construction of Ethnic Communities, 300–700*, TRW 2, ed. Walter Pohl and Helmut Reimitz (Leiden: E. J. Brill, 1998), 27–69; Guy Halsall, *Settlement and Social Organization: The Merovingian Region of Metz* (Cambridge: Cambridge University Press, 1995), 245–46.

15. Frans Theuws and Monica Alkemade, "A Kind of Mirror for Men: Sword Depositions in Late Antique Northern Gaul," in *Rituals of Power from Late Antiquity to the Early Middle Ages*, TRW 8, ed. Frans Theuws and Janet L. Nelson (Leiden: E. J. Brill, 2000), 401–76; Igor Kopytoff, "The Cultural Biography of Things: Commoditization as Process," in *The Social Life of Things*, 66–67.

16. Lynda L. Coon, *Sacred Fictions: Holy Women and Hagiography in Late Antiquity* (Philadelphia: University of Pennsylvania Press, 1997), 52–70; Bonnie Effros, "Symbolic Expressions of Sanctity: Gertrude of Nivelles in the Context of Merovingian Mortuary Custom," *Viator* 27 (1996): 1–10.

17. Krzysztof Pomian, "Collezione," in *Enciclopedia Einaudi* 3 (Turin: Giulio Einaudi Editore, 1978), 335–36.

18. Roth, "Archäologische Beobachtungen," 60–65.

hence worth stealing if the risk of being caught was relatively low. Clerics, by contrast, promulgated legislation with respect to interment only in the cases in which church property was threatened, such as when ecclesiastical vestments or liturgical objects were used as grave goods or when lay-persons sought the privilege of burial within the walls of a church or city.[19] They, too, were far from successful in achieving their objectives. Although both clerical leaders and lay elites attempted to defend the contents of their relatives' and colleagues' sepulchers against plunderers, it is important to note that they did not seek to regulate the actual choice and distribution of objects in Christian graves.

The focus of Chapter III is written evidence from grave sites, namely epigraphy. Besides pointing to the changing geographical distribution and decline in popularity of inscribed markers between the fourth and eighth centuries, this discussion evaluates the representational functions of funerary inscriptions: What apparent concerns for the deceased were expressed through above-ground markers, and how did these rites differ in urban and rural contexts?[20] What impact did imitation and reuse have on the content of Merovingian epigraphy? An investigation of markered burial from the late Roman period to the early eighth century suggests that inscriptions appeared primarily in ecclesiastical and monastic communities, as well as among elite families in cosmopolitan settings. These groups were on the whole more literate and well versed in late Roman customs. For the majority of the inhabitants of Gaul, however, the increasing rarity of epitaphs and the disorder of cemeterial topography from the seventh century

19. Bailey K. Young, "Merovingian Funeral Rites and the Evolution of Christianity: A Study in the Historical Interpretation of Archaeological Material" (Ph.D. diss., University of Pennsylvania, 1975), 52, 76–80.

20. Guy Halsall, "Social Change Around A.D. 600: An Austrasian Perspective," in *The Age of Sutton Hoo: The Seventh Century in North-Western Europe*, ed. Martin Carver (Woodbridge: Boydell Press, 1992), 269–70; Halsall, *Settlement and Social Organization*, 266–67.

onward point to alternate means of honoring the dead that left few lasting physical signs.[21]

Liturgical and other ceremonial rites constitute a fourth aspect of mortuary ritual preserved in written accounts in early medieval Gaul. In fact, the historical record represents the most concise source of information for the customs associated with funerals or anniversaries of the dead, since these rarely left permanent traces in the landscape. Because funerary practice was described mainly in religious texts written by clerics, however, an accurate rendering of these ritual activities among lay Christians before the eighth century is difficult. The objectives of Christian burial ritual were not solely religious. Nor was Christian concern with the afterlife a new development in commemorative rites, since the unwritten rites practiced previously also served important cosmological functions. Funerals were momentous occasions for the display of the physical remains of the deceased and thus the worldly and otherworldly relationships of the deceased as envisioned by families or religious communities. Because they had differing significance for individual participants, however, liturgical developments do not give us an accurate reading of the belief systems of contemporary Christians. We do not know what proportion of them were actually recited or by whom they were used other than clerics.

Chapters IV and V are dedicated, therefore, to an assessment of changing depictions of the afterlife from the fifth to the eighth century as well as the commemorative rites for the dead that emerged in response to growing fear of purgatorial suffering. Because the extant physical remains attest to activities, primarily feasting and sacrificial rites, that differed significantly from the customs sanctioned by clerics, I suggest that important distinctions

---

21. Patrick Périn, "Le problème des sarcophages-cénotaphes du haut moyen âge: A propos de la nécropole de Quarré-les-Tombes, site d'une bataille légendaire," in *La chanson de geste et le mythe carolingien: Mélanges René Louis* 2 (Saint-Père-sous-Vézelay: Musée archéologique régional, 1982), 824.

existed between clerical ideology and actual Christian practice. Since burials were performed by families and communities for the deceased, these customs varied considerably by region and evolved over time, as did those rites involving the deposition of grave goods. Such features point to the relative adaptability of funerary rites in response to individual and contemporary needs.[22] Commemorative activities for the dead often idealized or otherwise masked existing social and spiritual hierarchies in Gaul.[23]

In sum, from the sixth to the early eighth century, Merovingian wills, penitential texts, and epigraphical remains reveal changing sentiments toward the liturgical rites suitable for competitive and symbolic funerary display. Those that became prominent at the end of the Merovingian period gave participants more assurance of their progress toward salvation, a need made greater by the growing number of theological, hagiographical, and visionary tracts expressing fear of the torments suffered by sinners in the afterlife. Although liturgical texts were slow at first to offer hope to Christian families,[24] eventually they did through psalmody and Masses for the dead. Exactly how widespread these practices became is unknown due to the infrequent survival of documents attesting to them. But, generally speaking, just as families had used the contents, location, and external appearance of sepulchers to promote an idealized image of the status, iden-

22. But see Jack Goody, who argues that ritual is conventualized and obligatory, especially in literate societies, and thus masks belief instead of conveying the current value systems of those practicing it. Jack Goody, "Against 'Ritual': Loosely Structured Thoughts on a Loosely Defined Topic," in *Secular Ritual*, ed. Sally F. Moore and Barbara G. Myerhoff (Assen: Van Gorcum, 1977), 32–33.

23. Mark P. Leone, "Time in American Archaeology," in *Social Archaeology: Beyond Subsistence and Dating*, ed. Charles L. Redman, Mary Jane Berman, et al. (New York: Academic Press, 1978), 26–27.

24. Donald A. Bullough, "Burial, Community, and Belief in the Early Medieval West," in *Ideal and Reality in Frankish and Anglo-Saxon Society: Studies Presented to J. M. Wallace-Hadrill*, ed. Patrick Wormald (Oxford: Basil Blackwell, 1983), 186–87; Geary, "Exchange and Interaction," 79–82, 90–92; Paxton, *Christianizing Death*, 61–68; Effros, "Beyond Cemetery Walls," 8–11.

tity, and religious affiliation of the deceased in the fifth, sixth, and seventh centuries, in the eighth century they funded liturgical commemoration of the dead with the donation of moveable possessions or lands to churches.[25] Both choices represented means of accomplishing similar objectives in very different times.

In the early Carolingian period, clerical representatives hastened this trend by more frequently claiming the right to administer the ceremonies considered essential to Christian burial. They sought control over rites previously regulated by the deceased's kin group or monastic community. Families and monasteries focused their wealth and attention not so much on outfitting graves as on sponsoring Masses at the time of and subsequent to funerals.[26] Indeed, the context in which grave goods and sarcophagi had frequently been used to promote the status of deceased kin was radically altered for all but a small number of the elite who still commissioned epitaphs for use in churches or churchyards. A new form of commemorative expression thereafter gained ascendancy: the deceased could be preserved in public memory through the recitation of their names by ordained clerics. Most of these activities took place at the altar rather than in the graveyard. Although the liturgy honored the deceased as had grave goods and epigraphy, the performance of these rites no longer occurred in close proximity to the body of the deceased after the initial funeral.[27] By means of such conventions, Christian clerics were ultimately able to convince the faithful that they were the sole authorities permitted to exercise liturgical

25. Otto Gerhard Oexle, "Memoria und Memorialüberlieferung im früheren Mittelalter," *FS* 10 (1976): 87–94; Arnold Angenendt, "Theologie und Liturgie der mittelalterlichen Toten-Memoria," in *Memoria: Der geschichtliche Zeugniswert des liturgischen Gedenkens im Mittelalter*, MMS 48, ed. Karl Schmid and Joachim Wollasch (Munich: Wilhelm Fink Verlag, 1984), 174 ff.

26. Young, "Merovingian Funeral Rites," 76–77; McLaughlin, *Consorting with Saints*, 30–31.

27. Otto Gerhard Oexle, "Mahl und Spende im mittelalterlichen Totenkult," *FS* 18 (1984): 401–20; Oexle, "Memoria and Memorialüberlieferung," 90–91; Paxton, *Christianizing Death*, 92–102.

functions at funerals. These rites became the dominant form of commemoration at the time of and subsequent to burial and promoted clerical status by suggesting that the clergy alone determined membership in the celestial kingdom.[28]

---

28. For centuries, the achievement of these clerical objectives was considerably less than certain. On Charlemagne's policies regarding Saxon burial, see Bonnie Effros, "*De partibus Saxoniae* and the Regulation of Mortuary Custom: A Carolingian Campaign of Christianization or the Suppression of Saxon Identity?" *Revue belge de philologie et d'histoire* 75 (1977): 269–87.

CHAPTER I

The Symbolic Significance of Clothing for the Dead

Personal Adornment and Identity

C lothing and grooming had great symbolic significance in early medieval society. Recognition of this fact must underpin any examination of Merovingian burial practice as an expression of the complex relationships between an individual and his or her community, as well as between an individual and the cosmos. Although the customs associated with personal adornment often gained alternative meanings in the context of funerals, such garments, accessories, and other possessions were the same as those used in life. Written descriptions and archaeological evidence of the daily applications of dress, hairstyles, and personal objects thus provide insight into the practical functions and objectives of funerary rites.[1] They shed light on the totality of the systems in which these artifacts circulated.[2]

In life, just as in death, personal adornment communicated various aspects of an individual's identity to other members of his or her society. As has been proposed by Ellen-Jane Pader in her study of early Anglo-Saxon burial remains: "[B]odily adornment is seen as being a potential means of expressing and reinforcing one's sex role, social identity and

---

1. Igor Kopytoff, "The Cultural Biography of Things: Commoditization as Process," in *The Social Life of Things: Commodities in Cultural Perspective*, ed. Arjun Appadurai (Cambridge: Cambridge University Press, 1986), 66–68.

2. Cécile Barraud, Daniel de Coppet, André Iteanu, and Raymond Jamous, *Of Relations and the Dead: Four Societies Viewed from the Angle of Their Exchanges*, trans. Stephen J. Suffern (Oxford: Berg Publishers, 1994), 5, 18–24, 33–35.

group affiliation as well as being a form of protection from the elements, providing aesthetic pleasure and overcoming modesty."[3] To this list should be added the ability of particular styles of dress, possessions, and hairstyles to convey religious belief, personal idiosyncrasies, and an individual's place in the life cycle.[4] This form of expression is only effective, however, if the signs chosen to communicate are understood by viewers. The successful conveyance of symbolic messages through bodily adornment is therefore dependent to a large extent on the circumstances in which the display occurs, the manner in which it is accomplished, and its audience. Indeed, one group may react to the signs of another in a manner entirely different from that originally intended, with potentially positive or negative consequences.[5] Ceremonial occasions, for instance, may provide a larger audience or lend greater importance to symbolic objects or acts than would everyday situations. These "tournaments of value" are nonetheless not entirely distinct from more mundane encounters.[6]

In the Merovingian period, bodily adornment represented a particularly important sort of visual expression. It could serve either to reinforce and validate the social order or to challenge existing conventions. The grooming of hair, the choice of costume, and the possession of symbolic and ritual objects likewise communicated to contemporaries the many facets of an individual's relationship to the community and his or her place in a larger sphere. Not merely the product of blind tradition or obligation,[7] bodily adornment involved a continually changing set of signi-

---

3. Ellen-Jane Pader, *Symbolism, Social Relations, and the Interpretation of Mortuary Remains*, BAR International Series 130 (Oxford: BAR, 1982), 18 ff.

4. Polly Wiessner, "Style and the Changing Relations Between the Individual and Society," in *The Meaning of Things: Material Culture and Symbolic Expression*, One World Archaeology 6, ed. Ian Hodder (London: Unwin Hyman, 1989), 56–59.

5. Gabriella Schubert, *Kleidung als Zeichen: Kopfbedeckungen im Donau-Balkan-Raum* (Wiesbaden: Harrassowitz Verlag, 1993), 31–68.

6. Arjun Appadurai, "Introduction: Commodities and the Politics of Value," in *The Social Life of Things*, 20–22.

fiers that contributed to the way in which participants defined themselves and the dimensions of their community.[8] Yet, early medieval adornment also served ideological purposes by reinforcing and justifying the existing social hierarchy. In the case of relics, for instance, the repetition of liturgical rites accorded value to what might be perceived by modern viewers as seemingly useless or esoteric artifacts. They nonetheless promoted the status of those who possessed them.[9] Written descriptions of such displays similarly manipulated these value systems to the advantage of those who composed them. Hence, to understand the function of adornment, it is important to observe the context in which it was used.

Even with the additional witness provided by written texts describing clothing, material artifacts related to bodily adornment in the Merovingian period do not often lend themselves to a straightforward interpretation of individuals' motivations for dressing in a particular style. Historians and archaeologists have at their disposal very fragmentary evidence. Similarly, archaeological artifacts accompanying the deceased do not reveal to the present-day observer the individual motives behind burying corpses in this fashion. Documentary and archaeological materials nonetheless provide general indications of the potential of clothing or appearance to be manipulated and transformed for a variety of purposes.

In the early Middle Ages, personal adornment probably demarcated ethnic, social, or religious groups. Yet, even in the case of ethnicity, it is difficult to pin down a set of objective criteria by which different groups were identified. Stereotypical references to the qualities of a Frank or

7. Jack Goody, "Against 'Ritual': Loosely Structured Thoughts on a Loosely Defined Topic," in *Secular Ritual*, ed. Sally F. Moore and Barbara G. Myerhoff (Assen: Van Gorcum, 1977), 32–33.
8. Michael Mann, *The Sources of Social Power* I (Cambridge: Cambridge University Press, 1986), 1–3, 22–23.
9. Mark P. Leone, "Time in American Archaeology," in *Social Archaeology: Beyond Subsistence and Dating*, ed. Charles L. Redman, Mary Jane Berman, et al. (New York: Academic Press, 1978), 26–27; Kopytoff, "The Cultural Biography of Things," 82–83; Barraud et al., *Of Relations and the Dead*, 38.

Lombard, for instance, depended in large part on the author, the subject of
his discourse, and the reasons he sought to establish distinctions between
himself and another group.[10] The same is true of grave remains. Although
ethnic differences did exist, outward appearance represented just one of
many factors in social and cultural expression.[11] Religious and secular
leaders nonetheless cultivated and sought to institutionalize these distinctions as a means of reinforcing existing social realities.[12] Although clerics
were not separated by an insuperable gulf of belief and practice from their
congregations or the lay elites to whom they were born, they used their
belief and practice to accomplish a host of objectives, primary among them
a heightened status for clerics and members of monastic orders in a warrior-
dominated society.[13]

*Monetary Worth and Symbolism of Fabric,
Clothing, and Personal Possessions*

Most of our understanding of early medieval clothing, weaponry, and
personal possessions is based upon artifacts retrieved from excavated

10. Walter Pohl, "Telling the Difference: Signs of Ethnic Identity," in *Strategies of Distinction:
The Construction of Ethnic Communities, 300–700*, TRW 2, ed. Walter Pohl and Helmut Reimitz
(Leiden: E. J. Brill, 1998), 17–22, 27–61.
11. Fredrik Barth, introduction to *Ethnic Groups and Boundaries: The Social Organization of
Culture Difference* (Boston: Little, Brown & Co., 1969), 9–38. For an opposing perspective, see Max
Martin, "Fibel und Fibeltracht: Späte Völkerwanderungszeit und Merowingerzeit auf dem
Kontinent," in *Reallexikon der germanischen Altertumskunde* 8, 2d ed. (Berlin: Walter de Gruyter,
1994), 574–77.
12. Bonnie Effros, "Appearance and Ideology: Creating Distinctions Between Merovingian
Clerics and Lay Persons," in *Encountering Medieval Dress and Textiles: Objects, Texts, and Images*,
ed. Janet Snyder and Désirée Koslin (New York: Palgrave, forthcoming); L. Carless Hulin, "The
Diffusion of Religious Symbols Within Complex Societies," in *The Meanings of Things: Material
Culture and Symbolic Expression*, One World Archaeology 6, ed. Ian Hodder (London: Unwin
Hyman, 1989), 90–94.
13. Jean-Claude Schmitt, "'Religion populaire' et culture folklorique," *Annales ESC* 31 (1976):
941–48. In contrast, see M. Lauwers, "'Religion populaire,' culture folklorique, mentalités: Notes
pour une anthropologie culturelle du moyen âge," *Revue d'histoire ecclésiastique* 82 (1987): 221–58.

cemeteries. The evidence is far from satisfactory for the formulation of an accurate image of the bodily adornment of inhabitants of Gaul, since fabric and other organic materials have left little or no physical trace in these graves. Brooches, weapons, amulets, and clothing did more than just keep those who wore them warm, dry, and safe; they also played an ideological role in conveying to contemporaries various aspects of a person's identity. This image was to some degree consciously constructed and thus in part fictive. Rather than passively reflect that person's ethnicity or social status to the exclusion of all other features, personal adornment expressed the relationship of an individual to the rest of the community as mediated by age, religious belief, gender, status, sense of style, and ethnic and familial allegiances.[14] For a modern observer, much of this symbolic language can no longer be understood, particularly with respect to individual graves. The fact that burial deposits were usually made not by the deceased but by his or her kin complicates the interpretive process still further.

For this reason, the following discussion is not meant to be a comprehensive survey of Merovingian dress, which has already been undertaken elsewhere.[15] I seek instead to critique current attempts to apply written and archaeological evidence from burials to the faithful reconstruction of the habits and customs of early medieval populations. While archaeological studies have furnished important information about metallic and stone artifacts, for instance, they are unsuited to revealing much about the multiple

14. Pader, *Symbolism, Social Relations*, 18 ff.; Leone, "Time in American Archaeology," 26–27.
15. Most studies point to ethnicity as the dominant factor in choosing goods to be buried with the deceased. See most recently Max Martin, "Schmuck und Tracht des frühen Mittelalters" and "Gürtel und Bewaffnung des frühen Mittelalters," in *Frühe Baiern im Straubinger Land: Gaudemuseum Straubing*, ed. Max Martin and Johannes Prammer (Straubing: Druckerei Bertsch, 1995), 40–71, 72–85; Gudula Zeller, "Tracht der Frauen," Françoise Vallet, "Weibliche Mode im Westteil des merowingischen Königreiches," Frank Siegmund, "Kleidung und Bewaffnung der Männer im östlichen Frankenreich," and Patrick Périn and Michel Kazanski, "Männerkleidung und Bewaffnung im Wandel der Zeit," all in *Die Franken: Wegbereiter Europas* 2 (Mainz: Verlag Philipp von Zabern, 1995), 672–711.

ways in which a specific object might have been used over the course of its lifetime.[16] Room also exists for differences in interpretation of the types of garments to which such artifacts, often brooches and buckles, were affixed.[17] Although the use and style of clothing and accessories such as belt buckles varied by region and over time, apparently significant variation existed even within individual communities.[18] Written descriptions, art-historical remains, and archaeological deposits were all biased toward the inhabitants who could afford or chose to inter such durable and precious objects with deceased kin. By comparison, skeletons unaccompanied by grave goods attracted far less attention among contemporaries in the early Middle Ages and continue to do so among archaeologists and historians today.

Clothing customs of the living shared some, but not all, features with material found in conjunction with buried remains. Although individual objects deposited in sepulchers were not ordinarily distinguishable from similar items used by the living, they gained new symbolic meaning in this last and permanent application. Grave goods, particularly luxury artifacts, thus had "semiotic virtuosity"[19] and significant ideological potential.[20] Thus, while outstanding examples of mortuary objects may have provided a model for contemporaries to imitate, they should not be construed as the

16. Frans Theuws and Monica Alkemade, "A Kind of Mirror for Men: Sword Depositions in Late Antique Northern Gaul," in *Rituals of Power from Late Antiquity to the Early Middle Ages*, TRW 8, ed. Frans Theuws and Janet L. Nelson (Leiden: E. J. Brill, 2000), 419–27; Édouard Salin, *La civilisation mérovingienne d'après les sépultures, les textes et le laboratoire* 4 (Paris: Éditions A. et J. Picard et Cie., 1959), 105–7.

17. Zeller, "Tracht der Frauen," 672–83.

18. Edward James, *The Merovingian Archaeology of South-West Gaul* 1, BAR Supplementary Series 25(i) (Oxford: BAR, 1977), 48 ff.

19. Appadurai, "Introduction," 38–39.

20. Lotte Hedeager, "The Creation of Germanic Identity: A European Origin Myth," in *Frontières d'empire: Nature et signification des frontières romaines: Actes de la table ronde international de Nemours, 1992*, ed. Patrice Brun, Sander van der Leeuw, and Charles R. Whittaker (Namur: A.P.R.A.I.F., 1993), 128–30.

most reliable indicator of their value in these communities. Their selection for deposition in graves, as opposed to the majority of such goods that remained in circulation, meant that they were specifically chosen for this application. Such decisions may have been undertaken with a variety of objectives, whether to honor the deceased with a cherished possession or to outdo competing families with an extravagant funeral for deceased kin.

Modern approaches to early medieval artifacts tend only to aggravate these interpretive problems. When investigating the quality of goods used in personal adornment, archaeologists and historians have consistently undervalued poorly preserved garments relative to what they have perceived as more glamorous luxury goods such as swords and precious jewelry. Attention usually centers on the expense and workmanship of magnificent artifacts. One such item is Childeric I's gold arm ring, estimated by Heiko Steuer to have been worth at least 65 *solidi*, the gold coinage then in circulation.[21] This bracelet was the approximate monetary equivalent of nine horses or thirty-two bulls in the *Lex ribuaria*.[22] Despite its great beauty and precious contents, however, a unique past would have presumably made the bracelet's value still greater. It is thus difficult to determine to what degree such seemingly straightforward items were prized by their early medieval owners.

Less frequently acknowledged by modern scholars, in part due to fabric's fragility and general characterization as having been produced domestically by women, is the amount of energy that had to be expended in order to produce clothing in the early Middle Ages. Studies of garments from this period have been hampered by the fact that only occasionally do

---

21. Heiko Steuer, *Frühgeschichtliche Sozialstrukturen in Mitteleuropa: Eine Analyse der Auswertungsmethoden des archäologischen Quellenmaterials*, Abhandlungen der Akademie der Wissenschaften in Göttingen, philologisch-historische Klasse, 3d ser., no. 128 (Göttingen: Vandenhoeck & Ruprecht, 1982), 325.

22. Franz Beyerle and Rudolf Buchner, eds., *Lex ribuaria* 40,11, *MGH: Leges* 3,2 (Hannover: Impensis bibliopolii Hahniani, 1954), 94.

more than minuscule fragments of cloth survive, and hence expenditure
on fabric is overshadowed by the more durable brooches and buckles with
which it was fastened. Although outside the regional scope of this monograph, Hayo Vierck's study of unusually well preserved Saxon garments
from bog finds and his discussion of their manufacture in northern Europe
is instructive. He noted that each piece was woven individually upon a
loom rather than produced as a larger block of fabric to be divided later;
this strategy reduced the amount of work necessary for finishing garments. Vierck estimated that the labor entailed in a single seventh-century
"Anglian" luxury coat discovered in the Thorsberger Moor (Schleswig-
Holstein) was enormous: the cloth originally measured at least 1.68 m ×
2.36 m and required the work of two skilled weavers for at least a year.
The indigo used to dye this coat, which was not exceptional in its quality,
was imported to this region.[23]

   The information above is not meant to imply that early medieval people valued objects primarily on the basis of the cost of their production,
since this interpretation is overwhelmingly modern. Indeed, the situation
appears to have been very different. The biography of a particular garment
or weapon and thus the context in which it was acquired might have had far
more significance to the person who owned or used it.[24] Certain types of
luxury fabrics acquired through trade, theft, or exchange, for instance,
must have alluded to the far-off places from which they were brought.
Early medieval elites in Gaul apparently had access to decorated silks from
locations as distant as Constantinople and Persia. They employed this
intricately decorated material to wrap relics stored in altars, manufacture

   23. Hayo Vierck, "Trachtenkunde und Trachtgeschichte in der Sachsen-Forschung, ihre Quellen,
Ziele und Methoden" and "Zur seegermanische Männertracht," in *Sachsen und Angelsachsen:
Ausstellung des Helmsmuseums, Hamburgisches Museum für Vor- und Frühgeschichte 18. November 1978
bis 28. Februar 1979* (Hamburg, 1978), 234, 266–69.
   24. Kopytoff, "The Cultural Biography of Things," 82–83; Barraud et al., *Of Relations and the
Dead*, 38.

liturgical garments, and produce the clothing of those with extensive resources or connections. Linen, also, was regarded by some sixth-century abbots as too fine for the use of monks, who were obligated to take vows of humility.[25]

Recent excavations of a few exceptionally well preserved burials at Saint-Victor in Marseilles give a small glimpse, one that is normally inaccessible, of the extensive role silk and linen likely played in outfitting the dead in some circumstances, especially in an active port city. One of the finest examples of cloth in an early medieval grave was found in a stone tomb exhumed from the nave of the early church. On its exterior, the sarcophagus was decorated with Old and New Testament scenes, including the sacrifice of Abraham and Jesus delivering the Law to Peter and healing a blind man. Inside the undisturbed tomb were uncovered the late-fifth-century remains of a woman in her twenties. She was clothed in a decorated silk tunic and fringed cloak, and taffeta cloth covered her head; when she was laid to rest on a bed of herbs, her head was bedecked with a wreath of flowers. On her forehead was placed a gold cross.[26] Although not clothed in silk, a forty- to sixty-year-old man buried in a neighboring sixth-century tomb was dressed in leather shoes and a hooded linen tunic that descended below his knees. Belted at the waist, the linen fabric was decorated with gold thread. The man was also interred with a gold ring on his left hand.[27] More than a century later, at the monastery of Chelles in the Marne valley, the former queen Balthild (d. 680/681) was buried in a red semicircular cloak with yellow fringes, while the first abbess of the

---

25. "Ut monachus quamlibet delicati corporis linea ad nuda corporis non utatur: quia incongruum est ut carnem, quae semper vitio naturae superbit, mollibus foreat indumentis, et ei quasi minus validae blandiatur." Jacques-Paul Migne, ed., *S. Ferreolus Ucetiensis episcopus: Regula ad monachos* 31, in *PL* 66 (Paris: Apud editorem in via dicta d'Amboise, 1847), 970.

26. From the vegetal matter found in the grave, it is possible to suggest that the woman was buried in July. Raymond Boyer et al., *Vie et mort à Marseille à la fin de l'antiquité: Inhumations habillées des Ve et VIe siècles et sarcophage reliquaire trouvés à l'abbaye de Saint-Victor* (Marseilles: Imprimerie municipale, 1987), no. 20, pp. 45–93.

27. Boyer et al., *Vie et mort*, no. 5, pp. 26–44.

house, Bertilla (d. circa 704), was laid to rest in a brown silk tunic decorated with yellow stripes and edging.[28]

In late-seventh- and early-eighth-century elite graves, the majority of extant fabric remnants were imported. They survived because they were used to wrap relics, and hence should be regarded as the highest quality of cloth available in the West due to this distinguished application. One surviving fragment of silk, which portrays Castor and Pollux and is believed to be of Byzantine provenance, arrived at the church of St. Servatius in Maastricht possibly as early as the translation of this saint in 726.[29] The eighth- or ninth-century embroidered winding cloth, pillow, and shroud that accompanied the relics of Remigius (d. 533) originated from Iran or Byzantium. In addition, a piece of Byzantine white silk with a figure in blue holding two lions by the throat was used as a winding cloth for Victor, a soldier of the Theban legion whose remains were kept at Sens from the mid–eighth century.[30] Contemporary Continental examples of Anglo-Saxon embroidery on silk include the eighth- or early-ninth-century *velamina* and *casula* of Harlindis and Relindis.[31]

When the reliquaries of Chelles, Faremoutiers, Andenne, and Sens were opened at various points in the last two centuries, individual swatches of Eastern silk with a variety of patterns were discovered to have been used as wrappings for saints' remains. Except in the example of Sens, in which the relics were separated from their coverings in the process of saving

28. Jean-Pierre Laporte and Raymond Boyer, *Trésors de Chelles: Sépultures et reliques de la reine Balthilde († vers 680) et de l'abbesse Bertille († vers 704)*, Catalogue de l'exposition organisée au Musée Alfred Bonno (Chelles: Société archéologique et historique, 1991), 22–34.

29. Marielle Martiniani-Reber, *Lyon, Musée historique des tissus: Soieries sassanides, coptes et byzantines X^e–XIe siècles*, Inventaire des collections publiques françaises 30 (Paris: Éditions de la Réunion des musées nationaux, 1986), no. 84, pp. 98–99.

30. *Les trésors des églises de France*, 2d ed. (Paris: Caisse nationale des monuments historiques, 1965), nos. 154–56, 812; pp. 78–79, 431–32.

31. Mildred Budny and Dominic Tweddle, "The Early Medieval Textiles at Maaseik, Belgium," *Antiquaries Journal* 65 (1985): 353–89.

them from a fire, their unique value stems from the parchment inscriptions (*authentiques*) bound with thread to the silk-enveloped relics. In the early Middle Ages, these tags verified the identity of each relic. Now, however, their script also provides an approximate dating of each.[32] In the case of the relics at Chelles and Faremoutiers, scholars have ascertained that at least eight of the pieces of silk must have reached northern France before the end of the eighth century.[33] These luxury goods, in direct conflict with existing monastic Rules limiting nuns' clothing to coarser, undyed fabrics, gave special honor to the holy relics.[34]

Another important quality of early medieval clothing, fabrics, and objects such as weapons was their perceived amuletic and thus nonmonetary worth. Swords and other sorts of armament not only served practical functions but had referential significance beyond the immediate moment in which they were used.[35] In Merovingian society, just as in contemporary Ireland, Italy, and Byzantium, Christians believed that clothing could transmit the curative power of an individual, especially future saints, even in their absence.[36]

32. On Faremoutiers and Chelles, see Hartmut Atsma, Pierre Gasnault, Robert Marichal, and Jean Vezin, eds., *Authentiques de Chelles et Faremoutiers*, in *ChLA* 18 (Dietikon-Zurich: URS Graf Verlag, 1985), no. 669, pp. 84–108; Jean-Pierre Laporte, "Reliques du haut moyen âge à Chelles," *Revue d'histoire et d'art de la Brie et du pays de Meaux* 37 (1986): 45–50. On seventh- to eighth-century *authentiques* and silk wrappings at Andenne: André Dasnoy, "Le reliquaire mérovingien d'Andenne," *Annales de la Société archéologique de Namur* 49 (1958): 41–60. Those of Sens are for the most part of a later date. Maurice Prou and E. Chartraire, "Authentiques de reliques conservées au trésor de la cathédrale de Sens," *Mémoires de la Société nationale des antiquaires de France* 59 (1900): 129–72.

33. Jean-Pierre Laporte, "Tissus médiévaux de Chelles et de Faremoutiers," in *Tissu et vêtement: 5000 ans de savoir-faire, 26 avril–30 novembre 1986* (Guiry-en-Vezin: Musée archéologique départemental du Val-d'Oise, 1986), 155–60.

34. Effros, "Appearance and Ideology."

35. H. Jankuhn, "Axtkult," in *Reallexikon der germanischen Altertumskunde* 1, 2d ed. (Berlin: Walter de Gruyter, 1973), 562–66; Theuws and Alkemade, "A Kind of Mirror," 419–27.

36. Ludwig Bieler, ed., *Muirchú's Vita sancti Patricii* I.20,11–13, in *The Patrician Texts in the Book of Armagh*, Scriptores latini Hiberniae 10 (Dublin: Dublin Institute for Advanced Studies, 1979), 96–97; Alan Orr Anderson and Marjorie Ogilvie Anderson, eds., *Adomnán's Life of Columba*, rev. ed., ii,24 and ii,45 (Oxford: Clarendon Press, 1991), 128–29, 174–75; Adalbert de Vogüé, ed., *Grégoire le Grand, Dialogues* 1,2,5–6, SC 260 (Paris: Les Éditions du CERF, 1979), 28–29.

Garments were perceived as working in the manner of relics, in some cases when their wearers were not yet deceased.[37] Inanimate personal possessions thus had the capacity to convey something of the charismatic power of their saintly owners and were highly prized commodities in relic collections, along with bones, hair, and objects of Christ's passion.[38] Accounts of wonders associated with cloth persisted well into the Christian period due to the powerful symbolism of weaving and binding.[39]

The integrity of descriptions of miracles linked to clothing, however, was affected by their authors' ideological objectives. References to garments, just as other details included in hagiographical texts, did not present an unmodified reflection of the saint. Rather, they were intended to contribute to subjective recollections of the holy man or woman. When Gertrude, abbess of Nivelles, instructed the nuns just before her death in 659 to bury her in an old veil and hair shirt left behind by a devout pilgrimess, more than ascetic aspirations motivated her desire to be interred in rags. The perceived amuletic properties of garments worn and perhaps woven by the pilgrimess might grant the abbess a companion in the hour of her death.[40] In the hands of her biographer, the event likewise became an

For Byzantium, see Ewa Kuryluk, *Veronica and Her Cloth: History, Symbolism, and Structure of a "True Image"* (Oxford: Basil Blackwell, 1991), 75–78.

37. Valerie I. J. Flint, *The Rise of Magic in Early Medieval Europe* (Princeton: Princeton University Press, 1991), 307–8.

38. Jacques Dubois, "La malle de voyage de l'évêque Germain de Paris (†576)," *Bulletin de la Société nationale des antiquaires de France* (1983): 238–49; Jacques Dubois, "Utilisation religieuse du tissu," in *Tissu et vêtement: 5000 ans de savoir-faire*, 147–48; Prou and Chartraire, "Authentiques de reliques," 143–62.

39. Annette B. Weiner, *Inalienable Possessions: The Paradox of Keeping-While-Giving* (Berkeley and Los Angeles: University of California Press, 1992), 3–4; Lynda L. Coon, *Sacred Fictions: Holy Women and Hagiography in Late Antiquity* (Philadelphia: University of Pennsylvania Press, 1997), 41–44; Flint, *The Rise*, 226–31.

40. Bruno Krusch, ed., *Vita sanctae Geretrudis* B.7, in *MGH: SRM* 2, new ed. (Hannover: Impensis bibliopolii Hahniani, 1956), 461–62; Bonnie Effros, "Symbolic Expressions of Sanctity: Gertrude of Nivelles in the Context of Merovingian Mortuary Custom," *Viator* 27 (1996): 1–5.

opportunity for the rhetorical expression of Gertrude's humility and ultimately her power as saint.

Garments, Weapons, and Valuables in Wills and Legislation

Not only inherent worth but other less easily measured aspects of the value of clothing and personal possessions motivated detailed descriptions of garments in surviving wills and property law from the early medieval period. Individuals evidently had some freedom to choose whether to place objects in graves, bequeath them to heirs, or distribute them as alms to the poor. These practices stand in direct contradiction to the legal restrictions envisioned by early-twentieth-century historians in their construction of the concepts of *Heergewäte* and *Gerade,* by which personal possessions allegedly could not be passed down to family members.[41] This theory has now largely been discounted.[42]

Of the few extant wills from the Merovingian period, most were composed by bishops, a reflection mainly of the fact that their bequests stood a greater chance of being formally recorded and preserved. The original documents or copies made of them in large part survive from north of the Loire, which is surprising in light of the fragile papyri upon which they were originally composed but not in terms of the land transactions they recorded. Remigius, bishop of Reims, for example, instructed in his will circa 533 that his successor was to receive his white cloak for Easter, two dove-colored

---

41. Heinrich Brunner, "Der Todtentheil in germanischen Rechten," *Zeitschrift der Savigny-Stiftung für Rechtsgeschichte,* germanistische Abteilung 19 (1898): 118–37; Siegfried Rietschel, "Heergewäte und Gerade," *Reallexikon der germanischen Altertumskunde* 2, ed. Johannes Hoops (Strasbourg: Verlag von Karl J. Trübner, 1913), 467.

42. For the development of these interpretations, see Bonnie Effros, *Merovingian Mortuary Archaeology and the Making of the Early Middle Ages* (Berkeley and Los Angeles: University of California Press, forthcoming).

blankets, and three curtains.[43] He left the last set of possessions to adorn the dining hall, chapter house, and saltern on festival days. Unusual in its detailed yet formulaic description of items of clothing, Remigius's testament also indicated that his nephew Pretextatus Moderatus would inherit, among other objects, a traveling cloak and his carved episcopal staff. Pretextatus's son received a hooded cloak, the fringes of which Remigius had himself altered.[44] The archdeacon Ursi inherited two linen cloaks of different sizes, two delicate mantles, as well as a blanket and Remigius's best tunic.[45] Some wills, however, were not as explicit with respect to individual garments. Bertichramnus, bishop of Le Mans (586–616), left no precise inventory of personal artifacts in his last testament. Instead, his will stipulated generally that clothing, in addition to an unspecified amount of gold, be distributed to the poor, as was widely done in this period.[46] Gregory I noted in his *Dialogues*, for instance, that Boniface, bishop of Ferentis, when still a boy living with his mother, gave away his clothing to the poor.[47]

Members of the lay nobility, for whom only a very small number of wills survive, also engaged in bequests of items of personal adornment.

43. In the case of Remigius's will, only ninth- and tenth-century copies survive, and their contents are to a certain extent suspect, especially with respect to landed property. Dominic Janes, "Treasure Bequest: Death and Gift in the Early Middle Ages," in *The Community, the Family, and the Saint: Patterns of Power in Early Medieval Europe*, ed. Joyce Hill and Mary Swan (Turnhout: Brepols, 1998), 370–74.

44. "Futuro episcopo successori meo amphibalum album paschalem relinquo; stragola columbina duo, vela tria, que sunt ad hostia diebus festis triclinii, cellae et culinae." Bruno Krusch, ed., *Testamenta sancti Remigii*, in *MGH: SRM* 3 (Hannover: Impensis bibliopolii Hahniani, 1896), 337–38.

45. "Ursi archidiaconi familiaribus usus obsequiis, dono ei domitextilis casulam subtilem et aliam pleniorem, duo saga delicata, tappete quod habeo in lecto et tunicam quam tempore transitus mei reliquero meliorem." Krusch, *Testamenta sancti Remigii*, 339.

46. "Illud vero rogo atque iubeo abbatibus . . . quando fuerit mea commemoratio, pauperibus, aut in vestimentum aut in aurum erogetur." G. Busson and A. Ledru, eds., *Le testament de Saint Bertrand*, in *AHM* 2 (Le Mans: Société des archives historiques du Maine, 1902), 108.

47. "Nam ait quod eo tempore quo cum matre sua puer habitabat, egressus hospitio nonnumquam sine linea, crebro etiam sine tunica revertebatur, quia mox nudum quempiam repperisset, vestiebat hunc, se expolians." De Vogüé, *Grégoire le Grand, Dialogues* 1,9,16, *SC* 260, 88–91.

An elite woman, Erminethrudis, for instance, enjoined sometime between 590 and 630/645 that much of her clothing and other property be left to her surviving son.[48] Because the clerics at this time encouraged donations of wealth to individual religious foundations, churches, and the poor, however, she divided the moveable and immoveable possessions at her disposal among relations, servants, and those beneficiaries whom she believed would benefit her as a Christian and a member of a powerful family. From her personal possessions, she donated a bejeweled gold brooch to the basilica of St. Peter, a gold cross worth seven *solidi* to the basilica of Mary, an enameled gold seal ring worth four *solidi* to the basilica of St. Stephen, and a gold seal ring engraved with her name to the basilica of St. Gervais. She also bequeathed clothing to the brothers at Saint-Denis, Bondy, and Emilia, all houses located in the vicinity of Paris.[49]

Erminethrudis's will demonstrates the far-reaching influence a widow might exercise in conjunction with her possessions if no restrictions were placed upon her. If the various Germanic law codes (*leges*) constitute an accurate measure of obstacles faced by women in various parts of Gaul, such freedom of expression must have dwindled over the next century.[50] The early-ninth-century *Lex Thuringorum*, for example, allowed daughters to receive only money and servants and forbade them from inheriting landed property even when they had no male siblings.[51] According to the

---

48. Jean-Pierre Laporte, "Pour une nouvelle datation du testament d'Ermenthrude," *Francia* 14 (1986): 577; Janes, "Treasure Bequest," 368–70.

49. Hartmut Atsma and Jean Vezin, eds., *Testament d'Erminethrude*, in *ChLA* 14 (Dietikon-Zurich: URS Graf Verlag, 1982), no. 592, pp. 72–75.

50. Ingrid Heidrich, "Besitz und Besitzverfügung verheirateter und verwitweter freier Frauen im merowingischen Frankenreich," in *Weibliche Lebensgestaltung im frühen Mittelalter*, ed. Hans-Werner Goetz (Cologne: Böhlau Verlag, 1991),129–33; Ingrid Heidrich, "Von Plectrud zu Hildegard: Beobachtungen zum Besitzrecht adliger Frauen im Frankenreich und zur politischen Rolle der Frauen der frühen Karolinger," *RV* 52 (1988): 1–4.

51. "Hereditatem defuncti filius non filia suscipiat. Si filium non habuit, qui defunctus est, ad filiam pecunia et mancipia, terra vero ad proximum paternae generationis consangineum pertineat." Karl

same code, sons might inherit land, slaves, and money from their mothers, whereas daughters had hereditary rights primarily associated with personal apparel: namely, necklaces, brooches, decorative collars, earrings, clothing, bracelets, and other ornaments.[52] A male heir, aside from being entitled to the mail shirt from his father's fighting equipment, could expect to receive his parents' land.[53] The *Lex Francorum Chamavorum* specified that although sons were entitled to forest, land, servants, and property, daughters were to receive their mother's inheritance (*materna hereditate*).[54] Women evidently found it easier to bequeath and inherit objects associated with personal adornment than immoveable possessions.

Prior to the above-mentioned regulation of inheritance, late-sixth-century law codes issued in northern Gaul addressed the problem of the unlawful seizure of women's jewelry among a host of measures punishing theft. Not only did the *Pactus legis salicae* forbid entrance into any house without permission of its owner, in a statute directed at least in part at protecting domestic possessions,[55] but it also specified a penalty of three *solidi* for the theft of a woman's bracelet.[56] Legislation for equivalent crimes was harsher in the ninth-century *Lex Thuringorum;* one measure stipulated that thieves who stole women's adornments (*ornamenta muliebra*)

Friedrich von Richthofen, ed., *Lex Thuringorum* 26–27, in *MGH: Leges* 5 (Hannover: Impensis bibliopolii Hahniani, 1875–89), 123–25.

52. "Mater moriens filio terram, mancipia, pecuniam dimittat, filiae vero spolia colli id est murenulas, nuscas, monilia, inaures, vestes, armillas, vel quicquid ornamenti proprii videbatur habuisse." Von Richthofen, *Lex Thuringorum* 32, 127–28. With reference to Burgundian women, see Suzanne Fonay Wemple, *Women in Frankish Society: Marriage and the Cloister, 500–900* (Philadelphia: University of Pennsylvania Press, 1985), 47.

53. Von Richthofen, *Lex Thuringorum* 31, 126–27.

54. Rudolf Sohm, ed., *Lex Francorum Chamavorum* 42, in *MGH: Leges* 5 (Hannover: Impensis bibliopolii Hahniani, 1875–89), 275.

55. "Si quis casam alienam sine consilio domini sui traxerit, mallobergo alachiscido, MCC denarios qui faciunt solidos XXX culpabilis iudicetur." Karl August Eckhardt, ed., *Pactus legis salicae* C27,35, *MGH: Leges* 4,1, rev. ed. (Hannover: Impensis bibliopolii Hahniani, 1962), 109.

56. "Si quis mulierem brachilem furverit, mallobergo subto, sunt CXX denarii qui faciunt solidos III culpabilis iudicetur." Eckhardt, *Pactus legis salicae* C27,34, 109.

would be obligated to give the injured party three times the stolen goods' value, in addition to paying a fine of twelve *solidi*.[57]

Such laws appear to have been directed at preventing seizure of personal possessions from individuals who could not adequately protect them. Unarmed monks would have been similarly defenseless, although their vulnerability was not addressed by contemporary legislation, since presumably they had little to steal. As recorded by an anonymous hagiographical author in the mid–seventh century, however, robbers murdered the exiled Irish monk Foillan of Fosses and his companions during a pilgrimage near their monastery in northern Gaul. After the killers plundered and hid their bodies, they sold the monks' personal property to make some financial gain from the incident.[58] On presumably similar grounds, the *Pactus legis salicae* 14,11 and 14,9 specified that theft from a sleeping man or an unburied corpse constituted equally punishable offenses, with a fine of a hundred *solidi*. In the case of the sleeping man, this sum was in addition to the value of the object and the reward for the person who identified the thief.[59] Comparable legislation protecting the goods of those who were murdered existed in Alemannic regions. A penalty for the theft was added to the *wergeld*, or compensatory damages, owed for the individual killed.[60]

In dictating the appropriate punishment for theft from the yet unburied dead, the *Pactus legis salicae* differentiated between free and enslaved

---

57. Von Richthofen, *Lex Thuringorum* 38, 131.

58. Bruno Krusch, ed., *Additamentum Nivialense de Fuilano*, in *MGH: SRM* 4 (Hannover: Impensis bibliopolii Hahniani, 1902), 450–51.

59. Eckhardt, *Pactus legis salicae* C14,9 and C14,11, 68–69; Hermann Nehlsen, "Der Grabfrevel in den germanischen Rechtsaufzeichnungen: Zugleich ein Beitrag zur Diskussion um Todesstrafe und Friedlosigkeit bei den Germanen," in *Zum Grabfrevel*, 137–38.

60. "Si quis ingenuus ingenuum interficiet et ei aliquid de res suas sangulentas tullerit aut hoc auferit ad parentes, nihil est ad requirendum. Si enim vero non offerit, 40 solidos solvat." Karl Lehmann, ed., *Pactus Alamannorum* II,44, in *Leges Alamannorum*, in *MGH: Leges* 3 (Hannover: Impensis bibliopolii Hahniani, 1888), 23. In the *Leges Alamannorum*, items stolen, including weapons and clothing, were to be replaced, and the appropriate *wergeld* paid. Lehmann, *Leges Alamannorum* (E.codd.B) 49, 107–8.

victims in meting out penalties for crimes committed against them. Whereas a fine of a hundred *solidi* was promulgated for the theft of possessions from a deceased freeman, a fine of only fifteen to thirty *solidi* was the punishment for taking goods from the corpse of someone else's servant. The determination of the size of this latter penalty depended upon whether the property's value exceeded forty *denarii*, the equivalent of one *solidus*.[61] If someone killed a person and then robbed him, by contrast, he faced a fine of 62½ *solidi*.[62] In northeastern Gaul, early-seventh-century measures in the *Lex ribuaria* also conveyed its authors' outrage at the pillage of the unburied dead, but stipulated significantly lower penalties for those who admitted stealing from corpses than for those who did not. The accused party, if found guilty after denying complicity, was obligated to pay a hundred *solidi* and give a reward to the individual who reported the deed (*dilatura*).[63] Ripuarian statutes thus appear to have been directed at curbing the theft of personal effects and preventing the more general robbery of burial goods from corpses just prior to inhumation.[64]

In early-eighth-century versions of the law codes, these penalties were augmented. If a thief pillaged the body of a deceased person who had not yet been buried, the guilty party was obligated to forfeit two hundred *solidi*, return the stolen goods, and pay a reward. Until these requirements were satisfied and the relatives of the deceased received appropriate com-

---

61. "6. Si quis serum alienum mortuum in furtum expoliaverit et ei super XL denarios valentes tulerit, mallb. teofriomosido MCCCC den. qui fac. sol. XXXV culp. iudic. 7. Si quis spolia ipsa minus XL den. valuerit, teofriomosido, DC den. qui fac. sol. XV culp. iud." Eckhardt, *Pactus legis salicae* C6,35,6–7, 131.

62. Eckhardt, *Pactus legis salicae* C55,1, 205.

63. "Si quis autem hominem mortuum, antequam humetur, expoliaverit, si interrogatus confessus fuerit, bis trigenos solidos multetur. Si autem negaverit et postea convictus fuerit, bis quinquagenos solidos cum dilatura multetur, aut cum 6 iuret." Beyerle and Buchner, *Lex ribuaria* 55,1, 103–4.

64. "Si quis corpus mortuum, priusquam sepeliatur, expoliaverit, 100 sol. cum capitale et dilatura multetur." Beyerle and Buchner, *Lex ribuaria* 88,1, 132.

pensation, the thief was expelled from the community (*wargus sit*).[65] Restitution of the value of the deceased's property to free persons apparently constituted a subject of concern to the king and the members of the elite who backed this legislation. Kin of the deceased thereby sought to tighten their hold on goods to which they were officially entitled. In other words, they wished to maintain control over the heritable objects on a person at the time of his or her murder or otherwise unfortunate end, as well as those that adorned the deceased in preparation for burial.

In both Salian and Ripuarian legislation, the indemnities to be rendered by thieves to the relatives of the deceased were vastly disproportionate to the cost of the items stolen; the sums appear to have been linked more to the *wergeld* of the deceased than to the value of the property itself.[66] Not only did the punishment of robbery involve compensation for objects stolen, but it sought to reestablish a family's honor in response to the shameful act committed against it. This legislation provides evidence that contemporaries recognized that while legally defined status was not tied systematically to bodily adornment in the Merovingian period, clothing and personal possessions were markers critical to the expression of a family's standing. One might propose that the penalties underlined monarchs' recognition of the seriousness of these offenses, which had to be punished accordingly.[67] Merovingian kings, to some degree the arbiters of the promotion of free and nonfree

65. "Si autem eum ex homo traxerit et expoliaverit, 200 sol. cum capitale et dilatura culpabilis indicetur, vel wargus sit (hoc est expulsus) usque ad parentibus satisfecerit." Beyerle and Buchner, *Lex ribuaria* 88,2, 132; Nehlsen, "Der Grabfrevel," 135–36.

66. Nehlsen notes that the penalties of fifteen, thirty-five, and one hundred *solidi* were equivalent to the *wergeld* owed as indemnities for other crimes against the same groups. Nehlsen, "Der Grabfrevel," 137–39.

67. František Graus, "Sozialgeschichtliche Aspekte der Hagiographie der Merowinger- und Karolingerzeit: Die Viten der Heiligen des südalemannischen Raumes und die sogenannten Adelsheiligen," in *Mönchtum, Episkopat und Adel zur Gründungszeit des Klosters Reichenau*, Vorträge und Forschungen 20, ed. Arno Borst (Sigmaringen: Jan Thorbecke Verlag, 1974), 161–63.

individuals to the nobility through appointments in their personal service,[68] may have sought through law to guard the exclusiveness of these honors by prosecuting the illegal appropriation of precious tokens associated with the offices.

During the Merovingian period, nevertheless, few documents reveal any attempt to formalize links between items of personal dress and identity. While bodily adornment had great symbolic significance, any interpretation of that symbolism must be cautious due to the highly fragmentary nature of the material and written sources. Evidence gathered mainly from south of the Loire reveals that it was clerics who were most interested in regulating social demarcations through personal adornment. Restrictions on the appearance of clerics during their lifetimes helped visually to reinforce the wholly artificial separation between secular and religious life.[69] Although clothing and possessions played an important role in the expression of various aspects of identity among the laity, their employment was rarely directly regulated by secular law written in centers of power between the Loire and Rhine. Because economic, social, and political considerations already limited access to such objects and garments, wills and legal codes focused on protecting their transmission.

Hagiographical and Historical Representations of the Dead

Personal adornment also had symbolic significance in Merovingian funerary contexts described in historical and hagiographical sources. While the deposition of grave goods accounts for the majority of surviving material

68. Rolf Sprandel, "Dux und Comes in der Merowingerzeit," *Zeitschrift der Savigny-Stiftung für Rechtsgeschichte,* germanistische Abteilung 74 (1957): 74; František Graus, *Volk, Herrscher und Heiliger im Reich der Merowinger: Studien zur Hagiographie der Merowingerzeit* (Prague: Nakladatelství ceskoslovenské akademie ved, 1965), 201–3.

69. Peter Brown, *The Rise of Western Christendom: Triumph and Diversity, AD 200–1200* (Oxford: Blackwell Publishers, 1996), 152–53; Effros, "Appearance and Ideology."

evidence, written records of funerals also serve as an important interpretive source of at least elite burials. Their authors did not, however, seek to provide a faithful description of early medieval mortuary customs. Just as the rituals attested to in the archaeological record served multiple functions and thus cannot be easily discerned by modern scholars, a variety of objectives motivated historical and hagiographical works. In some senses, these texts are even less reliable than the material evidence because they were more easily manipulated by their authors. As with grave goods, written descriptions of funerary ceremony and of the grave goods themselves shaped communal memory of the identity and personality of the deceased.[70]

Lewis Binford has proposed that it is necessary to address two primary characteristics of social structure in research on funerary custom in any community. First, one must identify the aspects of the deceased's social persona deemed important at the time of death, and second, one should take into account the makeup of the social unit responsible for a formal acknowledgment of the deceased's status at the time of the disposal of the body. Binford has observed that these two components directly influence funerary ritual, including the corpse's treatment prior to burial, the structure chosen to house the body, as well as the grave goods deposited at the time of inhumation. The higher the social status of the deceased, the larger the number of individuals involved in and affected by funerary preparations.[71] While grave goods did not necessarily represent the possessions of the deceased, they were also not randomly chosen objects. Instead, their

70. Heinrich Härke, "'Warrior Graves'? The Background of the Anglo-Saxon Weapon Burial Rite," *Past and Present* 126 (1990): 22–43; Heinrich Härke, "Die anglo-amerikanische Diskussion zur Gräberanalyse," *AK* 19 (1989): 185–94.

71. Lewis R. Binford, "Mortuary Practices: Their Study and Potential," in *Approaches to the Social Dimensions of Mortuary Practices*, Memoirs of the Society for American Archaeology 25, ed. James A. Brown (Washington, D.C.: Society for American Archaeology, 1971), 17, 21; Arthur Alan Saxe, "Social Dimensions of Mortuary Practices" (Ph.D. diss., University of Michigan, 1970), 69–75.

selection reflected a kin group's concerns about the family's standing within the framework of a community's burial customs.[72]

Funerary rites and the objects that contributed to them helped to identify the relationships maintained by the deceased during his or her lifetime as well as the ones that would be established on entrance into the afterlife.[73] Historical sources of the sixth to eighth centuries give some impression of the grave goods employed in early medieval funerals in Gaul, but focus almost exclusively on elite burial and are thus not representative of popular norms. The anonymous author of the *Liber historiae Francorum*, for example, briefly described the garments in which two Merovingian kings were laid to rest. He noted that Sigibert (d. 575), who was buried by his brother and foe Chilperic I (d. 584) and possibly Chilperic's wife, was dressed in ornate clothing.[74] Chilperic himself was interred by Mallulfus, bishop of Senlis, in royal garments, the precise definition of which was not provided.[75] Because this historical work was composed approximately a century and a half after the events described, these details may have reflected early-eighth- instead of sixth-century expectations of royal custom. The author wanted to convey to readers that Sigibert and Chilperic I were buried honorably, in the robes of their office, by some of the most powerful men in their kingdoms. In this manner, the text witnessed that the royal dignity of the Merovingian kings was maintained at the time of their

72. Härke, "'Warrior Graves,'" 22–24; Steuer, *Frühgeschichtliche Sozialstrukturen*, 52–53.

73. Bailey K. Young, "Paganisme, christianisation et rites funéraires mérovingiens," *AM* 7 (1977): 36–37.

74. "Tunc egressus Chilpericus a Turnaco cum uxore sua ac populo, vestitum Sighiberto vestibus ornatis apud Lambrus vicum sepelivit." Bruno Krusch, ed., *Liber historiae Francorum* 32, in *MGH: SRM* 2 (Hannover: Impensis bibliopolii Hahniani, 1888), 296–97.

75. "Mallulfus itaque Silvanectinsis episcopus, qui in ipso palatio tunc aderat, indutumque eum [Chilpericum] vestibus regalibus, in nave (in villa quae dicitur Calla) levato, cum hymnis et psallentio cum Fredegunde regina vel reliquo exercitu Parisius civitate in basilica beati Vincenti martyris eum sepelierunt." Krusch, *Liber historiae Francorum* 32, 304; Alain Erlande-Brandenburg, *Le roi est mort: Étude sur les funérailles, les sépultures et les tombeaux des rois de France jusqu'à la fin du XIIIᵉ siècle*, Bibliothèque de la Société française d'archéologie 7 (Geneva: Droz, 1975), 7.

funerals.[76] While sixth-century kings' burials likely also involved lavish costume, eighth-century authors probably transposed anachronistic ideas upon these earlier events.

Contemporary accounts of nuns' burials were no more objective than descriptions of the funerals of kings. The way in which a virgin was laid to rest often constituted a final reflection of her humility and purity and the simplicity of her existence. Gregory of Tours's depiction of the burial of the nun Disciola (d. 583) at the monastery of Sainte-Croix, Poitiers, included the observation that the former queen and current inmate Radegund, the prestigious founder of the abbey, "could not find in her cupboard a wind-ing-sheet which was whiter than she [Disciola]. They wrapped her in clean linen and committed her to the grave."[77] In choosing a linen shroud as an appropriate funerary garment for the devout nun, Radegund chose a sparkling symbol of the nun's chastity. Notably, she chose this fine cloth rather than Disciola's monastic garb to envelop and protect the worthy corpse. Gregory does not indicate that there was anything incongruous about such luxury in death after a humble existence as a nun.

As noted above, nearly a century later, according to the *vita* of Gertrude of Nivelles (d. 659), the abbess informed her congregation that she wished to be laid to rest with humility. She requested burial in her own hair shirt as well as a veil formerly owned by a holy pilgrimess, who had used it to cover her head while stopping at the abbey.[78] Gertrude's choice of mortuary

---

76. Richard A. Gerberding, *The Rise of the Carolingians and the "Liber historiae Francorum"* (Oxford: Clarendon Press, 1987), 46.

77. "ut nullum lenteum reperire abbatissa [Radegundis] potuisset in prumptu, quod corpore candidior cerneretur; induta tamen lenteis mundis, sepulturae mandata est." Bruno Krusch, ed., *Gregorius episcopus Turonensis, Libri historiarum X* 6,29, MGH: SRM 1,1, rev. ed. (Hannover: Impensis bibliopolii Hahniani, 1951), 268. Translation taken from *Gregory of Tours, History of the Franks*, trans. Lewis Thorpe (London: Penguin Books, 1974), 357.

78. "Ita decrevit, ut in ipso sepulturae loco nullum lineum vel laneum vestimentum super se misissent preter unum velum vile multum, quod quaedam sanctimonialis peregrina ante dies multos direxerat ad caput operiendum, et ipsum cilicium subpositum, in pace deberet requiescere et alio

costume did not signal a break with the custom of grave goods,[79] but instead her assimilation of a late antique expression of piety and power in her desire to be buried in holy clothing.[80] This celebrated moment, the last image of the saint before interment, represented a critical point in her biographer's hagiographical oeuvre. The monastic house profited from such a portrayal because the clothing in which the saint was buried itself became a relic.[81]

The examples of Disciola and Gertrude illustrate that when archaeologists discover no tangible goods in a grave buried near saints' relics (*ad sanctos*), this absence may not necessarily signal rejection of the custom of grave goods. In fact, in some cases, virtually the opposite is true. No surviving written evidence suggests that contemporaries characterized their use as either pagan or Germanic. Indeed, sepulchers seemingly devoid of artifacts, especially in the interments of women, may have once contained valued holy or luxury fabrics.[82] Written accounts and archaeological remains consistently indicate that for those who made religious professions, both symbolic burial dress and a grave *ad sanctos* played an important role in communicating the spiritual status of the deceased. Such was the case of the fifth-century woman buried in silk and other finery, including a cross, in the church of Saint-Victor in Marseilles.[83]

---

nullo operiri velamine, exceptis his duobus, id est cilicio, quo erat induta, et panno veteri, quo cilicium ipsum tegebatur." Krusch, *Vita sanctae Geretrudis* B.7, 461–62.

79. Bailey K. Young, "Exemple aristocratique et mode funéraire dans la Gaule mérovingienne," *Annales ESC* 41 (1986): 379–83.

80. Effros, "Symbolic Expressions of Sanctity," 1–10; Kuryluk, *Veronica and Her Cloth*, 188–89.

81. Upon opening the tomb of Bishop Valerius of Saint-Lizier, it was found that "[l]auri etiam folia sub se habebat strata, de qua adsumens episcopus, multis infirmis praebuit medicinam. De vestimentis igitur, eius reliquias sumpsit; rursumque operto tumulo, venerandum deinceps antestitem honoravit, multaque miracula de his pignoribus cernens in posterum." Bruno Krusch, ed., *Gregorius episcopus Turonensis, Liber in gloria confessorum* 83, in *MGH: SRM* 1,2, new ed. (Hannover: Impensis bibliopolii Hahniani, 1969), 352.

82. Heli Roosens, "Reflets de christianisation dans les cimetières mérovingiens," *Les études classiques* 53 (1985): 132–34.

83. Boyer et al., *Vie et mort à Marseille*, no. 20, pp. 45–93.

For the sake of comparison, the unusually well preserved seventh-century sepulcher found during excavations of the crypt of St. Ulrich and St. Afra in Augsburg points to the significance of organic evidence ordinarily susceptible to decomposition. In this case, along with remnants of a wooden staff, archaeologists uncovered the remains of an approximately sixty-year-old man dressed in short leather boots, a wool cape, and linen clothing tied with a leather belt. Buried *ad sanctos,* this man may have been a cleric or simply a deceased member of an elite family that wished to commemorate him in the type of clothing likely worn by contemporary members of the clergy.[84] Staffs of the sort found here were employed not just by bishops, abbots, priests, and monks, but also by missionaries and pilgrims. Thus, even with organic remains, which normally would have decayed beyond recognition, no firm conclusions regarding their symbolic meaning can be drawn.

Occasionally artifacts engraved with written descriptions promoting the spiritual status of the deceased appear in graves of the Merovingian period. Contemporaries must have donated such goods with Christian significance to outfit sepulchers in commemoration of relatives or companions. Just as hagiographical texts preserved and promoted the deeds of the saints, the inscriptions on brooches and buckles conveyed very positive images of the deceased. They highlighted the merits of the faithful Christian presumably not just for the living but for eternity. One example of this practice is found on a silver brooch produced in a workshop in the Rhineland and brought to the region of the Danube in the seventh century; the inscribed piece, with niches possibly for relics, was included in the elite grave of a young woman buried in Wittislingen. Proclaiming Uffila's innocence and faith, the author of the passage wished her peace in the

---

84. Joachim Werner, "Die Gräber aus der Krypta-Grabung 1961/1962," in *Die Ausgrabungen in St. Ulrich und Afra in Augsburg 1961–1968* 1 (Munich: C. H. Beck'sche Verlagsbuchhandlung, 1977), 142–52.

afterlife.[85] By commemorating the deceased's devotion to Christianity, the brooch promoted her religious status and brought honor to her family and community. A much simpler eighth-century disk of inscribed bone now owned by the Rheinisches Landesmuseum in Trier served much the same purpose.[86] By praising Rotsuintda as a handmaid of God, the artifact offered consolation with hopes of her resurrection. Presumably, the amulet also aided her safe passage to the afterlife.

The act of interring the dead honored not only the deceased but also those who performed this public rite on their behalf. For most, the written sources suggest that family members prepared their bodies for burial. The funeral represented an opportunity for kin to express their solidarity or possibly disunity. For those in monastic houses, by contrast, the religious *familia,* not kin groups, constituted the most prominent of members' relationships. As a consequence, ecclesiastical measures by the late eighth century included rather specific guidelines as to the monastic costume in which abbesses and nuns were to be buried. In the Berlin Sacramentary Phillipps 1667, for instance, members of female religious houses were made responsible for washing and clothing corpses of their sisters and brethren for burial.[87] The funerals of prestigious individuals drew the ministrations of commensurately prestigious peers; for example, the early

85. Bernhard Bischoff has reconstructed the inscription: "UFFILA VIVAT IN DEO FILIX-INOCENS FUNERE CAPTA-QUIA VIVERE DUM POTUI-FUI FIDELISSEMA-PAUSA IN DEO." The piece was then signed: "WIGERIG FECIT." Bernhard Bischoff, "Epigraphisches Gutachten II," in *Das alamannische Fürstengrab von Wittislingen,* Münchner Beiträge zur Vor- und Frühgeschichte 2, ed. Joachim Werner (Munich: C. H. Beck'sche Verlagsbuchhandlung, 1950), 68–71.

86. The inscription on the Rotsuintda-Scheibe states: "IN $\overline{\text{XPO}}$ NOMINE ROTSVINTDA ANCELLA $\overline{\text{XPI}}$ SVM EGO / IN NOMINE PATRIS ET FILII $\overline{\text{SPV}}$.$\overline{\text{SCI}}$ AMEN ALLELVA." This object, Rheinisches Landesmuseum, #9,865, was likely originally placed on the deceased in her grave. It was found, however, in the Trier amphitheater. Wilhelm Reusch, ed., *Frühchristliche Zeugnisse im Einzugsgebiet von Rhein und Mosel* 97 (Trier: Unitas-Buchhandlung, 1965), 111–12, pl. 97.

87. Damien Sicard, *La liturgie de la mort dans l'Église latine des origines à la reforme carolingienne,* Liturgiewissenschaftliche Quellen und Forschungen 63 (Münster: Aschendorffsche Verlagsbuchhandlung, 1978), 6–11, 108–11.

Carolingian recension of the *vita* of Eligius of Noyon indicates that the former queen Balthild chose the silk garments for the bishop's interment.[88] Whether for the funeral of a lay or religious person, the garments in which the deceased was to be laid to rest were meant to evoke certain aspects of his or her vocation and achievements. Yet, interpreting the data requires significant caution due to the symbolic qualities of the garments and personal artifacts used to accompany the dead.[89] Since those burying the dead benefited from such final images, particularly those of the bodies of the saints, great incentive existed for the manipulation of these memories.

---

88. "Praeparabat etiam regina [Balthildis] vestimenta omnia olosirica nimium praetiosa, ut eum [Eligium] in die transmigrationis exueret illa quae dudum cum eo miserat indumenta et induerat ea quae tunc praeparabat nova." Bruno Krusch, ed., *Vita Eligii episcopi Noviomagensis* 2,48, in *MGH: SRM* 4 (Hannover: Impensis bibliopolii Hahniani, 1902), 727.

89. Pader, *Symbolism, Social Relations*, 18 ff.

CHAPTER 11

✦ • ✦

Lay and Clerical Regulation of
Grave Goods and Cemeteries

Implications of Legal Evidence for the Deposition of Mortuary Goods

Spurred by the expansion of the railways and the growth of the antiquities trade, antiquarians and archaeologists unearthed large numbers of early medieval grave goods in the late nineteenth and early twentieth centuries. In France, Germany, and Belgium, these finds eventually sparked both scholarly and public discussions of the identity of the populations using such burial practices in the early Middle Ages.[1] Because specialists studying documentary sources usually enjoyed privileged status over the amateur collectors, clerics, and civil servants who worked with material artifacts—and archaeologists and curators were more interested in the stylistic features of burial goods—the general interpretation of burial practice fell largely to historians. In 1898, the legal scholar Heinrich Brunner proposed that in Germanic antiquity it was customary for a dying person to leave one-third of his or her possessions for funerary rites and expenses. According to Brunner, the practice of *Todtentheil,* or "dead man's part," made it mandatory that all of the deceased's personal goods be deposited in their graves rather than be handed down to the next generation.[2] He hypothesized that

---

1. Bonnie Effros, *Merovingian Mortuary Archaeology and the Making of the Early Middle Ages* (Berkeley and Los Angeles: University of California Press, forthcoming).
2. Heinrich Brunner, "Der Todtentheil in germanischen Rechten," *Zeitschrift der Savigny-Stiftung für Rechtsgeschichte,* germanistische Abteilung 19 (1898): 118–37; Heinrich Brunner, *Deutsche Rechtsgeschichte* 1, 2d ed. (Leipzig: Verlag von Duncker & Humblot, 1906), 108–9.

Heergewäte and *Gerade,* the personal possessions of men and women such as weaponry and jewelry, respectively, could not be inherited.

Brunner's thesis created a new paradigm for understanding early medieval burial rites. German legal historians thereby sought to remove the taint of what might otherwise have been interpreted as pagan mortuary ritual; they could now explain the use of grave goods as resulting from legal strictures as opposed to religious practices. Followers of Brunner argued that this prehistoric custom was unique to the Germanic peoples and that its origins lay in an oral society independent of the complex legal traditions of Rome.[3] Legal specialists thus provided scholarly support for the identification of the Germanic inhabitants of western Europe by means of rituals involving their personal possessions. They believed that one could deduce from the contents of graves in Gaul whether the deceased were Franks or Gallo-Romans, since the latter could transmit their goods to heirs and therefore left their burial places relatively sparsely furnished.

Despite the certainty with which these concepts were regarded by legal historians at the beginning of the twentieth century, early medieval documents reveal disappointingly little about the perspectives of most individuals who participated in funerary rites or the ideologies that came into play at the graveside. Only one measure in the pre-eighth-century Germanic laws might be interpreted as containing a provision regulating property in the context of burial. Promulgated outside of Gaul, this particular piece of legislation indicates the slippery historical footing on which the early-twentieth-century premises of *Heergewäte* and *Gerade* rested. The *Pactus Alamannorum* stipulated: "If anyone should place in the earth for his own dead (anything) deriving from somebody else's property worth at least a *solidus,* he must pay forty *solidi.*" The law punished infractions involving

3. Clara Redlich, "Westgermanische Stammesbildungen," *Nachrichten aus Niedersachsens Urgeschichte* 36 (1967): 5–11; Albert J. Genrich, "Grabbeigaben und germanisches Recht," *Die Kunde* n.s. 22 (1971): 205–17.

burial of objects of lesser value with a fine of twelve *solidi*.[4] Legal historians traditionally interpreted this law as forbidding placement of the property of one person into the grave of another.[5] This reading, however, incorrectly relied upon the assumption that legislators conceived of property as belonging to individuals rather than collectively to kin groups.

Because we know that a family or clerical community was responsible for the funeral arrangements of their dead, this legal measure must have sought to curb only the burial of alien property: that which did not belong to the group and was possibly illegally acquired. Therefore, the *Pactus Alamannorum* did not oppose the deposition of items belonging to relations or heirs into the deceased's grave, even if the goods were of distant origin. Some historians and archaeologists have thus rightly discounted the concepts of *Heergewäte* and *Gerade* as influencing the choice of objects placed in the graves of the deceased, since neither these terms nor these practices were used by contemporaries.[6] This development has consequently led to serious reconsideration of the functions of grave goods.[7] The lack of formal prescriptions for funerary behavior points to the predominantly local and oral features of early medieval burial rites.

As noted above, the concept of *Todtentheil* allowed scholars to explain that the deposition of artifacts in the sepulchers of the deceased represented the expression of legal observance as opposed to religious sentiment. With

---

4. "Si quis superius mortuum suum de alienas res, qua valuerit solidos, in terra miserit, solvat solidos 40. Et si tremissis aut duos valuerit, solvat solidos 12 aut cum 12 medicus electus iuret." Karl Lehmann, ed., *Pactus Alamannorum* 11,42, in *Leges Alamannorum*, in *MGH: Leges* 3 (Hannover: Impensis bibliopolii Hahniani, 1888), 23.

5. Clara Redlich and Albert Genrich refer to these same measures as 16,1 and 16,2. Redlich, "Westgermanische Stammesbildungen," 5–8; Genrich, "Grabbeigaben und germanisches Recht," 219–20.

6. These hypotheses have only been slowly abandoned. Heinrich Härke, "The Nature of Burial Data," in *Burial and Society: The Chronological and Social Analysis of Archaeological Burial Data* (Århus: Århus University Press, 1997), 19.

7. Alain Dierkens, "La tombe privilégiée (ivᵉ–viiiᵉ siècles) d'après les trouvailles de la Belgique actuelle," in *L'inhumation privilégiée*, 47.

the rejection of this interpretation, however, historians and archaeologists had to seek other means to account for the scarcity of evidence for clerical involvement in funerary custom. Édouard Salin, for example, observed that clerical silence in this regard implied that grave goods were not perceived as pagan. If they had been widely believed to have been transported to the afterlife, presumably clerics would have opposed the practice more vigorously. Salin nonetheless characterized the eventual abandonment of burial goods as reflecting the Germanic population's Christianization.[8]

Like Salin, Bailey Young and Donald Bullough have observed that when clerics congregated at synods and councils south of the Loire, the interment of burial goods apparently did not represent cause for concern, as did many other sorts of rustic behavior.[9] In part, this reticence may have stemmed from the fact that the practice was not as prevalent among predominantly Gallo-Roman populations as among larger numbers of Franks further to the north. Yet, the distinct lack of reference to the practice was not only a consequence of ethnic demography. Only in cases in which burial rites threatened the integrity of church property, as when ecclesiastical articles were used in funerary ceremonies or as grave objects, did clerics pass measures modifying these customs. In 535, for instance, the Council of Clermont legislated against wrapping the dead in liturgical cloth or burying the dead with instruments necessary for Christian worship. While this application of the church's cloth honored and protected the deceased, it was seen by bishops as polluting the sacred altar.[10] At the

8. Édouard Salin, *La civilisation mérovingienne d'après les sépultures, les textes et le laboratoire* 2 (Paris: Éditions A. et J. Picard, 1952), 233–36.

9. Bailey K. Young, "Merovingian Funeral Rites and the Evolution of Christianity: A Study in the Historical Interpretation of Archaeological Material" (Ph.D. diss., University of Pennsylvania, 1975), 52, 76–80; Donald Bullough, "Burial, Community, and Belief in the Early Medieval West," in *Ideal and Reality in Frankish and Anglo-Saxon Society: Studies Presented to J. M. Wallace-Hadrill*, ed. Patrick Wormald (Oxford: Basil Blackwell, 1983), 189.

10. "[3.] Observandum, ne pallis vel ministeriis divinis defunctorum corpuscula obvolvantur." "[7.] Ne opertorio dominici corporis sacerdotes unquam corpus, dum ad tumulum evehetur, obtegatur

Diocesan Synod of Auxerre (561–605), the assembled bishops, in addition
to confirming earlier legislation at Clermont for both laypersons and deacons, proclaimed a ban on the interment of the eucharistic wafer and relics
with deceased Christians.[11] The synod sought to halt practices that might
impede the performance of liturgical services, deplete ecclesiastical coffers,
and challenge the clerical monopoly of these sacramental objects.

It is difficult to ascertain the uniformity of clerical efforts to enforce
these canons. Indeed, the measure promulgated at Auxerre differed significantly from the precedent established in Gregory I's widely read biography of Benedict of Nursia, in which the abbot gave advice to the family of
a monk whose body had twice been miraculously ejected from his tomb.
Gregory claimed that Benedict had instructed the dead man's kin to place
the viaticum on the monk's chest when they reburied him; the precaution
successfully freed his remains from further unrest.[12] Hagiographical evidence indicates that this practice may also have been taken up in Anglo-
Saxon England. The anonymous *vita* of Cuthbert, for instance, recorded
the special circumstances of his burial in ecclesiastical garments, with an
offering (*oblata*) placed on his chest.[13] In Merovingian Gaul, clerics' attitudes toward sacred objects in burial seem to have evolved over the course
of the seventh century. Although the written evidence describes mainly

---

et sacro velamine usibus suis reddeto, dum honorantur corpora, altaria polluantur." Charles de Clercq,
ed., *Concilia Galliae A.511–A.695*, *CCSL* 148A (Turnhout: Typographi Brepols editores Pontificii,
1963), 106–7.

 11. "[12.] Non licet mortuis nec eucharistia nec usculum tradi nec de vela vel pallas corpora
eorum involvi." "[13.] Non licet diacono de vela vel pallas scapulas suas involvi." De Clercq,
Concilia Galliae, 267.

 12. "Quibus [parentibus] vir Dei manu sua protinus communionem dominici corporis dedit,
dicens: 'Ite, atque hoc dominicum corpus super pectus eius ponite eumque sepulturae sic tradite.'"
Adalbert de Vogüé, ed., *Grégoire le Grand, Dialogues* 2,24,1–2, SC 260 (Paris: Les Éditions du
CERF, 1979), 210–13.

 13. Bertram Colgrave, ed. and trans., *Anonymous Life of St. Cuthbert* 13, in *Two Lives of Saint
Cuthbert* (Cambridge: Cambridge University Press, 1940), 130–31; Bullough, "Burial, Community,"
188–89.

clerical funerals, leaders of the clergy, judging from the high-profile cases
in which the mortuary rite was employed, desired to retain exclusive control
of liturgical objects. These sacramental artifacts were symbolic of clerics'
privileged status as religious authorities and represented an important
source of prestige in a gift-exchange society.

Visionary literature of the Merovingian period also provides an indication of attitudes toward the use of liturgical garments in the afterlife. As
with the legislation described above, its authors were primarily clerics.
The ideas expressed in these writings are therefore not necessarily representative of the beliefs of the laity. Visions were nonetheless influential in
shaping perceptions of the afterlife among Christian faithful. In the *vita* of
Austregisillus, bishop of Bourges (d. 624), for instance, the hagiographer
wrote that the saint was seen assisting in his own funeral with a fellow
deceased bishop dressed in white vestments (*candidis vestibus*).[14] Likewise,
two youths clothed in white ecclesiastical stoles appeared beside the
deathbed of Sisetrude, a seventh-century nun at Faremoutiers.[15] In the
Dialogues, Gregory I's description of a small boy at the deathbed of
Probus, the bishop of Rieti, included a similar reference. The youth grew
fearful when he saw the saints Juvenal and Eleutherius in white robes.[16]
Narratives involving demons and the sinful, by contrast, reduced descriptions to incomplete impressions of their dark and horrible appearance;
they excluded any mention of attire.[17] On the whole, visionary literature

14. Philippe Labbé, ed., *Vita (Liber prima) S. Austregisilli Bituricensis archiep.*, in *Novae bibliothecae manuscriptorum librorum* 2 (Paris: Apud Sebastianum Cramoisy, 1657), 354.

15. "Venerunt ergo duo iuvenes, candidis circumamicti stolis, animam [Sisetrudis] a corpore
segregantes." Bruno Krusch, ed., *Ionas, Vitae Columbani abbatis discipulorumque eius libri II* 2,11, in
MGH: SRG 37 (Hannover: Impensis bibliopolii Hahniani, 1905), 258.

16. "Subito aspexit [puer] intrantes ad virum Dei quosdam viros stolis candidis amictos, qui
eundem quoque candorem vestium vultuum suorum luce vincebant." De Vogüé, ed., *Grégoire le
Grand, Dialogues* 4,13,3, *SC* 265 (Paris: Les Éditions du CERF, 1980), 53–54.

17. Barontus recalled seeing "quattuor daemones nigerrimi nimis, qui me cupiebant dentibus et
unguibus lacerare crudeliter." Wilhelm Levison, ed., *Visio Baronti monachi Longoretensis* 7, in

promoted the positive connotations of sacred vestments in funerals and made their acquisition more desirable. By the eighth century, especially in northern regions of Gaul influenced by Anglo-Saxon clerics, clerical resistance to privileged burial with liturgical clothing had worn down. According to his *vita*, Hubert, bishop of Liège (d. 727), for instance, was interred in liturgical vestments.[18]

In the Merovingian kingdoms, then, neither secular nor canon law included more than one or two provisions regulating the type of objects that might be used in burial. The dearth of evidence prior to the eighth century implies that there was no consistent program among lay or clerical authorities to prescribe to families particular sorts of funerary rites. Hence, the abandonment of most grave goods in the late seventh century cannot be interpreted as a consequence of Christianization or of disenchantment with this rite due to greater "spiritual" awareness. Indeed, the first direct attempt to regulate burial rites in Gaul or neighboring regions, for which there is surviving evidence, was Charlemagne's legislation for the Saxons in the late eighth century.[19]

Despite the lack of clerical involvement in funerary rites, this discussion is not meant to imply that burial ritual had little spiritual significance for its participants as proposed by Guy Halsall, who has argued that the lack of interference by lay and clerical authorities meant that funerary

---

MGH: SRM 5 (Hannover: Impensis bibliopolii Hahniani, 1888), 382. Gregory I recounted that one man, upon his return from the dead, observed that "[t]aetri valde erant homines qui me docebant, ex quorum ore ac naribus ignis exiebat, quem tolerare non poteram." De Vogüé, *Grégoire le Grand, Dialogues* 1,12,2, *SC* 260, 114–15.

18. "Crastina die cum decore custodes illius induunt ei [Hugberti] albam et casulam, sicut solebat in sacerdotio." Wilhelm Levison, ed., *Vita Hugberti episcopi Traiectensis*, in *MGH: SRM* 6 (Hannover: Impensis bibliopolii Hahniani, 1913), 492.

19. Alfred Boretius, ed., *Capitulatio de partibus Saxoniae* 7 and 22, in *MGH: Leges* 2, *Capitularia* 1,26 (Hannover: Impensis bibliopolii Hahniani, 1883), 69–70; Bonnie Effros, *"De partibus Saxoniae* and the Regulation of Mortuary Custom: A Carolingian Campaign of Christianization or the Suppression of Saxon Identity?" *Revue belge de philologie et d'histoire* 75 (1997): 269–87.

ritual acted primarily as an arena for social competition. Yet he has rightly played down the ability of archaeological remains to convey to scholars useful information regarding belief during the Merovingian period.[20] Indeed, in cemeterial excavations, little differentiates burial custom among pagans from those rites practiced by Christian families. Both groups continued for centuries to use the same grave sites and to deposit similar goods in the sepulchers of relatives. The main exceptions existed among elite burials, whether in funerary chapels or those incorporating gold-foil crosses (*Goldblattkreuᵹe*), particularly in Alemannic regions.[21]

Although archaeological remains cannot in most cases provide direct evidence of religious belief, some funerary rituals nevertheless left evidence that they fulfilled important spiritual needs.[22] The votive *Goldblattkreuᵹe*, for instance, appear to have been sewn directly onto the clothing of the corpse just before burial. Marked by needle holes along their length rather than constructed with a loop for hanging, they were far too delicate to have been worn during an individual's lifetime. Of course, the *Goldblattkreuᵹe* had not only spiritual but also social implications,[23] revealing both the religious affiliation of the deceased and the resources of surviving kin. Grave artifacts inscribed with prayers and feasting rituals likewise expressed religious belief and identity in the context of burial rites. The small quantity of

20. Guy Halsall, "Burial, Ritual, and Merovingian Society," in *The Community, the Family, and the Saint: Patterns of Power in Early Medieval Europe*, ed. Joyce Hill and Mary Swan (Turnhout: Brepols, 1998), 325–38; Guy Halsall, *Settlement and Social Organiᵹation: The Merovingian Region of Metᵹ* (Cambridge: Cambridge University Press, 1995), 247–65.

21. Rainer Christlein, "Der soziologische Hintergrund der Goldblattkreuze nördlich der Alpen," in *Die Goldblattkreuᵹe des frühen Mittelalters*, Veröffentlichungen des Alemannischen Instituts Freiburg i. Br. 37, ed. Wolfgang Hübener (Bühl: Verlag Konkordia, 1975), 73–83.

22. Cécile Barraud, Daniel de Coppet, André Iteanu, and Raymond Jamous, *Of Relations and the Dead: Four Societies Viewed from the Angle of Their Exchanges*, trans. Stephen J. Suffern (Oxford: Berg Publishers, 1994), 33–35.

23. Hayo Vierck, "Folienkreuze als Votivgaben," in *Die Goldblattkreuᵹe des frühen Mittelalters*, 134–42; Ernst Foltz, "Technische Beobachtungen an Goldblattkreuzen," in *Die Goldblattkreuᵹe des frühen Mittelalters*, 16–17.

clerical legislation affecting the deposition of grave goods did not mean that the commemorative rite lacked spiritual significance.

Economic resources, political allegiances, ethnic customs, and ritual considerations informally shaped families' choices of what sorts of personal possessions and clothing to inter with the dead. Rather than address these matters, which were decided locally, the large majority of surviving legislation from the Merovingian period served instead to safeguard various categories of property rather than regulate burial rites. These laws also restricted the choice of locations associated with interment. We will thus turn now to a discussion of the legal evidence, since it is one of the few types of sources that provide at least normative guidelines protecting the deposition of grave goods and regulating the choice of appropriate burial places.

The Protection of Grave Goods by Lay and Religious Authorities

As discussed above, measures in Frankish legislation related to funerary custom concentrated on punishing the theft of objects from the unburied dead and furnished graves. They also sought to prevent any manner of disturbing the deceased subsequent to burial, even if such acts were not performed with malicious intent. In the eyes of jurists, the exhumation and theft of grave objects constituted heinous crimes and entailed greater indemnities than robbery of property from the living or the unburied dead (matters examined in the last chapter). While not all measures acknowledged that the main offense was larceny and not simply violation of the peace of the dead, the penalties were among the most severe in Frankish legislation. The fourteenth section of the sixth-century recension of the *Pactus legis salicae*, for instance, levied an indemnity of two hundred *solidi* against those convicted of exhuming and robbing a corpse.[24] Beyond the

---

24. "Si quis hominem mortuum effoderit vel expoliaverit, malb. tornechallis sive odocarina sunt, den. vIIIM qui fac. sol. cc culp. iud." Karl August Eckhardt, ed., *Pactus legis salicae* C6 14,9, *MGH: Leges* 4,1, rev. ed. (Hannover: Impensis bibliopolii Hahniani, 1962), 68–69.

high fine, those who did not admit their guilt faced the status of *wargus*, to be interpreted during this period as exile from the community.[25] Any persons or family members who offered hospitality to the thief before the deceased victim's relatives consented to his or her rehabilitation were to be fined fifteen *solidi*.[26] Relying heavily on its Salic predecessor and model, Ripuarian legislation punished grave robbers with a two-hundred-*solidi* penalty and *wargus* status. The guilty party was obligated to pay a reward (*dilatura*) to the person who reported the deed.[27]

Although directly influenced by measures 3,16,1 and 9,38,3 and 9,38,7 of the Theodosian Code,[28] Frankish legislation does not seem to have shared the same concerns with necromancy in conjunction with grave robbery as expressed in Roman penal laws and addressed again in eleventh-century legislation.[29] Burgundian law constituted the only exception to this view.

25. Hermann Nehlsen, "Der Grabfrevel in den germanischen Rechtsaufzeichnungen: Zugleich ein Beitrag zur Diskussion um Todesstrafe und Friedlosigkeit bei den Germanen," in *Zum Grabfrevel*, 139–46. For an opposing interpretation, see Georg Christoph von Unruh, "Wargus, Friedlosigkeit und magisch-kultische Vorstellungen bei den Germanen," *Zeitschrift der Savigny-Stiftung für Rechtsgeschichte*, germanistische Abteilung 74 (1957): 2–34.

26. "Si quis corpus iam sepultum effoderit et expoliaverit, malb. tornechale wargo sit usque de illa quae cum parentibus illius defuncti convenerit ut ad ipso pro eo rogent ut ei inter homines liceat accedere. Et quaecumque antea aut panem aut hospitalitatem dederit sive uxor sua propria, DC den. qui fac. sol. XV culp. iud. Si tamen auctor sceleris se admisisse aut effodisse probatur, malb. thornechale sunt den. VIIIM qui f. sol. CC cul. id." Eckhardt, *Pactus legis salicae* C6 55,5, 206–7.

27. "Si autem eum ex homo traxerit et expoliaverit, 200 sol. cum capitale et dilatura culpabilis iudicetur, vel wargus sit, usque ad parentibus satisfecerit." Franz Beyerle and Rudolf Buchner, eds., *Lex ribuaria* 88,2, *MGH: Leges* 3,2 (Hannover: Impensis bibliopolii Hahniani, 1954), 132; Nehlsen, "Der Grabfrevel," 135–36.

28. Theodor Mommsen and Paul M. Meyer, eds., *Codex Theodosianus libri XVI cum Constitutionibus Simmondianis et Leges novellae ad Theodosianum pertinentes* 1,2 (Berlin: Apud Weidmannos, 1905), 155–56, 495–97; Ian Wood, "Sépultures ecclésiastiques et sénatoriales dans la vallée du Rhône (400–600)," *Médiévales* 31 (1996): 16–18; Ian Wood, "The Code in Merovingian Gaul," in *The Theodosian Code*, ed. Jill Harries and Ian Wood (Ithaca: Cornell University Press, 1993), 161–69.

29. Dieter Harmening, *Superstitio: Überlieferungs- und theoriegeschichtliche Untersuchungen zur kirchlich-theologischen Aberglaubensliteratur des Mittelalters* (Berlin: Erich Schmidt Verlag, 1979), 205; Folke Ström, *On the Sacral Origins of the Germanic Death Penalties*, Kungl. Vitterhets Historie och Antikvitets Akademiens Handlingar, Del. 52 (Stockholm: Wahlström & Widstrand, 1942), 89–90.

There, grave robbery, like sorcery and adultery, provided legal grounds for a man to divorce his wife;[30] the law did not indicate, however, that a man had to denounce his wife in this manner if he did not desire a separation. No similar provisions existed for a woman who wished to divorce her husband. They appeared only in the early-sixth-century *Lex romana Burgundionum*, a code that remained more faithful to its Roman antecedent than others of the period.[31] Such accusations must have served to get rid of unwanted spouses regardless of their guilt. No Frankish king passed any comparable law, demonstrating the selective approach by which monarchs in Gaul adopted measures affecting graves from the Theodosian Code.

Laws against grave robbery promulgated in Alemannic regions differed considerably from those of the Franks.[32] So did Visigothic measures, which were among the earliest of the codes and especially harsh in the punishment of slaves who violated sepulchers: they were to be burned alive. More specific as to procedure than the Frankish corollaries, Visigothic statutes also stipulated that goods stolen from a sepulcher were to be returned, not to the deceased's grave, but to heirs.[33] Goods were thus no longer legally the property of an individual once deceased, even if interred with him or

---

30. "Si quis vero uxorem suam forte dimittere voluerit et ei potuerit vel unum de his tribus criminibus adprobare, id est adulterium, maleficium vel sepulchrorum violatricem, dimittendi eam habeat liberam postestatem; et iudex in eam, sicut debet in criminosam, proferat ex lege sententiam." Ludwig Rudolf de Salis, ed., *Leges Burgundionum* 34,3, *MGH: Leges* 2,1 (Hannover: Impensis bibliopolii Hahniani, 1892), 68; Wood, "Sépultures ecclésiastiques," 16–18; Salin, *La civilisation mérovingienne* 2, 385–86.

31. Nehlsen, "Der Grabfrevel," 118–19.

32. "Si quis liberum de terra effodierit, quidquid ibi tulerit novem geldos restituat, et 40 solidos conponat. Feminam autem cum 80 solidos conponat, si eam effodierit; res autem quas tulerit, sicut furtiva conponat." Lehmann, *Leges Alamannorum* (E.codd.B) 50,1, 108.

33. The *Lex Visigothorum* (Antiqua) 11.2,1 stated: "Si quis sepulcri violator extiterit aut mortuum expoliaverit et ei aut ornamenta vel vestimenta abstulerit, si liber hoc fecerit, libram auri coactus exolvat heredibus et que abstulit reddat. Quod si heredes non fuerint, fisco nostro cogatur inferre et preterea c flagella suscipiat. Servus vero, si hoc crimen admiserit, cc flagella suscipiat et insuper flammis ardentibus exuratur, reddistis nihilhominus cunctis, que visus est abstulisse." Karl Zeumer, ed., *Leges Visigothorum, MGH: Leges* 1 (Hannover: Impensis bibliopolii Hahniani, 1902), 403.

her. The measure thus throws into doubt the idea of the survival of the personality of the dead in Visigothic law. Kin selected objects to be buried with the dead without being constrained by whether such goods had constituted personal possessions of the deceased.[34]

A parallel for this interpretation of Visigothic views of the ownership of grave goods may be found in Cassiodorus's account of the Ostrogothic king Theodoric's sanction (507/511) of the taking of gold and silver from graves "that do not have a master."[35] Theodoric's advice did not constitute an invitation to rob all burial sites indiscriminately on the grounds that the living benefited from riches more than the dead. Rather, if one translates *dominus* as the patron or heir of the deceased, Theodoric sought to limit the appropriation of gold to the resting places of corpses lacking guardians, whether kin or spiritual, such as local clergy, who might otherwise lay claim to these goods.[36] How accurately scholars may use this example to interpret Frankish law is more difficult to ascertain, since the relevant measures in the *Pactus legis salicae* and the *Lex ribuaria* did not specify to whom the stolen goods should be returned.

By contrast, no clerical measures directed specifically against the theft of mortuary goods survive prior to the eight *Libri paenitentiales simplices* composed in the first half of the eighth century. Each penitential contained passages punishing the violation of graves and requiring confessed Chris-

---

34. Heinrich Härke, "'Warrior Graves'? The Background of the Anglo-Saxon Weapon Burial Rite," *Past and Present* 126 (1990): 22–24, 42–43; Joseph A. Tainter, "Mortuary Practices and the Study of Prehistoric Social Systems," in *Advances in Archaeological Method and Theory* 1, ed. Michael B. Schiffer (New York: Academic Press, 1978), 125.

35. "Aurum enim sepulcris iuste detrahitur ubi dominus non habetur: immo culpae genus est inutiliter abditis relinquere mortuorum, unde se vita potest sustentare viventium." Theodor Mommsen, ed., *Cassiodorus senator, Variae* 4,34, *MGH: Auctores antiquissimi* 12 (Berlin: Apud Weidmannos, 1894), 129.

36. Hermann Nehlsen has instead interpreted this case as permitting the theft of gold by a private individual. Nehlsen, "Der Grabfrevel," 112–14.

tians to do penance for five years, three of them on bread and water.[37] The *Iudicium poenitentiale* contained an equivalent measure.[38] Merovingian hagiographical works, however, occasionally referred to specific incidents involving the violation of saints' graves. Gregory of Tours, for instance, recounted that according to an inscription on the tomb of the late antique bishop Helius of Lyons, his relics miraculously clung to the rustic thief who had disturbed his grave. The saint, moreover, did not allow the man to be punished in accord with secular law.[39] His public humiliation was considered to be sufficient penalty, a lenient alternative to harsh measures in Roman legislation.[40] In a seventh-century hagiographical text commemorating the life of Gaugericus, bishop of Cambrai (d. 623/624), a thief named Launericus was caught red-handed trying to pillage his tomb. After being alerted in his sleep by a vision from the saint, one of the custodians of the church, Baudegisilus, reached the tomb in time to rescue the bishop's grave goods. Launericus fled to sanctuary in the basilica of Saint-Quentin and was eventually pardoned a few years before his death.[41] Despite their

37. These penitential measures included *Burgundense* 15, *Bobbiense* 14, *Parisiense simplex* 9, *Sletstatense* 14, *Oxoniense I* 12, *Floriacense* 15, *Hubertense* 16, and *Sangallense simplex* 23. Raymund Kottje, Ludger Körntgen, and Ulrike Spengler-Reffgen, eds., *Paenitentialia minora: Franciae et Italiae saeculi VIII–IX, CCSL* 156 (Turnhout: Typographi Brepols editores Pontificii, 1994), 25–33.

38. E. A. Lowe, "The Vatican MS. of the Gelasian Sacramentary and Its Supplement at Paris," *JTS* 27 (1926): fol. 50r, 365–66.

39. The bishop Nicetius recounted the following story to Gregory: "Nocte autem sequenti veniens quidam paganus, lapidem qui sarcofagum tegebat revolvit, erectumque contra se corpus sancti conatur spoliare. At ille extensis lacertis constrictum ad se hominem fortiter amplexatur et usque mane, populis expectantibus, tamquam constipatum loris, ita miserum brachiis detenebat. Igitur iudex loci violatorem sepulchri iubet abstrahi ac legalis poenae sententia condemnari; sed non laxabatur a sancto. Tunc intellegens voluntatem defuncti, facta iudex de vita promissione, laxatur et sic incolomis redditur." Bruno Krusch, ed., *Gregorius episcopus Turonensis, Liber in gloria confessorum* 61, in *MGH: SRM* 1,2, new ed. (Hannover: Impensis bibliopolii Hahniani, 1969), 333–34.

40. Okko Behrends, "Grabraub und Grabfrevel in römischen Recht," in *Zum Grabfrevel,* 85–86.

41. The anonymous author insinuated that Launericus's premature death was related to the despicable crime: "Contigit quadam nocte, instigante parte adversa, veniente quidam homo nomine

theme of clerical moderation, such hagiographical vignettes warned against desecrating the resting places of the saints.

In a number of cases recounted by Gregory of Tours, thieves suffered more severe retribution for stealing costly ornaments from the exterior of holy graves. At the church of Saint-Denis, a thief took the gold and bejeweled shroud covering the saint's sarcophagus. A second robbery involved the golden dove that also decorated its exterior. Although the first man returned the shroud, he died within a year of his crime. The second man was found dead at the scene. Gregory attributed both perpetrators' deaths to divine punishment.[42] He related a similar tale of efforts to steal a bejeweled cross from the top of a tomb. The would-be thief fell into a deep sleep and thus could not complete the crime.[43] Unlike the standard remedy of secular measures against grave robbery, clerical descriptions of comparable acts did not refer to royal intervention. This marked reticence likely stemmed from fear that a king might benefit from such a precedent to interfere in bishops' or abbots' households. Clerical leaders and saints actively defended the contents of their tombs against plunderers just as their lay contemporaries did, but they did so independently of the monarch.

Heavy penalties for grave theft and the descriptions of the more lavishly appointed graves of the Merovingian period make it impossible to ignore

Launericus, nocte in ipsa basilica ingressus, sepulchrum beati pontificis [Gaugerici] furtu sceleris expoliavit. Apparuit beatus pontifex per visionem custodi, cuius sollicitudo de ipsa basilica habebatur, nomine Baudegisilo. . . . Continuo ipse custos surrexit a somno et in eclesiam secundum visionem quam viderat velociter introivit, ad beati pontificis sepulchrum accessit, latronem ipsum invenit; retentis spoliis, latronem ad basilicam sancti Quintini fugere permisit: excussatus exinde egressus est et paucos postea vixit annos." Bruno Krusch, ed., *Vita Gaugerici episcopi Camaracensis* 15, in *MGH: SRM* 3 (Hannover: Impensis bibliopolii Hahniani, 1896), 657–58; Karl Heinrich Krüger, "Grabraub in erzählenden Quellen des frühen Mittelalters," in *Zum Grabfrevel*, 171.

42. Bruno Krusch, ed., *Gregorius episcopus Turonensis, Liber in gloria martyrum* 71, in *MGH: SRM* 1,2, 85–86.

43. Bruno Krusch, ed., *Gregorius episcopus Turonensis, Liber de virtutibus S. Juliani* 20, in *MGH: SRM* 1,2, 573. See also Bruno Krusch, ed., *Vita Eligii episcopi Noviomagensis* 2,65, in *MGH: SRM* 4 (Hannover: Impensis bibliopolii Hahniani, 1902), 733.

the considerable resources invested by heirs in funerals. Although the deceased's kin likely did not purchase or acquire goods specifically for burial, they deposited with the deceased desirable artifacts that they might otherwise have kept for themselves.[44] While the placement of particular grave goods in the sepulcher was in some cases sentimental, it also brought recognition of a family's identity among contemporaries. These objects helped to define the relationship of the deceased to the community now that he or she had entered the afterlife.[45] No surviving Merovingian records, however, indicate legislative efforts to restrict such goods to particular status or ethnic groups.[46]

Most important, the deposition of grave goods theoretically rendered moveable property physically inaccessible to the living after the funerary ceremony had come to a close. Krzysztof Pomian has argued generally that objects such as grave goods or offerings were rarely intended to reenter regular economic circulation. In his estimation, such violations would only have been committed in dire circumstances.[47] Yet did survivors of the deceased truly abandon all hopes of regaining buried artifacts? Judging from the regularity with which early medieval sepulchers were violated, valued mortuary objects remained too attractive to be forgotten by families who owned them.

44. Ross Samson, "Social Structures from *Reihengräber:* Mirror or Mirage?" *Scottish Archaeological Review* 4 (1987): 116–26.

45. Bonnie Effros, "Beyond Cemetery Walls: Early Medieval Funerary Topography and Christian Salvation," *EME* 6 (1997): 1–23.

46. Walter Pohl, "Telling the Difference: Signs of Ethnic Identity," in *Strategies of Distinction: The Construction of Ethnic Communities, 300–700,* TRW 2, ed. Walter Pohl and Helmut Reimitz (Leiden: E. J. Brill, 1998), 17–22, 27–61; František Graus, "Sozialgeschichtliche Aspekte der Hagiographie der Merowinger- und Karolingerzeit: Die Viten der Heiligen des südalemannischen Raumes und die sogenannten Adelsheiligen," in *Mönchtum, Episkopat und Adel zur Gründungszeit des Klosters Reichenau,* Vorträge und Forschungen 20, ed. Arno Borst (Sigmaringen: Jan Thorbecke Verlag, 1974), 161–63.

47. Krzysztof Pomian, *Collectors and Curiosities: Paris and Venice, 1500–1800,* trans. Elizabeth Wiles-Portier (Cambridge: Polity Press, 1987), 11–13.

The lucrative nature of grave robbery must have accounted for the popularity of the practice despite the risks and penalties it involved. Gregory of Tours suggested that Duke Gunthramn Boso may have developed an interest in a childless relative's lavish burial furnishings after participating in her funeral at Metz circa 589. Although she had been buried with numerous grave goods, many of them possibly former possessions, Boso may have desired them whether or not they rightfully belonged to him. He thus sent his servants secretly to plunder the contents of her sarcophagus.[48] The undertaking did not turn out happily. Monks who had witnessed the robbery in the church reported the crime to the king. Following the scandal's disclosure, the duke's servants fearfully returned the stolen goods by placing them on the monastery's altar.[49] Childebert II, who did not favor Gunthramn Boso, charged him with grave robbery as defined by Salic law. After two years as a fugitive, Boso was executed by the king.[50]

Although theft of grave goods merited severe punishment, it remained very tempting. Aggrieved heirs could theoretically have authorized or even secretly perpetrated the grave robberies for which we have evidence today. Attempts to make sense of the discrepancy between archaeological evidence for the frequency of thefts and the severity of the penalties have

---

48. Gunthramn Boso knew of the wealth in the grave from his participation in his female relative's funeral: "Discedentibus autem multis e civitate cum episcopo et praesertim senioris urbis cum duci. . . ." Bruno Krusch, ed., *Gregorius episcopus Turonensis, Libri historiarum X* 8,21, in *MGH: SRM* 1,1, rev. ed. (Hannover: Impensis bibliopolii Hahniani, 1951), 387–88.

49. "Ante paucus autem dies mortua propinqua uxoris eius [Bosonis Guntchramni] sine filiis, in basilicam urbis Metinsis sepulta est cum grandibus ornamentis et multo auro. . . . venerunt pueri Bosonis Guntchramni ad basilica, in qua mulier erat sepulta. Et ingressi, conclusis super se osteis, detexerunt sepulchrum, tollentes omnia ornamenta corporis defuncti, quae reperire potuerant. . . . Sed timentes [pueri], ne, adprehensi in via, diversis subegerentur poenis, regressi sunt ad basilicam. Posueruntque quidem res super altarium." Krusch, *Gregorius episcopus Turonensis, Libri historiarum X* 8,21, 387–88.

50. Guy Halsall, "Female Status and Power in Early Merovingian Central Austrasia: The Burial Evidence," *EME* 5 (1996): 1–2.

not been entirely satisfactory. Albert Genrich has viewed such attitudes toward these burial customs as somewhat hypocritical, but has anachronistically interpreted the objects left behind by thieves as an attempt to appease the dead.[51] Heiko Steuer has offered an alternative interpretation of rampant grave robbery: he attributes such incidents to the financial strains resulting from a tradition that was no longer meaningful to participants.[52] Yet, he assumes that disenchantment with grave goods stemmed from deeper insight into Christianity, or "spiritualization," among early medieval peoples, a hypothesis not easily defended. As a consequence, reasons for the heightened determination of individuals in the sixth century to seize funerary objects in the face of harsh penalties remain unclear. Whatever the cause, as the level of grave robbery steadily grew in the Merovingian kingdoms and adjacent regions, it contributed to waning interest in the deposition of grave goods and the search for more effective means of commemorating the dead.

Archaeological evidence suggests that stealing from cemeteries escalated in frequency from the first third of the sixth century until the first half of the seventh century. At Köln-Müngersdorf, a cemetery active from 500 to 700, Fritz Fremersdorf observed that 46 of 149 graves (30.87 percent) were pillaged not long after being filled.[53] In his survey of *Grabfrevel,* Helmut Roth has estimated that an average of 39 percent of the graves

---

51. Genrich, "Grabbeigaben und germanisches Recht," 220–21.

52. Heiko Steuer, *Frühgeschichtliche Sozialstrukturen in Mitteleuropa: Eine Analyse der Auswertungsmethoden des archäologischen Quellenmaterials,* Abhandlungen der Akademie der Wissenschaften in Göttingen, philologisch-historische Klasse, 3d ser., no. 128 (Göttingen: Vandenhoeck & Ruprecht, 1982), 498–99. No evidence for such an economic motive for abandoning this rite exists in England, where a similar decline in the use of grave goods took place. Heinrich Härke, "Early Saxon Weapon Burials: Frequencies, Distributions, and Weapon Combinations," in *Weapons and Warfare in Anglo-Saxon England,* Oxford University Committee for Archaeology 21, ed. Sonia Chadwick Hawkes (Oxford: Oxford University Committee for Archaeology, 1989), 49–52, 55–59.

53. Fritz Fremersdorf, *Das fränkische Reihengräberfeld Köln-Müngersdorf* 1, Germanische Denkmäler der Völkerwanderungszeit 6 (Berlin: Walter de Gruyter, 1955), 18–19, 29–31.

investigated were robbed by contemporaries during the Merovingian period. Among what he describes as Frankish inhumations, the figure was 56 percent. By the second half of the seventh century, the practice had decreased in proportion with the steady drop in the use of burial goods in the Merovingian kingdoms.[54] The reliability of these figures is nonetheless not altogether certain, however, since some of the disorder characterized as robbery may have actually been caused by the collapse of wooden coffins. Yet, even half the number of documented thefts would indicate marked changes in attitudes toward grave goods during these two centuries.

Heiko Steuer has additionally observed that fewer graves were pillaged in small cemeteries than in large ones. He has thus noted that members of relatively small communities who buried their dead at a particular site must have been able to detect and prevent the theft of grave goods from the deceased of kin and neighbors. In sizeable communities, where more social interaction occurred under the cloak of anonymity, thieves were more difficult to track. Perhaps the incidence of grave robbery increased when rival communities shared a single cemeterial site or attacked those of their competitors. Even in large necropoleis, however, burial theft seems to have remained subject to a degree of social control, since thieves normally left some of the most well-endowed graves untouched.[55] Bullough thus posits that selective pillaging may have been motivated by more severe punishments for stealing from elite burials.[56] The incidence of grave robbery was highest both in regions with unstable populations facing catastrophe and in areas where powerful local nobility made it impossible for dependent families to protect their burial places. In the latter scenario,

54. Helmut Roth, "Archäologische Beobachtungen zum Grabfrevel im Merowingerreich," in *Zum Grabfrevel*, 60–65.

55. Steuer, *Frühgeschichtliche Sozialstrukturen*, 499. Alternatively, these unpillaged graves may point to the difficulty of systematically robbing a complete cemetery that was used over the course of multiple generations and did not offer thieves the advantage of headstones to guide their excavation.

56. Bullough, "Burial, Community," 192–94.

Steuer has linked disregard for burial customs to consolidation of the manorial system.[57]

It is necessary to supplement Steuer's hypothesis with the observation that thieves typically appear to have worked soon after the inhumation of a corpse or at least at a site with which they were familiar. Many grave robbers must have known at least the sex of the interred individual even before they began to dig, since they tended to excavate female graves only in the area near the head and neck, while they explored the length of male burials for armament. By limiting their excavations to the specific portions of the sepulchers that they recognized would produce the richest yields, they wasted little time in their endeavors.[58] These activities were thus symptomatic not only of the breakdown of the social fabric but also of less concern with or respect for the functions of grave goods.

Helmut Roth and Ursula Koch have additionally noted that thieves in Merovingian Gaul as well as further east consistently avoided certain goods, including amulets, rings, ornaments inscribed with Christian symbols, less valuable weapons such as arrow tips and lances, and single brooches from sets of four.[59] Some of these artifacts may still have had recognizable religious and amuletic significance, serving to identify the deceased as a Christian and protect his or her body from harm. If so, this practice resulted

57. Heiko Steuer, "Grabraub, archäologisches," in *Reallexikon der germanischen Altertumskunde* 12, ed. Johannes Hoops, 2d ed. (Berlin: Walter de Gruyter, 1998), 516–23; Heiko Steuer, "Archaeology and History: Proposals on the Social Structure of the Merovingian Kingdom," in *The Birth of Europe: Archaeology and Social Development in the First Millennium A.D.*, Analecta romana instituti danici supplementum 16, ed. Klavs Randsborg (Rome: L'Erma di Bretschneider, 1989), 116–20.

58. Roth, "Archäologische Beobachtungen," 54–58, 65–67; Genrich, "Grabbeigaben und germanisches Recht," 219–20; Joachim H. Schleifring, "Antiker Grabraub: Ausgrabungsbefunde als Nachweis von Grabraub und Grabfrevel," *Das Rheinische Landesmuseum Bonn: Berichte aus der Arbeit des Museums* 3 (1991): 33–36.

59. Helmut Roth, "Bemerkungen zur Totenberaubung während der Merowingerzeit," *AK* 7 (1977): 287–90; Ursula Koch, "Beobachtungen zum frühen Christentum an den fränkischen Gräberfeldern von Bargen und Berghausen in Nordbaden," *AK* 4 (1974): 259–66; Roth, "Archäologische Beobachtungen," 68–73.

from the fact that Christians in the West continued to attach great significance to the physical well-being of the dead. Although the theological
teachings of Augustine had minimized the importance of the funerary
treatment of the Christian faithful's mortal remains, Yvette Duval has
argued that the general population did not share this view even in late
antiquity. Augustine's belief that the mutilated and burned relics of martyrs
would experience complete bodily resurrection did not become widespread.[60] Thieves may thus have purposely left behind in plundered graves
Christian-inspired objects and those with amuletic functions, since these
items protected the material remains of the faithful until the Last Judgment.
They seem to have respected the role of objects with *Chi-Rho* insignia or
inscriptions, which were intended to identify the deceased as a Christian
until the time of the reunion of spirit with flesh, more than other sorts of
grave goods. Yet, the presence of simple decorative motifs such as crosses
does not necessarily represent proof of Christian belief, since those
designs must have been popular regardless of the faith of those who
employed them.[61]

Other items left behind by grave robbers included those of relatively
little worth, such as arrows, and objects of unwieldy size, such as lances.
That such goods remained in plundered sepulchers should come as no
great surprise in light of the hazards faced by thieves in these ventures: the
steep penalties for such crimes precluded any unnecessary risks. The last
category of goods left by thieves, single brooches from sets of four, how-

60. "Neque istud pia fides nimium reformidat, tenens praedictum nec absumentes bestias resurrecturis corporibus obfuturas, quorum capillus capitis non peribit." Gustave Combes, ed., *De cura
gerenda pro mortuis*, in *Oeuvres de Saint Augustin*, 1st ser., pt. 2, Bibliothèque augustinienne (Paris:
Desclée de Brouwer et Cie., 1937), 390–91; Yvette Duval, *Auprès des saints corps et âme:
L'inhumation "ad sanctos" dans la chrétienté d'Orient et d'Occident du III* et VII* siècle* (Paris: Études
augustiniennes, 1988), 3–26.

61. Alain Dierkens, "Interprétation critique des symboles chrétiens sur les objets d'époque
mérovingienne," in *L'art des invasions en Hongrie et en Wallonie: Actes du colloque tenu au Musée
royal de Mariemont du 9 au 11 avril 1979*, Monographie du Musée royal de Mariemont 6 (Morlanwelz:
Musée royal de Mariemont, 1991), 110–16.

ever, invites a number of methodological questions. Roth and Koch assert that they were able to determine that the deceased whose tombs were robbed had been buried with complete sets of four brooches. Their conclusions appear to be based upon the presumption that contemporary costumes were largely identical and that corpses attired in clothing were always buried with four brooches, thus making it possible to predict what was "missing." The accuracy of such expectations cannot be substantiated conclusively.

Likewise, the prevalence of grave robbery in a particular cemetery cannot be used to propose dates by which missionaries succeeded in Christianizing the burial customs of local inhabitants. Along these lines, Helmut Roth has argued that, "[d]uring the Merovingian period, a distinctive sort of grave robbery first made its appearance, a development that can only be explained as a consequence of the knowledge and further spread of Christianity and its ideas. Because a general familiarity with Christian belief systems, in which grave goods for the dead had no more place, caused these pagan practices and imagination to lose their unique efficacy."[62] This thesis rests exclusively upon a general conception of grave goods as a non-Christian practice. As we have seen, however, surviving clerical texts that touched upon funerary rites did not express any negative attitudes toward burial dress, nor did they encourage theft. No evidence exists, furthermore, that burial objects were linked to the destination of the spirit in the afterlife. The only material goods mentioned in visionary literature were linen garments in which souls of saints were occasionally depicted, and it is not clear that they were viewed as the actual ones in which they had been buried or simply represented an analogy for their purity. The acceptance of the practice of grave goods by lay Christians and clerics is best substantiated through their legal efforts to protect grave goods and the integrity of Christians' bodies until the final resurrection.

---

62. Roth, "Archäologische Beobachtungen," 74.

Defense of the Resting Places of the Dead

Among early medieval clerics and lay officials, attention to the violation of graves went beyond prevention of and restitution for the robbery of mortuary goods (described above). Written sources indicate that besides defending from pillage artifactual material placed in sepulchers, early medieval leaders were concerned to protect the human remains of Christians. Late antique and early medieval Christians in the West attached great significance to the physical resting places of the deceased.[63] In the Novels of Theodosius and Valentinian Augustus of 447, for instance, laws addressed fears that dishonor to or destruction of burial places disturbed the peace of the dead.[64] Arthur Nock consequently proposed that concern with the violation of the tombs was stronger in the Near East than in Rome. In the West, by contrast, legislation against grave robbery was based on a defense of human dignity rather than a fear of sacrilege.[65]

Occasionally, early medieval epigraphical anathemas from the Italian peninsula testified to the belief that the failure to bury a body properly contributed to the likelihood that the individual would not be resurrected at the Last Judgment.[66] Directed against violation of the integrity of the deceased's resting place, such inscriptions sought the protection of both the saints and the living. On the joint gravestone of Guntelda (*famula Christi*), her son, and grandson, from the last decade of the sixth century at Como, for instance, the epitaph proclaimed: "I beseech all of you

---

63. Combes, *De cura gerenda pro mortuis* 4, 390–91; Duval, *Auprès des saints*, 3–26.

64. "Quis enim nescit quietos sollicitari funestis ausibus manes et horribilem violentiam defunctorum cineribus inferri?" Mommsen and Meyer, *Leges novellae* 23,1–9, in *Codex Theodosianus libri XVI* 2, 114–17.

65. Arthur Darby Nock, "Tomb Violations and Pontifical Law," in *Essays on Religion and the Ancient World* 2, ed. Zeph Stewart (Cambridge: Harvard University Press, 1972), 531–33.

66. At the Roman cemetery of St. Agnese, one epitaph read: "male pereat, insepultus / iaceat, non resurgat, / cum Iuda partem habeat, / si quis sepulcrum / hunc violarit." Ernst Diehl, ed., *ILCV* 2,3845, new ed. (Dublin: Weidmann, 1970), 291.

Christians and you, the guardian blessed Julian, on account of God and the feared day of Judgment, that it never be permitted that this sepulcher be violated but rather that it should be preserved until the end of the world."[67] Other stones, such as an inscription at St. Vitalis, Ravenna, from after the sixth century, warned that any violations of the sepulcher would be punished with the penalty meted out to Judas: the perpetrator would not be resurrected at the Last Judgment.[68]

Clerics and lay Christians in early medieval Gaul, by contrast, do not appear to have voiced such concerns as readily as those in Italy in late antiquity and the early Middle Ages. Although Pope John II (d. 535) sent a letter condemning the profanation of graves to Caesarius of Arles (d. 542), who subsequently communicated to other Gallic bishops the message that the disturbance of human remains was thenceforth to incur the severe penalty of excommunication, this legislation is not known to have made a measurable impact.[69] Curses were likewise less frequently inscribed on Merovingian epitaphs. Since the majority of approximately 2,500 surviving burial inscriptions from Gaul, with the exception of those from Trier, come from regions south of the Loire, areas in which stone tombs were frequently reused by Christians as early as the fourth century, this

---

67. The latter part of this inscription stated: "Adiuro vus omnes, X̄p̄iani, et te, / custude beati Iuliani, p(er) d(e)o et p(er) tre / menda die iudicii, ut hunc sepulcrum / nunquam ullo tempore violetur, / sed coseruet(ur) usque ad finem mundi, / ut posim sine impedimento in vita / redire, cum venerit, qui iudicaturus / est vivos et mortuos." Diehl, *ILCV* 2,3863, 295. Münz, "Anathema und Verwünschungen auf altchristlichen Monumenten," *Annalen des Vereins für nassauische Alterthumskunde und Geschichtsforschung* 14 (1875): 172–73; Duval, *Auprès des saints,* 179.

68. "✝ in n̄. patris et filii et spiritum s̄c̄i hic / requiescit in pace Dominicus prb. de / serviens basilice s̄c̄i Vitalis marty / ris. et si quis hunc sepulchrum vi.olave / rit, partem abea(t) cum Iuda traditorem / et in die iudicii non resurgat partem suam / cum infidelibus ponam." Diehl, *ILCV* 2,3850, 292.

69. "[V]iolatoris vero sepulchri lecit augustorum principum capitaliter damnit sententia, tamen, si qui in hoc facinus fuerint reperti superstites, ab eclesiastica communione priventur; quia nefas est, ut eis christianorum non obserretur consorcium, qui temeritatis auso humatorum ceneris reddere praesumpserint inquietus." W. Gundlach, ed., *Epistolae arelatenses genuinae* 35 in *MGH: Epistolae* 3 (Berlin: Apud Weidmannos, 1892), 54.

attitude is not surprising. Surviving anathemas were written at a relatively late date, such as on the right post of the entryway into the Hypogeum of Dunes at Poitiers.[70] Such harshly worded warnings sought, as did their counterparts in Italy, to protect the dead. These admonitions against disturbing the integrity of the graves and the peace of the dead should also be understood as including reference to the theft of funerary goods and destruction of burial monuments.

Although the application of Frankish legislation was evidently haphazard, it made clear that even in more benign circumstances than grave robbery, great care was to be taken with existing graves. Salic measures likely took their immediate cue from contemporary ecclesiastical measures rather than the Theodosian Code, since the latter focused on the spoliation of stone and on pollution resulting from contact between the living and the dead.[71] The *Pactus legis salicae* specified that during the construction of a church the peace of any buried remains was not to be disturbed.[72] This law was enacted primarily against those who sought to reuse funerary stone or dislodge graves in the course of building a new church on an old foundation.[73] It may have also constituted an attempt to exclude the graves of non-Christian ancestors from new basilicas. The *Lex ribuaria*, which did not mention the circumstances of the disturbance, also forbade

70. The final line, improved by Carol Heitz, reads: "SI QUIS. QUI. NON. HIC. / AMAT.ADORARE. D(omi)N(u)M IH(eus)M XP(istu)M. ET DISTRUIT. OPERA / ISTA SIT. ANATHEMA / MARANTHA / USQUID. IN SEMPITERNUM." Carol Heitz, "L'Hypogée de Mellebaude à Poitiers," in *L'inhumation privilégiée*, 91–96; Edmond Le Blant, ed., *Nouveau recueil* 247 (Paris: Imprimerie nationale, 1892), 257–59.

71. Mommsen and Meyer, *Codex Theodosianus libri XVI* 1,2, at 9,17,1–5, 463–65; Bonnie Effros, "Monuments and Memory: Repossessing Ancient Remains in Early Medieval Gaul," in *Topographies of Power in the Early Middle Ages*, TRW 6, ed. Mayke de Jong and Frans Theuws (Leiden: E. J. Brill, 2001), 103–10.

72. This measure was not included in the earliest recensions of the Salic code, but only in those dating from later in the Merovingian period: "Si quis basilicas expoliaverit desuper hominem mortuum, malb. chereotasino sol. XXX culp. iud." Eckhardt, *Pactus legis salicae* C6 55,6, 209; Salin, *La civilisation mérovingienne* 2, 368; Paul Rops, "Les 'basilicae' des cimetières francs," *Annales de la Société archéologique de Namur* 19 (1890): 3.

73. Nehlsen, "Der Grabfrevel," 161.

the exhumation of any deceased. It sanctioned an extraordinarily high fine of two hundred *solidi* for such violations.[74]

Eighth-century penitential measures repeated such concerns. As mentioned above, the *Iudicium poenitentiale* sentenced those guilty of unspecified grave violation to five years of penance, three of which were to be spent on bread and water.[75] Because penitential penalties were stipulated well after grave goods had ceased to be commonly used, however, these punishments did not constitute a direct response to the theft of mortuary objects. Instead, they served primarily to defend corpses from general violation.[76] These measures thus differed significantly from provisions in the eighth-century penitential attributed to Theodore of Canterbury, since the Anglo-Saxon text specifically sanctioned the expulsion of pagan remains from Christian churches.[77] Preventing the integration of pagan and Christian burial places among the recently converted population represented an issue of more immediate concern among clerics in Anglo-Saxon England than in contemporary Gaul.[78]

Pre-eighth-century legislation protecting remains of the dead also differed from measures passed during the Carolingian era. Only in the ninth century, when increasing numbers of Christians were being buried in

74. "Si quis mortuum effodire praesumpserit, quater quinquagenos solid. multetur aut cum 12 iuret." Beyerle and Buchner, *Lex ribuaria* 55(54),2, 104; Nehlsen, "Der Grabfrevel," 135.

75. "Siquis sepulcru violaverit v an pent III ex his in pan et aq." Lowe, "The Vatican MS.," fol. 50r, 365–66; Salin, *La civilisation mérovingienne* 2,210, 387. This legislation is virtually identical to the eight *Libri paenitentiales simplices: Burgundense* 15, *Bobbiense* 14, *Parisiense simplex* 9, *Sletstatense* 14, *Oxoniense I* 12, *Floriacense* 15, *Hubertense* 16, and *Sangallense simplex* 23. Kottje, Körntgen, and Spengler-Reffgen, *Paenitentialia minora*, 25–28.

76. Steuer, "Grabraub, archäologisches," 516–23.

77. "[4.] In ecclesia in qua mortuorum infidelium sepeliuntur sanctificare altare non licet sed si apta videtur ad consecrandum inde evulsa et rasis vel lotis lignis eius reaedificetur. [5.] Si autem consecratum prius fuit missas in eo caelebrare licet si religiosi ibi sepulti sunt. Si vero paganus sit mundare et iactare foras melius est." Paul Willem Finsterwalder, ed., *Die Canones Theodori Cantuariensis und ihre Überlieferungsformen* U2,1,4–5 (Weimar: Hermann Böhlaus Nachfolger, Hof-Buchdruckerei, 1929), 311–12.

78. Effros, "Monuments and Memory," 97–98, 116–18.

church graveyards, did clerics voice greater opposition to the violation of the resting places of the deceased. They then outlined more clearly which activities were forbidden with respect to the exhumation of corpses. In his capitulary of 857, for instance, Hincmar of Reims (d. 882) portrayed the removal or transfer of Christian remains from existing sepulchers as unacceptable under any circumstances, including translations authorized by priests. Even if approached by the family of the deceased, priests were not to disturb the bodies of the faithful in any manner.[79] This very strict approach, which was likely not widely implemented, nonetheless suggests that clerics, rather than the families of the deceased, had by this time gained more control over the disposition of burial. This legislation also resembled the Theodosian Code 9,17,7, which forbade the movement of bodies and particularly the transfer of the holy dead.[80] Hincmar likened the disinterment of human remains to casting a person from his or her home,[81] and explained why such activities were detestable: "[I]t is a sacrilege to throw a body out of its sepulcher in an undevout and irreligious manner on account of selfishness. That is where someone resting in peace must await the Lord's call, so that he may be resurrected at the coming of the judgment of the just."[82] In his eyes, a body was ideally to remain undis-

---

79. "Ipse tamen sacerdos, memor ordinis sui, provideat et congruam cuique sepulturam, et ne scandalum, quantum vitari potest, fiat suis parochianis. Et provideat, sicut de ministerio suo et coram Deo et coram saeculo vult gaudere, ut nullius Christiani corpus de sepulcro suo ejiciatur, et nec sepulcra confringantur, vel caminatae sicut solent inde fiant." Jacques-Paul Migne, ed., *Hincmarus archiepiscopus Rhemensis, Capitula synodica* 3,2, in *PL* 125, 2d ser. (Paris: Apud editorem in via dicta d'Amboise, 1852), 794; Salin, *La civilisation mérovingienne* 2,209, 387.

80. "Humatum corpus nemo ad alterum locum transferat; nemo martyrem distrahat, nemo mercetur. Habeant vero in potestate, si quolibet in loco sanctorum est aliquis conditus, pro eius veneratione quod martyrium vocandum sit addant quod voluerint fabricarum." Mommsen and Meyer, *Codex Theodosianus libri XVI* 1,2, 466.

81. "[Q]uia sicut crudele est quemquam de domo sua expellere, et misericordiae opus est, egenum et vagum iuxta Dominicum dictum in domum recipere." Migne, *Hincmarus archiepiscopi Rhemensis, Capitula synodica* 3,2, 794.

82. "[I]ta sacrilegum est, corpus indevote ac irreligiose propter cupiditatem a sepulcro eiicere, ubi quisque Dominicam vocationem, ut in adventu iusti iudicis resurgat, in pace quiescens debuerat exspectare." Migne, *Hincmarus archiepiscopus Rhemensis, Capitula synodica* 3,2, 794.

turbed until the Last Judgment regardless of the wishes of kin, even if they desired to create a family burial plot. The expulsion of a baptized corpse from a grave thus constituted sacrilegious disregard for an individual's well-being in the afterlife.[83]

During the Merovingian period, by contrast, authorities addressed the protection of not only the bodies but the tombs themselves. Concern about would-be violators was especially pronounced among the elite who desired to inter their dead in stone sarcophagi. Particularly in southern Gaul, where such practice had traditionally served as a form of privileged burial, the shortage and expense of tombs grew severe following the fifth century.[84] Not only were sarcophagi of the Roman era appropriated for reuse by early medieval Christians and altered as necessary, but more recent tombs and epitaphs were also reused.[85] These circumstances and the wish to be buried near loved ones led some kin groups in northeastern Gaul, too, to inter their dead in the existing graves of family or possibly other community members rather than deprive them of a desirable burial place. Such was the case, for instance, at the Merovingian necropolis of Lavoye (Meuse), where Bailey Young has documented multiple burials at individual grave sites.[86] In some cemeteries in Burgundy, Normandy, and the region of Paris, as many as three layers of stone or plaster tombs have been found stacked atop one another.[87]

83. Luce Pietri, "Les sépultures privilégiées en Gaule d'après les sources littéraires," in *L'inhumation privilégiée*, 134; Duval, *Auprès des saints*, 35 ff.; Effros, "Beyond Cemetery Walls," 6–8.

84. René Louis and Gilbert-Robert Delehaye, "Le sarcophage mérovingien considéré sous ses aspects économiques et sociaux," in *Actes du 105ᵉ Congrès national des Sociétés savantes, Caen 1980: La Normandie: Études archéologiques*, Section d'archéologie et histoire de l'art (Paris: Comité des travaux historiques et scientifiques, 1983), 280–84; Nehlsen, "Der Grabfrevel," 122 ff. See Chapter III below for a discussion of sarcophagi and the reuse of epitaphs.

85. See, for example, Nancy Gauthier, ed., *RICG* 1,13 (Paris: Éditions du CNRS, 1975), 136–39; Diehl, *ILCV* 1,149, 39.

86. Michel Fixot, "Les inhumations privilégiées en Provence," in *L'inhumation privilégiée*, 118–19; Bailey K. Young, *Quatre cimetières mérovingiens de l'Est de la France: Lavoye, Dieue-sur-Meuse, Mezières-Manchester et Mazerny*, BAR International Series 208 (Oxford: BAR, 1984), 27–28.

87. Salin, *La civilisation mérovingienne* 2, 187–89.

Families could also elect to move or dispose of remains discovered in confiscated tombs, sepulchers lined with stones, or coffins. Alain Dierkens has observed twenty double and ten triple burials at Tombois (Franchimont, Namur). Some required the superpositioning of bodies over one another, while others involved the removal of remaining bones to a corner of the grave in order to accommodate a new corpse.[88] At Audun-le-Tiche, approximately 45 percent of the graves were reused.[89] Some families may have removed only selected bones from graves so that they could be buried with relations at another site in the same or a more distant cemetery.[90] Although reoccupation has been observed most frequently when the deceased was buried in a stone or wood structure, the reuse of plain earth graves has also been documented in cemeteries in which this custom was predominant, such as at Dieue-sur-Meuse.[91] Even in a grave lacking structural protection, reburial appears to have offered some advantage over digging a new sepulcher.[92]

As reinhumation and multiple interments became more common in the sixth century, they started to attract the attention of ecclesiastical authorities at councils held south of the Loire. The fifteenth canon of the Synod of Auxerre (561–605) forbade adding bodies to existing graves.[93] Likewise,

---

88. Alain Dierkens, "A propos des cimetières mérovingiens de Franchimont (Belgique, Province de Namur)," in *Actes du 105ᵉ Congrès national des Sociétés savantes, Caen 1980*, 304.

89. Alain Simmer, *Le cimetière mérovingien d'Audun-le-Tiche (Moselle)*, Association française d'archéologie mérovingienne, Mémoire 2 (Paris: Éditions Errance, 1988), 97–101.

90. Joël Serralongue and Cécile Treffort, "Inhumations secondaires et ossements erratiques de la nécropole de Combes, à Yvoire (Haute-Savoie): Analyse archéologique et questions historiques," *Pages d'archéologie médiévale en Rhône-Alpes* 2 (1995): 106–10.

91. Young, *Quatre cimetières*, 46.

92. Michel Colardelle, *Sépulture et traditions funéraires du Vᵉ au XIIIᵉ siècle après J.-C. dans les campagnes des Alpes françaises du nord (Drôme, Isère, Savoie, Haute-Savoie)* (Grenoble: Publication de la Société alpine de documentation et de recherche en archéologie historique, 1983), 48.

93. "Non licet mortuum super mortuum mitti." De Clercq, *Concilia Galliae*, 267.

participants in the Second Council of Mâcon (585) proclaimed in canon seventeen that if such a violation had been perpetrated, the family responsible for the care of the tomb would be permitted to eject the newly deposited corpse from it.[94] In the eyes of religious authorities, both the positioning of bodies over one another and the disposal of older remains were unacceptable. Nevertheless, since the latter practice was likely against the will of the tomb's owner, the ecclesiastical council stipulated that laying one body on top of another in a sepulcher constituted a less reprehensible violation than ridding a tomb of the remains of its current occupant without the permission of those responsible for it.[95]

The integrity of an individual's grave reflected the well-being of the deceased's soul and signaled the status of surviving kin. Regarding the former, some perceived the souls of multiple occupants of single tombs or mass burials as having suffered misfortune. This was certainly the case in the murder and mass burial of the Irish monk Foillan and his companions on 30 October 652. According to the anonymous author of the *Additamentum Nivialense de Fuilano,* after robbers killed the monks, their four bodies were thrown into a single ditch in a pig sty.[96] Just as today, willful disrespect for the dead constituted a conscious violation of their peace in the afterlife. The inability to identify the precise location of a deceased rela-

94. "Quod si factum fuerit, secundum legum auctoritatem superimposita corpora de eisdem tumulis reiactentur." De Clercq, *Concilia Galliae,* 246; Nehlsen, "Der Grabfrevel," 122; Duval, *Auprès des saints,* 37.

95. "Comperimus multos necdum marcidata mortuorum membra sepulchra reserare et mortuos suos superimponere vel aliorum, quod nefas ist, mortuis suis relegiosa loca usurpare, sine voluntate scilicet domini sepulchrorum." De Clercq, *Concilia Galliae,* 246; Nehlsen, "Der Grabfrevel," 122; Salin, *La civilisation mérovingienne* 2,181, 375.

96. "Sed beato viro [Fuilano] Deo gratias clamante, ne vox illius diutius audiretur, venerandum illius capud amputarunt atque in proximo tecto, ubi grex porcorum commanebat, facta fossa nuda ac dilacerata sepelierunt impiae IIIIor corpora [de Fuillano et fratribus suis] in unum." Bruno Krusch, ed., *Additamentum Nivialense de Fuilano,* in *MGH: SRM* 4 (Hannover: Impensis bibliopolii Hahniani, 1902), 450–51.

tion, moreover, implied that family members might not be able—or, for that matter, feel compelled—to pay respects to the deceased.[97]

From its earliest recension in the early sixth century, the *Pactus legis salicae* contained more severe penalties than did ecclesiastical councils for disturbing the deceased by burying additional bodies in the same sepulcher. In particular, Salic law instructed that thirty-five *solidi* would be forfeited by perpetrators engaged in the illicit action, whether the deceased lay in a wood coffin or stone sarcophagus.[98] The expulsion of a baptized corpse from its burial place constituted sacrilege, since it entailed absolute disregard for the soul of that individual in the afterlife. This legislation also addressed the significant repercussions of grave violations for the living: these acts violated the honor of the family of the deceased. With both of these factors in mind, the harsh sentence of *wargus* enumerated in the *Pactus legis salicae* meant that those who disrupted the integrity of a sepulcher or committed related crimes theoretically faced complete exile from the Christian community. Authorities viewed this high penalty as warranted by the serious circumstances in which the acts occurred.[99] It is unknown, however, how effectively these measures were enforced.

Preserving Christian Bodies for the Resurrection

In accord with apparent disregard for legal measures protecting the integrity of sepulchers is the relatively rare expression of such concerns in

---

97. Pietri, "Les sépultures privilégiées," 134–35. See Gregory of Tours's account of mass burials that resulted from the plague in Clermont-Ferrand in 571. Krusch, *Gregorius episcopus Turonensis, Libri historiarum X* 4,31, 166–68.

98. "Si quis hominem mortuum super alterum in naupho aut in petra miserit, malb. edulcus sol. XXXV culp. iud." Eckhardt, *Pactus legis salicae* C6 55,4, 209; Krüger, "Grabraub in erzählenden Quellen des frühen Mittelalters," 182; Duval, *Auprès des saints,* 35 ff.; Pietri, "Les sépultures privilégiées," 134.

99. Nehlsen, "Der Grabfrevel," 139–46. But see von Unruh, "Wargus, Friedlosigkeit," 2–34.

contemporary epigraphy. Christian burial inscriptions of the Merovingian period focused less often on punishment of grave violations than on the anticipated resurrection of the faithful at the grave site. Typical of the epitaphs of persons deemed holy by contemporaries was the fifth-century grave inscription of Eufrasius, proclaiming: "Here rests in peace the blessed Eufrasius, who lived seventy years, two months, and seven days. He will be resurrected on the day when his maker comes from heaven."[100] The inscription, which is no longer extant, noted that Eufrasius's physical remains would lie in his sepulcher until they were reunited with his soul in heaven. A later epitaph of an anonymous abbess, dated by Bernhard Bischoff to the first half of the eighth century, likewise made clear the importance of the flesh in the absence of the spirit. While the holy woman's soul flew directly to heaven, her body awaited Christ's coming in its sepulcher.[101] The biographer of the *Vita sanctae Eustadiolae* expressed similar sentiments on behalf of the saint.[102]

In Merovingian hagiographical works, accounts of the preservation and sweet aroma of corpses often testified to the sanctity of recently deceased holy men and women. Since late antiquity the relics of saints, the models of heroic Christian death, had been identified with the perfumes and glory of paradise. In the course of translation ceremonies bringing attention to the *praesentia* of holy remains, the foci of the festivities were often

100. "Hic pausat Eufra/sius ben[e]dictus in / pace, qui vixit an(nos) / LXX mens(es) II et dies VII. / Surr(ecturu)s die caelo cum / venerit auctor." Françoise Descombes, ed., *RICG* 15,146 (Paris: Éditions du CNRS, 1985), 486–89; Edmond Le Blant, ed., *Inscriptions chrétiennes de la Gaule antérieures au VIIIe siècle* 2,398 (Paris: A l'Imprimerie impériale, 1865), 44.

101. "Dum ad eius hinc sancta anima pernix revolavit auctorem, hoc sacro templo in pace felix conditur antro. Hic remoratura paululum desiderabilem sanctis Christi praestolatur adventum, ut hinc resurrectura postmodum rapiatur obviam Christo dein . . . semper suo cum Domino regnatura per aevum." Bernhard Bischoff, "Epitaphienformeln für Äbtissinnen (achtes Jahrhundert)," in *Anecdota novissima: Texte des vierten bis sechzehnten Jahrhunderts* (Stuttgart: Anton Hiersemann Verlag, 1984), III,152.

102. Philippe Labbé, ed., *Vita sanctae Eustadiolae abbatissae*, in *Novae bibliothecae manuscriptorum librorum* 2 (Paris: Apud Sebastianum Cramoisy, 1657), 378.

unblemished corpses.[103] Gregory I therefore observed in his *Dialogues* that the body of the martyred bishop Herculanus of Perugia remained untouched by decay forty days after his death. In fact, the severed head of the bishop was discovered to have been reunited with the rest of his body, leaving no trace of his wounds. By contrast, the corpse of a child buried at the same time in that location had rapidly decomposed.[104] Such descriptions made the burial places of saints very special, places associated with triumph over decomposition and the healing of the sick.

With exposure to Christian teaching or ceremonies about the saints, some of the faithful aspired to similarly ideal burials. The application of practices intended to hinder bodily decay indicates that some Christians viewed the physical well-being of deceased kin as evidence of their standing with God before the Last Judgment. The prevalent technique for embalming in late antiquity and the early Middle Ages, which was far less sophisticated than mummification as practiced in ancient Egypt, involved the use of linen bandages and various herbs. Myrrh was especially noted for its success in retarding putrefaction.[105] This practice might be applied in the burials of the holy as well as of those whose families had the necessary resources. When Gregory of Tours described the discovery of a long-deceased girl in a damaged sarcophagus in the church of St. Venerandus, Clermont, for instance, he observed that she appeared as if she were only recently dead. Most interestingly, he concluded that her great beauty was

---

103. Peter Brown, *The Cult of Saints: Its Rise and Function in Latin Christianity* (Chicago: University of Chicago Press, 1981), 76; Martin Heinzelmann, *Translationsberichte und andere Quellen des Reliquienkultes*, Typologie des sources du moyen âge Occidental 33 (Turnhout: Brepols, 1979), 83–84.

104. De Vogüé, *Grégoire le Grand, Dialogues* 3,13,2–3, SC 260, 300–303.

105. M. E. A. Pigeon, "De l'embaumement des morts à l'époque mérovingienne," *Bulletin archéologique du Comité des travaux historiques et scientifiques* (1894): 139–42. Pigeon considered all descriptions of corpses releasing pleasant scents to be evidence of preservative techniques.

not a miraculous sign of her holiness but the result of the successful application of spices to preserve her body.[106]

With respect to holy women, Gregory also recalled that prior to the funeral of Radegund of Poitiers, at which he officiated in 587, so many spices had been used to wrap her body that the coffin had to be expanded to accommodate them.[107] Although the bishop offered no actual identification of the spices used, thus making it impossible to determine whether the vast resources of the former queen came into play, one may speculate that practical reasons, in addition to any symbolic considerations, justified their use. Specifically, an unusually long interval separated the time of death from the burial ceremony, a delay caused by the Poitevan bishop Maroveus's refusal to perform the funeral. At the nuns' request, Gregory of Tours traveled to Poitiers to officiate in Maroveus's place.[108] Other references to preservative efforts include a description of the delightful aroma given off by the body of Gibitrude—a nun in Burgundofara's (d. circa 641/655) monastery of Faremoutiers (Evoriacas)—which may have been prepared with balsam prior to burial.[109] Jonas of Bobbio made similar observations regarding the corpse of Domma, another member of the community,

106. "In quo [sepulchro] apparuit puella iacens, ita membris omnibus solidata, quasi nuper ab hoc saeculo fuisset adsumpta. Nam facies manusque eius cum reliquis artubus integrae erant cum ingenti caesaries longitudine; sed credo, eam aromatibus fuisse conditam." Krusch, *Gregorius episcopus Turonensis, Liber in gloria confessorum* 34, 768–69; Bonnie Effros, "Symbolic Expressions of Sanctity: Gertrude of Nivelles in the Context of Merovingian Mortuary Custom," *Viator* 27 (1996): 8–9.

107. "Nam providentia abbatissae capsam ligneam fecerat, in qua corpus aromatibus conditum incluserat, et ob hoc fossa sepulturae spatiosior erat, ita ut, ablatis duorum sepulchrorum singulis spondis, ac de latere iuncta capsa cum sanctis artubus locaretur." Krusch, *Gregorius episcopus Turonensis, Liber in gloria confessorum* 104, 366.

108. Bonnie Effros, "Images of Sanctity: Contrasting Descriptions of Radegund of Poitiers by Venantius Fortunatus and Gregory of Tours," *UCLA Historical Journal* 10 (1990): 47.

109. "Quae ita felicem exitum peregit [Gibitrudis], ut intra cellulam, qua corpus iacebat exanime, balsama crederes desudare." Krusch, *Ionas, Vitae Columbani abbatis discipulorumque eius libri* II 2,12, 261.

although he did not link its balsam scent to embalming but to a miracle reflecting heavenly recognition of the nun's sanctity.[110]

A number of archaeological excavations have corroborated the actual use of these techniques, not all of which were necessarily costly, on at least the most prestigious graves of the Merovingian period. A fifth-century tomb found at Saint-Victor at Marseilles contained the remains of a female wearing silk garments and wrapped in linen, spices, and herbs, including incense, nettles, and thyme. The deceased's head was adorned with a wreath of leaves and rested on a cushion of flowers. Multiple bouquets were also deposited in the sepulcher.[111] The skeleton found at Saint-Germain-des-Prés in the eighteenth century and attributed to Bilichild, the daughter of Sigibert III (d. 656), was observed to have been protected by a cushion of herbs cradling the skull.[112] Following analysis of the grave of Saint-Denis often referred to as that of Queen Aregund, Michel Fleury and Albert France-Lanord have proposed it probable that the corpse was submerged in a preservative solution and that a similar fluid was injected into her mouth. These steps resulted in the partial embalming of her remains.[113]

All of the aforementioned examples of preservation techniques from the fifth through seventh centuries derive from an era during which graves are more easily dated due to the presence of burial goods. It is thus possible that the practice may have lasted longer in the medieval period than currently documented. Spices purchased by monasteries such as Corbie in the eighth

110. "Eratque hora diei nona, qua odor suavissimus cellam [Dommae] repleverat. Balsami odor flagrabat e pectore, sicque per totam supervenientem noctem, sic per subsequentem diem usque ad aliam horam nonam et odoris suavitas et cantus modolamina perseverarunt." Krusch, *Ionas, Vitae Columbani abbatis discipulorumque eius libri II* 2,16, 267–68.

111. Raymond Boyer, "Le sarcophage à sa découverte," in *Premiers temps chrétiens en Gaule méridionale: Antiquité tardive et haut moyen âge IIIème–VIIIème siècles* (exhibition catalogue) (Lyons: Association lyonnaise de sauvetage des sites archéologiques médiévaux, 1986), no. 142b, p. 82.

112. Jacques Bouillart, *Histoire de l'abbaye royal de Saint Germain des Prez* (Paris: Grégoire Dupuis, 1724), 252.

113. Michel Fleury and Albert France-Lanord, "La tombe d'Aregonde," *Les dossiers d'archéologie* 32 (1979): 31.

century, for instance, may have been intended for more than medicinal purposes and cooking;[114] they may also have served in preparing monks' or elite patrons' burials. Embalming enabled the deceased to be transported when necessary, and assuaged fears regarding the decomposition of human corpses prior to the final resurrection of the flesh. Such practices also reflected the social and spiritual status to which the deceased's kin aspired.

Maintaining Boundaries Between the Living and the Dead

A final sense in which early medieval legislation affected burial related to the growing attraction of interment in close proximity to the saints. Resting places *ad sanctos,* normally situated within funerary churches, sparked controversy as a consequence of the late antique interdiction, enshrined in the Theodosian Code, of burial within city walls (*intra muros*). In the imperial period, for instance, only those persons designated by the Senate as having sacrificed their lives for the empire or who had defended its borders were permitted to receive burial within urban limits. This honor was thus usually reserved for emperors or consuls, such as Constantine, who was interred in Constantinople.[115] According to the Theodosian Code 9,17,6, however, the vast majority of the population was to be laid to rest in urns or sarcophagi outside inhabited spaces.[116]

Permission for the translation of martyrial relics into urban churches became more common late in the fourth century as a growing number of religious communities moved into cities. They sought the sort of security

---

114. Jean Lestocquoy, "Épices, médecine et abbayes," in *Études mérovingiennes,* 179–86.
115. Bernhard Kötting, "Die Tradition der Grabkirche," in *Memoria: Der geschichtliche Zeugniswert des liturgischen Gedenkens im Mittelalter,* MMS 48, ed. Karl Schmid and Joachim Wollasch (Munich: Wilhelm Fink Verlag, 1984), 69–70.
116. "Omnia quae supra terram urnis clausa vel sarcofagis corpora detinentur, extra urbem delata ponantur, ut et humanitatis instar exhibeant et relinquant incolarum domicilium sanctitatem." Mommsen and Meyer, *Codex Theodosianus libri XVI* 1,2, 465.

that could not be assured in rural or suburban locations, yet desired to continue to venerate and promote relics in their possession.[117] Bishops also recognized the importance of highlighting the holy remains in their control. Ambrose's famous translation of the relics of Gervasius and Protasius into Milan in 385 was a crucial precedent for this development, due in part to the publicity that resulted from imperial resistance to the ceremony. The bishop's orchestrated celebration increased relics' visibility among the urban Christian population.[118] Barriers against *intra muros* interment grew more porous as the cult of saints rose in significance, particularly in episcopal centers. Yet such taboos did not disappear overnight. Because early medieval cathedrals and monastic houses for women were usually located within city walls for administrative purposes and the protection they afforded, long-standing measures against burial *intra muros* had a great impact on the burial of clerics and nuns. For this reason, even the former queen and monastic founder Radegund (d. 587) was buried beyond the city walls. Her sisters, who were not allowed on any condition to leave the monastery, thus protested that they would need to violate their vows of claustration in order to visit her grave.[119]

Relics nonetheless represented only one component of the presence of the dead in Roman towns and cities. Burial sites in the vicinity of saints were also perceived as privileged, due both to the exclusivity of graves *ad sanctos* and to their exposure to large numbers of the Christian faithful

---

117. Jill Harries, "Death and the Dead in the Late Roman Empire," in *Death in Towns: Urban Responses to the Dying and the Dead, 100–1600,* ed. Steven Bassett (London: Leicester University Press, 1992), 62–65; Kötting, "Die Tradition," 74–78.

118. Neil B. McLynn, *Ambrose of Milan: Church and Court in a Christian Capital* (Berkeley and Los Angeles: University of California Press, 1994), 209–17; Daniel H. Williams, *Ambrose of Milan and the End of the Nicene-Arian Conflicts* (Oxford: Oxford University Press, 1995), 219–23; Brown, *The Cult of Saints,* 33 ff.

119. Krusch, *Gregorius episcopus Turonensis, Liber in gloria confessorum* 104, 364–66; Hartmut Atsma, "Les monastères urbains du Nord de la Gaule," *Revue d'histoire de l'église de France* 62 (1975): 184–85.

coming to church services.[120] By the seventh century, bishops such as Eligius of Noyon were honored with sepulchers near the altar.[121] However, changes in this direction were not always embraced by religious leaders. Jonas of Bobbio's mid-seventh-century *vita* of Vaast of Arras (d. 650), for instance, referred to the bishop's objection to burial within city walls. The conflict between Vaast and his followers on this subject was resolved only when the bier upon which Vaast was carried during his funeral resisted all attempts by the brethren to move it from the cathedral. This miracle sanctioned Vaast's interment in the church despite his apparent wishes to the contrary while he was still alive.[122]

The Carolingian Synod of Aachen's (809) short-lived effort to revive more strict measures against burial *intra muros* harked back to late antique, rather than early medieval, precedents. The early-ninth-century canon differed markedly from seventh-century laws that had not sought to ban graves from city limits but instead granted church burial only to those who had received the bishop's permission.[123] The fourteenth canon of the Synod of Auxerre (561–605) also prohibited interments from taking place in baptisteries.[124] Reversing restrictions on interment in churches, however, the Synod of Mainz in 813 definitively allowed *intra muros* burial for

120. Gisella Cantino Wataghin, "The Ideology of Urban Burials," in *The Idea and Ideal of the Town Between Late Antiquity and the Early Middle Ages*, TRW 4, ed. Gian Pietro Brogiolo and Bryan Ward-Perkins (Leiden: E. J. Brill, 1999), 158–63.

121. Krusch, *Vita Eligii episcopi Noviomagensis* 2,48, 727.

122. Bruno Krusch, ed., *Vita Vedastis episcopi Atrebatensis duplex* 9, in *MGH: SRM* 3 (Hannover: Impensis bibliopolii Hahniani, 1896), 412–13; Cécile Treffort, "Du *cimiterium christianorum* au paroissial: Évolution des espaces funéraires en Gaule du VIe au Xe siècle," in *Archéologie du cimitière chrétien: Actes du 2e colloque ARCHEA (Orléans, 29 septembre–1er octobre 1994)* (11th supplement of the *Revue archéologique du Centre de la France*), ed. Henri Galinié and Elisabeth Zadora-Rio (Tours: FÉRACF, 1996), 56–57; Megan McLaughlin, *Consorting with Saints: Prayer for the Dead in Early Medieval France* (Ithaca: Cornell University Press, 1994), 109–10; Effros, "Beyond Cemetery Walls," 15–17.

123. "Ut intra septa monastyrii (non) baptizetur nec missae defunc(to)rum saecularium in monastyrio (celebr)entur nec saecularium cor(pora) (ib)idem sepeliantur, forsitan (per)miso ponteficis." Charles de Clercq, ed., *Concilium incerti loci (post a.614)* c.6, in *Concilia Galliae*, 287.

124. De Clercq, *Concilia Galliae*, 267.

bishops, abbots, and lay faithful (*fideles laici*).[125] Burials in these churches were usually centrally located or situated just outside of the sanctuaries.

While most Christians could not expect privileged resting places near the saints, their burial sites were nonetheless influenced and transformed by increasingly permissive attitudes toward interment *intra muros*. Christian graves in the eighth, ninth, and tenth centuries occurred in greater numbers around local parish churches in or near villages. Clerics thereby gained more authority over the disposition of Christian graves in church grave-yards than had ever been the case in rural row grave cemeteries.[126] These developments have nonetheless been notoriously difficult to document archaeologically due to the repeated occupation of precisely the same sites in subsequent centuries.[127] Written sources have not proved much more revealing. Although the few surviving eighth-century sacramentaries contained Masses to be performed specifically near graves, they included no liturgy for the consecration of Christian cemeteries.[128] The earliest extant benedictions of burial places date from the tenth century,[129] demonstrating the slow pace at which clerical prerogatives in burial became unquestioned institutional features of funerary practice.

125. Christian Sapin, "Architecture and Funerary Space in the Early Middle Ages," in *Spaces of the Living and the Dead: An Archaeological Dialogue*, American Early Medieval Studies 3, ed. Catherine E. Karkov, Kelly M. Wickham-Crowley, and Bailey K. Young (Oxford: Oxbow Books, 1999), 39–45; Kötting, "Die Tradition," 74–78.

126. Patrick Périn, "Le problème des sarcophages-cénotaphes du haut moyen âge: A propos de la nécropole de Quarré-les-Tombes, site d'une bataille légendaire," in *La chanson de geste et le mythe carolingien: Mélanges René Louis* 2 (Saint-Père-sous-Vézelay: Musée archéologique régional, 1982), 824; Richard Morris, *The Church in British Archaeology*, CBA Research Report 47 (London: CBA, 1983), 54–62.

127. Alain Dierkens, "Un aspect de la christianisation de la Gaule du Nord à l'époque mérovingienne: La 'Vita Hadelini' et les découvertes archéologiques d'Anthée et de Franchimont," *Francia* 8 (1980): 621–22; Colardelle, *Sépulture et traditions*, 84–87, 369.

128. Bullough, "Burial, Community," 189–90.

129. Cécile Treffort, *L'église carolingienne et la mort: Christianisme, rites funéraires et pratiques commémoratives*, Collection d'histoire et d'archéologie médiévales 3 (Lyons: Presses universitaires de Lyon, 1996), 141–42.

This sword (spatha), *from grave 5 at Flonheim (Rheinhessen), was probably never considered a fighting weapon, since the fine workmanship on the golden grip and cloisonné decoration would have rendered it impractical in battle. The burial likewise included a massive gold belt buckle inlaid with precious stones, a purse decorated with bird heads, a large crystal bead, a short blade, and other weaponry. The grave has been dated to circa 500. Hermann Ament,* Fränkische Adelsgräber von Flonheim in Rheinhessen, *Germanische Denkmäler der Völkerwanderungszeit, ser. B, vol. 5 (Berlin: Gebrüder Mann Verlag, 1970), 43–66. Photograph of Inv. F1981 reproduced with permission of the Museum der Stadt Worms.*

Rock-crystal balls such as this possibly had status-linked or amuletic functions. Found in late 1885 at Flonheim by the Altertumsverein Worms, the ball and a meter-long chain lay in grave 6 with other burial goods, including a bead necklace, four brooches, belt decorations, a Roman coin, a glass bottle, and a bone comb. The sepulcher dated to the sixth century and is presumed to have belonged to a woman. Ament, Fränkische Adelsgräber, *78–82. Photograph of Inv. F247 reproduced with permission of the Museum der Stadt Worms.*

This luxurious assemblage of grave goods from sepulcher 319 at the cemetery of Lavoye (Meuse) is thought to have belonged to a man buried in the late fifth century. Patrick Périn, "Die archäologischen Zeugnisse der fränkischen Expansion in Gallien," in Die Franken: Wegbereiter Europas *1 (Mainz: Philipp von Zabern, 1996), 227–32. Photograph reproduced with permission of the Musée des antiquités nationales, Saint-Germain-en-Laye.*

Excavated from the early medieval cemetery of Wanquetin (Pas de Calais) in 1894, this openwork belt fitting (châtelaine) *of copper alloy, 8.9 cm in length, dates to roughly the seventh century. It was originally a part of the collection of Léandre Cottel, but later passed into the hands of the antiquarians Oswald Dimpre in Abbeville and then Stanislas Baron in Paris. Jacques Seligmann, a Parisian antiquities dealer, acquired it for J. Pierpont Morgan who purchased it in 1910. After Morgan's death in 1913, his son donated it on his behalf as part of a larger collection of Gallo-Roman and Merovingian antiquities to The Metropolitan Museum of Art. Patrick Périn, "Aspects of Late Merovingian Costume in the Morgan Collection," in* From Attila to Charlemagne: Arts of the Early Medieval Period in The Metropolitan Museum of Art, *ed. Katharine R. Brown, Dafydd Kidd, and Charles T. Little (New York: The Metropolitan Museum of Art, 2000), 258–59. The Metropolitan Museum of Art, Gift of J. Pierpont Morgan, 1917. (17.192.162) Photograph © 2000 The Metropolitan Museum of Art.*

This earring of sheet gold, with garnet and silver-bead settings, is 4.5 cm in diameter and likely dates to the second half of the sixth century. Although its original provenance is unknown, the piece was acquired by Jacques Seligmann on behalf of J. Pierpont Morgan in 1910 and donated to The Metropolitan Museum of Art by Morgan's son in 1917. Périn, "Aspects of Late Merovingian Costume," 244. The Metropolitan Museum of Art, Gift of J. Pierpont Morgan, 1917. (17.191.1) Photograph © 2000 The Metropolitan Museum of Art.

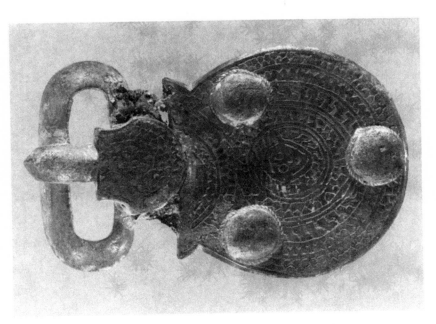

This tinned copper-alloy buckle with cast relief dates from roughly 600 and has a length of 9.6 cm. While the buckle's original provenance is unknown, its design is typical of Neustrian regions between the Île-de-France and the Channel. The artifact was acquired by J. Pierpont Morgan through his dealer Jacques Seligmann as part of a larger collection, that which was donated by Morgan's son to The Metropolitan Museum of Art in 1917. Decoration of the buckle consists of zigzag patterns surrounding a stylized face surmounting a cross, perhaps suggesting an image of Christ. Périn, "Aspects of Late Merovingian Costume," 252–53. The Metropolitan Museum of Art, Gift of J. Pierpont Morgan, 1917. (17.191.223) Photograph © 2000 The Metropolitan Museum of Art.

This assemblage of high-quality grave goods was presumably buried with a woman in grave 2587 in the late fifth or early sixth century at the cemetery of Arcy–St. Restitue. The objects include a pair of silver earrings decorated with garnets, a bird-shaped brooch, a large, late Roman bead of glass paste, two jasper beads, and a ceramic vessel with a diameter of 8.1 cm and height of 6.5 cm. Photograph reproduced with permission of the Musée des antiquités nationales, Saint-Germain-en-Laye.

These two nearly identical Merovingian digitated bow fibulae of silver gilt (with measurements of 8.8 cm × 5 cm and 8.7 cm × 4.9 cm) are decorated with five projecting tabs set with garnets. Each has a triangular foot plate terminating in a stylized animal mask. They are thought to date from the fifth or sixth century and resemble a brooch owned by the Walters Art Museum in Baltimore (54.2443). Although their provenance is unknown, the brooches are typical of those from northeastern France and the Rhine valley. The brooches were acquired by the Saint Louis Art Museum at the Parke-Bernet Galleries auction of the collection of the late antiquities dealer Joseph Brummer in April 1949. Robert G. Calkins, A Medieval Treasury: An Exhibition of Medieval Art from the Third to the Sixteenth Century *21 (Ithaca: Andrew Dickson White Museum of Art, Cornell University, 1968), 113. Photograph of 57:1949 and 58:1949 reproduced with permission of the Saint Louis Art Museum.*

This brooch dates from roughly the seventh century and was discovered in a cemetery in Charnay (Saône-et-Loire). With a diameter of 5.5 cm, the gold frame decorated with garnet and glass insets surrounds a late antique cameo depicting the head of a woman. Photograph of 34702 reproduced with permission of the Musée des antiquités nationales, Saint-Germain-en-Laye.

This *late-sixth-century* plaque-boucle *of 13 cm in length was possibly found in either Chalon-sur-Saône or Saône-et-Loire. As noted in its inscription, it depicts the prophets Daniel and Habakuk with their arms upraised in the lions' den. Outfitted with small pockets possibly for the reception of relics, the buckle's edge contains an inscription expressing confidence in the resurrection of the faithful. Helmut Roth,* "Kunst der Merowingerzeit," *in* Die Franken: Wegbereiter Europas 2 *(Mainz: Philip von Zabern, 1996), 638. Photograph of 17698 reproduced with permission of the Musée des antiquités nationales, Saint-Germain-en-Laye.*

Dated to the early seventh century, this glass bell beaker has incurved walls and a pointed base. It was excavated from an unidentified site in France and is now housed in The Metropolitan Museum of Art, having been donated on behalf of J. Pierpont Morgan, who had amassed this collection, in 1917. Vera I. Evison, "The Frankish Glass Vessels," in From Attila to Charlemagne: Arts of the Early Medieval Period in The Metropolitan Museum of Art, *ed. Katharine R. Brown, Dafydd Kidd, and Charles T. Little (New York: The Metropolitan Museum of Art, 2000), 270–79. The Metropolitan Museum of Art, Gift of J. Pierpont Morgan, 1917. (17.191.351) Photograph © 2000 The Metropolitan Museum of Art.*

CHAPTER III

✣ • ✣

Grave Markers as *Memoria*

Early Medieval Epigraphical Evidence: An Introduction

E pigraphical remains represented an integral component of burial traditions during the Merovingian period because funerary inscriptions, like grave goods and liturgical ceremony, actively expressed contemporary values and beliefs. More than 2,500 epitaphs of Christians are extant from late antique and early medieval Gaul.[1] In comparison to most means of remembering the dead, inscribed stones were more permanent in their fulfillment of commemorative and ideological functions, since they could remain standing for generations. The limited literate circles in which this custom operated and the visibility of existing epigraphy in churches and cemeteries may explain why its evolution over the centuries was slower than other aspects of the burial rite. Ian Morris nonetheless cautions against privileging this accessible feature of funerary custom over those more difficult to document in historical or archaeological evidence, since it was far less common than grave goods.[2]

1. Mark A. Handley, "Beyond Hagiography: Epigraphic Commemoration and Saints' Cults in Late Antique Trier," in *Revisiting Late Roman Gaul*, ed. Ralph Mathisen and Danuta Shanzer (London: Ashgate, 2001), 187–200.
2. Ian Morris, *Death-Ritual and Social Structure in Classical Antiquity* (Cambridge: Cambridge University Press, 1992), 32, 156–72. Morris's discussion of early medieval Christian attitudes toward lavish display, which he characterizes as highly negative, is not reflective of the evidence in Gaul. Bailey K. Young, "Exemple aristocratique et mode funéraire dans la Gaule mérovingienne," *Annales ESC* 41 (1986): 379–407; Bonnie Effros, "Symbolic Expressions of Sanctity: Gertrude of Nivelles in the Context of Merovingian Mortuary Custom," *Viator* 27 (1996): 1–10.

Although now removed in most cases from their original contexts, early medieval epitaphs were symbolic of elite status due to their expense, their association with literate culture, and the exclusive locations in which they were often erected. The custom also provided greater continuity for the commemoration of ancestors, since funerary inscriptions and carvings in stone preserved an idealized image of the deceased for subsequent generations. For this reason, contemporaries may have viewed epigraphy as more effective in the long term than other types of burial customs. This bias was particularly strong among members of urban populations, where the transmission of oral tradition was not as reliable as in smaller settlements.[3] Above-ground display involving stone walls, crosses, and decorated sarcophagus covers also occurred in the vicinity of rural aristocratic churches, such as that at Audun-le-Tiche (Moselle), which dates to the second half of the seventh century.[4] While even the most lavish grave goods disappeared from view once buried, the erection of an inscribed stone monument ensured the long preservation of at least limited details of the lives of the deceased. The impression they made upon a community was no longer constrained by the firsthand memories of families or acquaintances.

Epigraphical data must nevertheless be assessed with the awareness that in late antiquity and the early Middle Ages, inscriptions were not used by most families in commemoration of the dead; they were also far more prevalent in the fifth century than in the eighth. The majority of individuals who tended to employ epitaphs inhabited and thus were buried near urban spaces of Roman origin and Christian ecclesiastical centers, especially toward the beginning of this period.[5] The majority of surviving inscrip-

3. Guy Halsall, *Settlement and Social Organization: The Merovingian Region of Metz* (Cambridge: Cambridge University Press, 1995), 271–72.

4. Alain Simmer, *Le cimetière mérovingien d'Audun-le-Tiche (Moselle)*, Association française d'archéologie mérovingienne, Mémoire 2 (Paris: Éditions Errance, 1988), 7–10; Alain Simmer, "La nécropole mérovingienne d'Audun-le-Tiche," *CA* 35 (1987): 31–40.

5. Ingrid Heidrich, "Südgallische Inschriften des 5.–7. Jahrhunderts als historische Quellen," *RV* 32 (1968): 169–71, 180–83; J. M. C. Toynbee, *Death and Burial in the Roman World* (Baltimore:

tional material in Gaul originates from south of the Loire, especially in
Poitou and the Auvergne in southwestern Gaul and in the Rhône valley.
Exceptions to this general rule occurred typically in more densely inhabited
areas in the Moselle valley, including the former imperial city of Trier,
which ranked only after Rome and Carthage in the number of surviving
epitaphs (887 to date) in the late Roman West.[6] Centers of royal power,
such as Paris, and episcopal seats along the Rhine, such as Mainz and
Cologne, were also important repositories of funerary inscriptions.[7] Interestingly enough, despite a brief resurgence in the popularity of epigraphy
in the sixth century, a fair number of monastic houses, particularly those
outside of the Rhône valley, have not produced evidence of its use. This
lacuna may be due in part to the intensive level of occupation and building
at these sites in more recent centuries.[8]

Whereas epigraphy was most common in urban centers, lavish burials
of a different sort, namely those with grave goods rife with symbols of
imperial authority, usually occurred in rural contexts in which the Roman
administration had completely disintegrated during the fifth century.[9] In
northern and northwestern Gaul, even in former Roman centers such as
Metz, the erection of funerary steles had not historically been customary.
Even fewer were carved following the disruption caused by Frankish
incursions. The dichotomy between rural and suburban burials was
nonetheless not necessarily a reflection of wealth, population density, or
ethnicity. Stone carving was not limited to cities, since the custom served

Johns Hopkins University Press, 1971), 273–74; Ramsay MacMullen, "The Epigraphic Habit in the
Roman Empire," *American Journal of Philology* 103 (1982): 241.

  6. Handley, "Beyond Hagiography," 188–189.
  7. Edward James, *The Merovingian Archaeology of South-West Gaul* 1, BAR Supplementary
Series 25(i) (Oxford: BAR, 1977), 19.
  8. Hartmut Atsma, "Die christliche Inschriften Galliens als Quelle für Klöster und
Klösterbewohner bis zum Ende des 6. Jahrhunderts," *Francia* 4 (1976): 1–57.
  9. Guy Halsall, "Towns, Societies, and Ideas: The Not-So-Strange Case of Late Roman and
Early Merovingian Metz," in *Towns in Transition: Urban Evolution in Late Antiquity and the Early
Middle Ages*, ed. Neil Christie and Simon T. Loseby (Aldershot: Scolar Press, 1996), 244–45.

a variety of functions. Rural communities in pagan and Christian Ireland, for instance, had long used inscribed stone monuments to commemorate their dead.[10] Of eighteen surviving fourth-century Christian epitaphs in Britain, the majority have been identified as coming from the north and west.[11]

Nor was the use of epitaphs confined to members of the population with Roman ancestry, for many stones commemorated individuals with Germanic names. Even those inscribed with Roman names might have belonged to families of Germanic origin that had assimilated to Gallo-Roman customs. The use of Roman names regardless of ethnic background, for instance, was particularly common among clerics: a sixth-century bishop of Cambrai, Gaugericus, had a Roman name but Germanic parents.[12] Persons of Gallo-Roman heritage are also known to have adopted Germanic names under certain circumstances.[13] An individual's ethnicity might change over the course of his or her lifetime, particularly when the alteration of one's identity provided some sort of political advantage.[14] Epigraphy thus preserved a record of some of the most effective bids for power in early medieval communities and as such was practiced mainly by those of significant means—who recognized the utility of its application.

10. Ann Hamlin, "Early Irish Stone Carving: Content and Context," in *The Early Church in Western Britain and Ireland: Studies Presented to C. A. Ralegh Radford*, BAR British Series 102, ed. Susan M. Pearce (Oxford: BAR, 1982), 283–96; Pádraig Lionard, "Early Irish Grave Slabs," *Proceedings of the Royal Irish Academy* 61C (1961): 95–169.

11. Mark A. Handley, "The Origins of Christian Commemoration in Late Antique Britain," *EME* 10 (2001): 181–82, 195–99.

12. Heidrich, "Südgallische Inschriften," 180–82; Nancy Gauthier, *L'évangélisation des pays de la Moselle: La province romaine de Première Belgique entre antiquité et moyen-âge (IIIᵉ–VIIIᵉ siècles)* (Paris: Éditions E. de Boccard, 1980), 244–48.

13. Jörg Jarnut, "Selbstverständnis von Personen und Personengruppen im Lichte frühmittelalterlicher Personennamen," in *Personennamen und Identität: Namengebung und Namengebrauch als Anzeiger individueller Bestimmung und gruppenbezogener Zuordnung*, Grazer grundwissenschaftliche Forschungen 3, Schriftenreihe der Akademie Freisach 2, ed. Reinhard Härtel (Graz: Akademische Druck- und Verlagsanstalt, 1997), 50–54.

14. Patrick J. Geary, "Ethnic Identity as a Situational Construct in the Early Middle Ages," *Mitteilungen der Anthropologischen Gesellschaft in Wien* 113 (1983): 15–26; Patrick Amory, "The Meaning and Purpose of Ethnic Terminology in the Burgundian Laws," *EME* 2 (1993): 25.

The most basic requirements for those who wished to have a burial inscription were access to someone sufficiently literate to compose or copy the desired text and the presence of and resources to pay stonecutters, who likely belonged to a workshop. Some sort of literacy, or at least respect for those who exhibited it, was also desirable among the intended audience. Although none of these features was indigenous to the Germanic population prior to contact with Rome, they soon imitated their Roman neighbors. In Roman Britain, as on the Continent, their exposure to inscribed monuments occurred first in suburban cemeteries and churches. Town dwellers erected funerary inscriptions more frequently than their rural counterparts due to higher literacy levels and the greater variety of funerary traditions characteristic of population centers.[15] Clerics did not mandate uniformity in the practice,[16] and Christian epitaphs served not only to honor the dead but also to elevate the status of surviving kin, as they had among pagans. Former loci of imperial influence, such as Lyons, Arles, and Vienne, therefore witnessed the greatest continuity of Roman tradition. These cities retained a senatorial class long after the Roman administration had disappeared from the countryside, and thus represented logical enclaves for the preservation and use of epigraphy.[17]

Funerary Inscriptions in Imperial Rome

Even in imperial Rome, burial in conjunction with a commemorative marker was an expensive and hence relatively exclusive privilege. Cremations were

15. Simon Esmonde Cleary, "Town and Country in Roman Britain?" in *Death in Towns: Urban Responses to the Dying and the Dead, 100–1600,* ed. Steven Bassett (London: Leicester University Press, 1992), 34–40.
16. Donald A. Bullough, "Burial, Community, and Belief in the Early Medieval West," in *Ideal and Reality in Frankish and Anglo-Saxon Society: Studies Presented to J. M. Wallace-Hadrill,* ed. Patrick Wormald (Oxford: Basil Blackwell, 1983), 177–201; Bonnie Effros, "Beyond Cemetery Walls: Early Medieval Funerary Topography and Christian Salvation," *EME* 6 (1997): 1–23.
17. Raymond Van Dam, *Leadership and Community in Late Antique Gaul* (Berkeley and Los Angeles: University of California Press, 1985), 152–56.

identified in much the same way as the burial of corpses, since the ashes of those who could afford the expense might be stored in urns or niches in mausolea, tomb structures, or *columbaria*. Some were also honored with an inscription.[18] In her study of Roman literacy, Elizabeth Meyer has observed that the erection of a commemorative inscription in pagan Rome was often directly linked to an heir's moral obligation to honor his benefactor, the deceased testator. Due to this responsibility, epitaphs not only granted significant attention to the deceased but also provided written recognition of the identity of the commemorator.[19] These witnesses must have been considered important, since families holding membership in *collegia* frequently received aid with such burial expenses.[20] During the principate, epitaphs primarily identified members of the deceased's nuclear family as having erected the stone. The families named therein benefited from the honor and publicity associated with the carving of the epitaphs. The main exceptions to the practice were among military men distant from their families.[21] To avoid uncertainty as to whether a gravestone would be erected for them, some individuals commissioned their own monuments.

In the second and third centuries, citizens were the only persons permitted to compose wills enforceable by Roman law and thus enjoyed relative exclusivity in the use of stone monuments. Such a marker represented a *de facto* monumental legal document attesting to the right of the deceased and his or her descendants to that grave.[22] Freedmen and freedwomen, by contrast,

18. Arthur Darby Nock, "Cremation and Burial in the Roman Empire," in *Essays on Religion and the Ancient World* 1, ed. Zeph Stewart (Cambridge: Harvard University Press, 1972), 277–93; Toynbee, *Death and Burial*, 50.

19. Elizabeth Anne Meyer, "Literacy, Literate Practice, and the Law in the Roman Empire, A.D. 100–600" (Ph.D. diss., Yale University, 1988), 123 ff., 189–91.

20. John R. Patterson, "Patronage, *Collegia*, and Burial in Imperial Rome," in *Death in Towns*, 17–23.

21. Richard P. Saller and Brent D. Shaw, "Tombstones and Roman Family Relations in the Principate: Civilians, Soldiers, and Slaves," *JRS* 74 (1984): 125–26.

22. Werner Eck, "Römische Grabinschriften: Aussageabsicht und Aussagefähigkeit im funerären Kontext," in *Römische Gräberstraßen: Selbstdarstellung-Status-Standard: Kolloquium in*

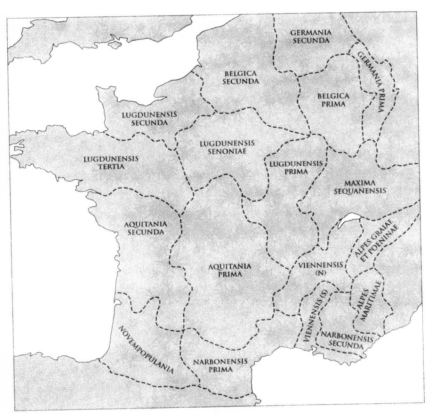

This map depicts the frontiers of the Roman provinces of Gaul, upon which early medieval episcopal sees were based. Map designed by Franz Siegmeth on the basis of information provided in Nancy Gauthier, ed., RICG *1 (Paris: Éditions du CNRS, 1975).*

required the permission of their patron for the erection of an independent tombstone. Alternatively, they might be included along with kin and slaves in family tombs or mausolea. Roman inscriptions thus primarily served to highlight the status possessed or aspired to by the deceased's social unit. The prominent place given to the titles of Roman offices (*honores*) in contemporary epigraphy demonstrated the importance of the permanent display of sociopolitical achievement.[23] Once Roman citizenship became less exclusive, however, the popularity of epitaphs as an effective means of conveying these values correspondingly decreased. Presumably there was no longer as great a need to publish a position that had lost some of its attraction as an honor of limited distribution.[24]

As has been noted by Gabriel Sanders, the monumental component of this burial custom was an important incentive for erecting epitaphs.[25] Contemporaries recognized that epigraphy increased the likelihood of the survival of a person in at least name long beyond his or her death.[26] Addressed to the general public, commemorative inscriptions constituted the silent *laudatio funebris* of the families who could afford them. Scholars thus should not underestimate epigraphy's influential role in late antique and early medieval society. Although not an accurate reflection of contemporary language usages, the Vulgar Latin employed in such compositions could be understood in Gaul as late as the Merovingian period.[27] Early

---

München von 28. bis 30. Oktober 1985, Bayerische Akademie der Wissenschaften, philosophisch-historische Klasse, Abhandlungen, n.s. 96, ed. Henner von Hesberg and Paul Zanker (Munich: Verlag der Bayerische Akademie der Wissenschaften, 1987), 76; Meyer, "Literacy," 189–91.

23. Martin Heinzelmann, *Bischofsherrschaft in Gallien: Zur Kontinuität römischer Führungsschichten von 4. bis zum 7. Jahrhundert: Soziale, prosopographische und bildungsgeschichtliche Aspekte*, Beihefte der Francia 5 (Munich: Artemis Verlag, 1976), 36 ff.; Meyer, "Literacy," 78–81.

24. Elizabeth Anne Meyer, "Explaining the Epigraphic Habit in the Roman Empire—The Evidence of Epitaphs," *JRS* 80 (1990): 83–91.

25. Gabriel Sanders, "Les inscriptions latines païennes et chrétiennes: Symbiose ou métabolisme," *Revue de l'Université de Bruxelles* (1977): 47–56.

26. Augustine of Hippo made his own observations of this phenomenon in his sixth sermon on Saint Stephen: "Propterea enim eos (versus) ibi scribere voluimus, ut qui vult legat, quando vult legat. Ut omnes teneant, ideo pauci sunt: ut omnes legant, ideo publice scripti sunt. Non opus est ut quaeratur codex: camera illa codex vester sit." Jacques-Paul Migne, ed., *Sanctus Aurelius Augustinus, Sermonum classes quatuor* 319,8, in *PL* 38 (Paris: Apud editorem in via dicta d'Amboise, 1845), 1442.

27. Betty I. Knott, "The Christian 'Special Language' in the Inscriptions," *Vigiliae Christianae* 10 (1956): 65–67. For a discussion of the *scripta latina rustica*, see Marc van Uytfanghe, "L'hagiographie et son public à l'époque mérovingienne," in *Studia patristica* 16,2, Texte und Untersuchungen zur Geschichte der altchristlichen Literatur 129 (Berlin: Akademie-Verlag, 1985),

medieval epigraphy acted as a powerful form of expression, acculturation, and instruction just as it had among the inhabitants of the Roman Empire.[28]

Tombstones of the Roman era often included the names of the individuals who had commissioned them; for modern historians, these identify the persons who took responsibility for choosing the types of rites to be performed at the funerals these stones marked. The same individuals likely also regulated the level of expenses incurred in carrying out the ceremonies. By comparison, others playing significant roles in the funerary rituals, such as the women thought to have been responsible for washing and preparing bodies for burial, were not recognized in such a public fashion. Female relatives' contributions to mortuary rites were thereby underrepresented on inscribed stones.

Because many epitaphs were sponsored as a part of testamentary obligations, immediate family members were most interested in the expression of the deceased's status, since they were the ones to benefit from this display. Brent Shaw has observed that 80 to 82 percent of the relationships recorded on tombstones of Roman civilians of the first through third centuries were of nuclear families. Dedications made between husband and wife and between parents and children outnumbered those commissioned by siblings.[29] Among soldiers removed from immediate contact with their kin, unrelated heirs (55 percent) and companions (*amici*) (8 percent), as opposed to nuclear (29 percent) and extended (3 percent) families, tended to commission inscriptions. Significant geographical separation from relatives must have caused a weakening of family ties as well as serious logistical difficulties in commemorating the deceased with an epitaph.[30] However, such negative

---

57–60; Marc van Uytfanghe, "Latin mérovingien, latin carolingien et *rustica romana lingua:* Continuité ou discontinuité?" *Revue de l'Université de Bruxelles* (1977): 66 ff.

28. Sanders, "Les inscriptions," 47–56; MacMullen, "The Epigraphic Habit," 246.

29. Brent D. Shaw, "Latin Funerary Epigraphy and Family Life in the Later Roman Empire," *Historia: Zeitschrift für alte Geschichte* 33 (1984): 465–66.

30. Saller and Shaw, "Tombstones," 131–34, 142–44.

evidence cannot be used to prove that soldiers in particular regions were foreign; the lack of epitaphs might have been due to regional custom rather than distance from relatives.[31] Unlike the difficult task of determining the identity of those who outfitted graves with burial goods, then, funerary inscriptions provided more precise information regarding who received credit publicly for making funeral arrangements. From Roman epigraphical evidence, it may be inferred that the nuclear, rather than an extended, kin group also took the leading role in the deposition of typical grave offerings such as Charon's *obol*, ceramic vessels, and food and drink.[32]

Children under the age of ten, slaves, and the rural masses all constitute demographic categories underrepresented in surviving inscriptions.[33] These individuals may be classified as those perceived as too young to merit a separate stone, those incapable of raising sufficient funds for this rite, or those far removed from the population centers that favored tomb inscriptions. Most markedly absent from Roman epitaphs were infants under the age of twelve months. Whereas it is believed that approximately 28 percent of newborns died before their first year, only 1.3 percent of more than sixteen thousand surviving tombstones from the Italian peninsula, for example, commemorate the death of an infant of that age.[34] This statistic does not necessarily imply that these children were denied a formal burial. Since this group is also largely absent from archaeological finds, however, they were likely laid to rest in a manner different from that used for the rest of the imperial-period population.

Prior to the time of Augustus, many slaves had simply been cast into mass graves (*puticuli*), since it was thought that they would not experience

---

31. J. C. Mann, "Epigraphic Consciousness," *JRS* 75 (1985): 204–6.

32. Toynbee, *Death and Burial*, 50–54. Toynbee's explanation of such rites as efforts to make the deceased feel at home or to keep them "alive" is difficult to substantiate in late Roman sources.

33. Saller and Shaw, "Tombstones," 127–30.

34. Peter Garnsey, "Child Rearing in Ancient Italy," in *The Family in Italy from Antiquity to the Present*, ed. David I. Kertzer and Richard P. Saller (New Haven: Yale University Press, 1991), 51–53.

the afterlife. City administrators were eager to bury the poor to avoid the health risks associated with abandoned corpses, but their obligations beyond this action were minimal.[35] Unless they were buried with or by their masters or a rich patron, slaves—and, for that matter, many of the poor—received no epitaph.[36] By contrast, freedmen and freedwomen produced a quantity of formulaic inscriptions disproportionate to their number. Their objective in investing in stone epitaphs, which could be commissioned only with their patrons' permission, was the assurance of continued recognition of their status as freed.[37] This population also sought to emulate the behavior of the wealthy patricians whom they served. By subtly omitting in some instances precise information regarding their unfree origins, however, they publicly and forcefully expressed their new status to future generations.[38]

For all of these reasons, epigraphy does not constitute a reliable source for statistical demographic analysis in any particular region or epoch.[39] Just as grave goods communicated an idealized identity, burial inscriptions allowed individuals commissioning them to display desired values and status to their contemporaries and descendants.[40] Economic hardship, varying cultural traditions, literacy rates, or any number of other factors

35. Éric Rebillard, "Les formes de l'assistance funéraire dans l'Empire romain et leur évolution dans l'antiquité tardive," *An Tard* 7 (1999): 269–82.

36. Burkhard Gladigow, "*Naturae deus humanae mortalis*: Zur sozialen Konstruktion des Todes in römischer Zeit," in *Leben und Tod in den Religionen: Symbol und Wirklichkeit*, ed. Gunther Stephenson (Darmstadt: Wissenschaftliche Buchgesellschaft, 1980), 126–28; Nock, "Cremation and Burial," 278.

37. They expressed this desire by means of a formula such as "libertis libertabusque posterisque eorum." Werner Eck, "Aussagefähigkeit epigraphischer Statistik und die Bestattung von Sklaven im kaiserzeitlichen Rom," in *Alte Geschichte und Wissenschaftsgeschichte: Festschrift für Karl Christ zum 65. Geburtstag*, ed. Peter Kneissl and Volker Losemann (Darmstadt: Wissenschaftliche Buchgesellschaft, 1988), 135–39.

38. Brent D. Shaw, "The Age of Roman Girls at Marriage: Some Reconsiderations," *JRS* 77 (1987): 40–41.

39. But see Brent D. Shaw, "The Cultural Meaning of Death: Age and Gender in the Roman Family," in *The Family in Italy from Antiquity to the Present*, 73–79.

40. Mann, "Epigraphic," 204–6; Morris, *Death-Ritual*, 158–61.

related to the local reuse of stone in subsequent centuries may also have affected the distribution of epitaphs. The families who tended to incorporate inscriptions in their funerary rites nonetheless shared the wish to benefit from community recognition of their standing as citizens or freed persons.

Christian funerary inscriptions, despite their origin in and coexistence with pagan epigraphy, emerged as a recognizably different tradition during the third century.[41] Their presence should not, however, be viewed as evidence for the spread of Christianity, since the practice was not necessarily adopted by the faithful. As late as the fifth century, Christian epitaphs might allude to paradise as the Elysian fields.[42] Although the practice of listing commemorators on the gravestone did not entirely cease, the emphasis of Christian funerary epigraphy was upon praise of the virtues of the deceased and confident proclamation of the soul's resurrection at the Last Judgment. Direct borrowing of liturgical passages, particularly the Psalms and the *acclamatio,* was also common in Christian epitaphs.[43] Early in their development, grave inscriptions of Christians therefore rapidly lost their legal wording. They concentrated less on worldly events than on matters pertaining to the afterlife. While still communicating an ideal vision of the deceased and limited to much the same demographic groups due to the expense of a carved stele, Christian epitaphs employed a rather different set of adjectives than pagan stones to express identity and edify the faithful.[44]

41. Gabriel Sanders, "Les chrétiens face à l'épigraphie funéraire latine," in *Assimilation et résistance à la culture gréco-romaine dans le monde ancien: Travaux du VIᵉ Congrès international d'études classiques (Madrid, septembre 1974),* ed. D. M. Pippidi (Bucharest: Editura Academiei, 1976), 290–94.

42. Françoise Descombes, ed., *RICG* 15,50 (Paris: Éditions du CNRS, 1985), 291–93.

43. Edmond Le Blant, "Les bas-reliefs des sarcophages chrétiens et les liturgies funéraires," *RA* n.s. 38 (1879): 224–25.

44. Charles Pietri, "Grabinschrift II (lateinisch)," in *Reallexikon für Antike und Christentum* 12 (Stuttgart: Anton Hiersemann, 1983), 551 ff.; Meyer, "Literacy," 180–82; Sanders, "Les chrétiens," 297–98.

Elizabeth Meyer and Ingrid Heidrich have drawn attention more specifically to the simplification of names, the lack of information about family
background, and a decrease in the use of titles on early Christian epitaphs.[45]
Of a person's three names standard in the Roman period, the *praenomen*
was used only by old aristocratic families by the second century, as was the
case with the *nomen* by the third century. Solely the *cognomen* survived into
the medieval period. Members of the elite, by contrast, continued to hold
multiple names until at least the fifth century and in some instances as late
as the second half of the sixth century.[46] In conjunction with these changes,
tombstones ceased to function as an expression of an heir's moral obligation. A declining number of living persons added their names to burial
inscriptions. Of the Christian funerary epitaphs from the fourth through
seventh centuries, 97 percent referred to the nuclear family of the deceased
as sponsoring the epitaph. This figure was significantly higher than among
pagans (80–82 percent).[47] In the inscription composed by Sidonius
Apollinaris in honor of his grandfather, for example, the bishop noted
twice that he, as a less immediate relation, still had the right to erect an
epitaph.[48] Although nuclear families continued to take primary responsibility for commissioning inscribed gravestones, as indicated on the few
epitaphs that acknowledged their sponsors, public recognition of this duty
evidently became far less important.

  Brent Shaw has characterized Christian epigraphy as evolving from the
expression of horizontal personal relationships of the deceased to an ideology focusing on vertical relationships *ad caelestem.*[49] Epitaphs therefore

45. Meyer, "Literacy," 188–90; Heidrich, "Südgallische Inschriften," 168.
46. Heinzelmann, *Bischofsherrschaft*, 15–20.
47. Shaw, "Latin Funerary," 465–69, 481–82.
48. W. B. Anderson, ed. and trans., *Sidonius Apollinaris, Poems and Letters* 3,12, Loeb Classical
Library 445 (Cambridge: Harvard University Press, 1965), 44–47.
49. Shaw, "Latin Funerary," 465–69, 481–82.

aid modern historians in documenting the origins of cults of saints only later attested to in late antique and early medieval hagiographical sources, like that of Eucharius, bishop of Trier in the second half of the third century.[50] Yet, inscriptions of this sort were aimed primarily at contemporaries and descendants in an effort to promote family status and religious identity through exclusive burial locations. When appropriate, Christian epitaphs thus made note of their close physical proximity to holy relics; the saints with whom families allied themselves varied in accordance with the relics present in their region. Larger cities such as Trier, Lyons, and Vienne hosted multiple saints, so families' choices of cemeteries devoted to particular cults revealed this important feature of their local allegiances.[51] Burial *ad sanctos* represented an important expression of the deceased's status, and thereby his or her family's honor, in a language comprehensible not just to community members but to literate Christians from anywhere in western Christendom who viewed the epitaph.[52] Funerary inscriptions reminded readers of the presence of the individual buried in a church or cemetery so that he or she would not be forgotten by contemporary or subsequent generations.

Changes in Fifth- and Sixth-Century Funerary Epigraphy in Gaul

A comparison of fourth-century Latin Christian burial inscriptions in Gaul with their pagan counterparts yields evidence of a rapid deterioration in the standards of epigraphy. Rather than signal a decline in the

---

50. Handley, "Beyond Hagiography," 189–190.

51. Mark A. Handley, "The Early Medieval Inscriptions of Britain, Gaul, and Spain: Studies in Function and Culture" (Ph.D. dissertation, University of Cambridge, 1998), 122–46, 286–87.

52. Yvette Duval, *Auprès des saints corps et âme: L'inhumation "ad sanctos" dans la chrétienté d'Orient et d'Occident du IIIe au VIIIe siècle* (Paris: Études augustiniennes, 1988), 66, 72, 83; Yvette Duval, "Sanctorum sepulcris sociari," in *Les fonctions des saints dans le monde occidental (IIIe–XIIe siècle): Actes du colloque organisé par l'École française de Rome, 27–29 octobre 1988,* Collection de l'École française de Rome 149 (Palais Farnèse: École française de Rome, 1991), 340–46.

wealth of the average family employing epitaphs,[53] the changes in epitaphs'
contents reflected a larger trend in literacy and writing styles. By no means,
however, should these developments be attributed to Christianity alone.[54]
During the instability of the fifth century, the rarity of epigraphy in Gaul
became even more pronounced as the supply of cut stone and the numbers
of the functionally literate minority dwindled. In his late-nineteenth-century
survey of Christian epitaphs in Gaul, Edmond Le Blant documented growing
inconsistency in the orthography, grammar, and paleography of funerary
inscriptions from the fourth through the seventh century.[55] The introduction of less formal types of script than the *monumentalis* for inscriptions in
the first century B.C.E. led to the proliferation of other hands, such as
Roman cursive in the third century and uncial in the fourth century. These
styles contributed to the irregularity and lack of clarity of many lapidary
inscriptions,[56] as did the early appearance of Vulgar Latin on these steles.[57]
In the meantime, regional differences in inscriptions also grew more marked,
as evidenced, for example, by the distinctiveness of those in Vienne in the
Burgundian kingdom.[58]

Although changes in written expression and the decline of epitaphs'
popularity during the fifth and sixth centuries had important repercussions, they did not signal the end everywhere of the effectiveness of Latin
epigraphy as a powerful vehicle of funerary commemoration. Just as in
imperial Rome, epitaphs were likely produced in local workshops. Cities
such as Trier, Arles, and Vienne may have had multiple workshops training

53. Shaw, "The Age," 42.
54. Sanders, "Les chrétiens," 294; Morris, *Death-Ritual,* 165; Meyer, "Literacy," 188–90.
55. Edmond Le Blant, "Paléographie des inscriptions latines du IIIe siècle à la fin du VIIe," *RA* 3d
ser. 29 (1896): 177–97, 345–55; 30 (1897): 30–40, 171–84; 31 (1897): 172–84.
56. Bernhard Bischoff, *Latin Paleography: Antiquity and the Middle Ages,* trans. Dáibhí Ó
Cróinín and David Ganz (Cambridge: Cambridge University Press, 1990), 54 ff.
57. Pietri, "Grabinschrift II," 551–52.
58. Mark A. Handley, "Inscribing Time and Identity in the Kingdom of Burgundy," in *Ethnicity
and Culture in Late Antiquity,* ed. Stephen Mitchell and Geoffrey Greatrex (London: Duckworth &
the Classical Press of Wales, 2000), 83–102.

stonecutters and plying their trade at particular cemeteries.[59] Those honored by such means were nearly twice as likely to be men as women. Mark Handley has estimated that roughly 63 percent of early medieval grave inscriptions recorded male names and 37 percent female names. Except among children, the ages of the deceased were often rounded to the nearest number ending in zero or five. He attributes this practice to the difficulty of calculating a person's age in an era when dates were based on regnal or consular years. Accurate rendering of the deceased's age thus appears to have been relatively unimportant to contemporaries.[60] As in the case of grave goods, women of child-bearing age and men of fighting age or possessing heritable property were frequently those buried with the most lavish displays. In epigraphical terms, those most likely to receive epitaphs were thus women recorded as being between the ages of twenty and fifty and men between twenty-five and sixty-five.[61]

Epitaphs in Gaul have been documented as belonging primarily to Catholic Christians. Little remains, for instance, in the way of Arian epitaphs.[62] Evidence exists, however, that members of Jewish communities patronized the same workshops as Catholics in times of relative safety.[63] The form taken by epitaphs and their distribution varied significantly. As may be seen in the following maps, for instance, burial steles continued to be erected in the region of Vienne from the late fifth to the seventh century; a high number of the inscriptions were distinguished from those

---

59. Handley, *The Early Medieval Inscriptions*, 208–19, 224–27.

60. Handley, *The Early Medieval Inscriptions*, 44–69.

61. Guy Halsall, "Female Status and Power in Early Merovingian Central Austrasia: The Burial Evidence," *EME* 5 (1996): 1–24; Handley, *The Early Medieval Inscriptions*, 61–68.

62. Handley, *The Early Medieval Inscriptions*, 112, 120.

63. Mark A. Handley, "'This Stone Shall Be a Witness' (Joshua 24.27): Jews, Christians, and Inscriptions in Early Medieval Gaul," in *Christian-Jewish Relations Through the Centuries*, Journal for the Study of the New Testament, suppl. ser. 192, Roehampton Papers 6, ed. Stanley E. Porter and Brook W. R. Pearson (Sheffield: Sheffield Academic Press, 2000), 239–54; Effros, "Beyond Cemetery Walls," 21.

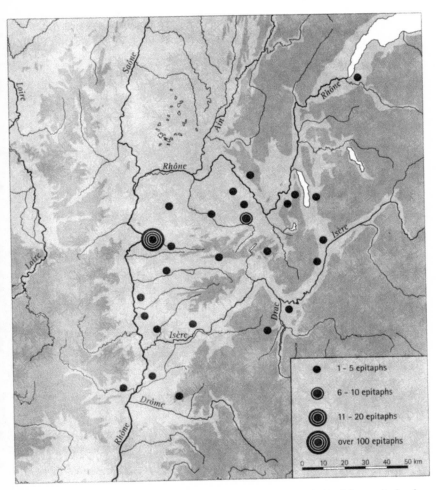

This map roughly illustrates the distribution of epigraphy in Viennoise du Nord that can be dated to the late fifth and mid-sixth centuries. Those fragments that could not be dated by Descombes have been excluded. Vienne, which had the largest concentration of surviving burial inscriptions, preserved far more evidence of the use of epigraphy in this period than the neighboring cities of Valence, Grenoble, and Geneva. Map designed by Franz Siegmeth on the basis of information provided in Descombes, RICG 15.

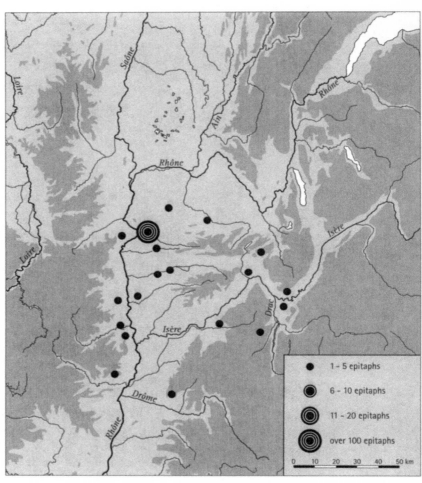

*From the second half of the sixth century in Viennoise du Nord, the city of Vienne still preserved
the most evidence for the continued use of epigraphy. On the whole, however, the various sites at
which inscriptions were still extant were clustered more closely together than in the prior period.
Geneva, Valence, and Aoste, by contrast, no longer revealed the commemorative rite's
survival. Map designed by Franz Siegmeth on the basis of information provided in Descombes,
RICG 15.*

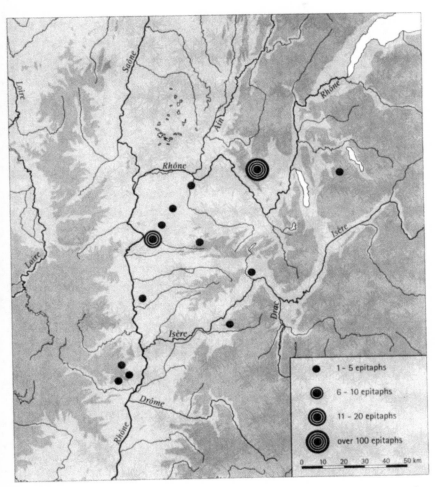

During the seventh century in Viennoise du Nord, Vienne was no longer the leading repository of epitaphs, but rather Briord seems to have gained a greater number of burial inscriptions than Vienne. This unprecedented change possibly owed to Briord's importance as a religious and pilgrimage center. Inhabitants of other small Rhône communities appear to have adopted the rite for the first time, demonstrating the importance of local idiosyncrasies of burial custom. Map designed by Franz Siegmeth on the basis of information provided in Descombes, RICG 15.

found in neighboring cities, such as Lyons, by their incorporation of consular dates. Mark Handley has suggested that the practice represented a
means of conveying shared identity in the Burgundian kingdom in the late
fifth and sixth centuries. The custom of dating in this fashion continued well
after the Frankish conquest, underlining the role of epigraphy in the
expression of civic allegiance.[64]

Bishops, especially those in Gallo-Roman strongholds of the Rhône
valley, were foremost among those who continued to commission epitaphs.
Of the forty sixth-century funerary poems composed by Venantius Fortunatus, for instance, eleven were dedicated to bishops. Although they
survive only in manuscript form, they reflect the conventions of inscribed
stones of the same period. They were likely intended for carving or painting,
perhaps in an abbreviated form, in a funerary context.[65] In the sixth century,
leading members of the clergy, despite hagiographers' effusive praise of
their ascetic intentions, clearly favored some of the more worldly aspects
of pagan epigraphy. As opposed to the comparatively modest epitaphs
lauding the humility of their fifth-century Christian predecessors, episcopal
inscriptions unabashedly proclaimed the religious reputation and public
standing of such cosmopolitan Christians.

Religious and hierarchical propaganda remained an integral part of elite
epigraphy into the late sixth century.[66] Notwithstanding their relative
anonymity as compared with earlier pagan epitaphs, the inscriptions of
high-status Christians were the few that continued to convey their family's
identity. In comparison to the prose inscriptions of the general population,
which Gabriel Sanders has described as vibrant and reflecting contempo-

---

64. Handley, "Inscribing Time and Identity," 91–93.

65. Judith W. George, *Venantius Fortunatus: A Latin Poet in Merovingian Gaul* (Oxford:
Clarendon Press, 1992), 85–87.

66. Heinzelmann, *Bischofsherrschaft*, 59 ff.; MacMullen, "The Epigraphic Habit," 238–41;
Descombes, *RICG* 15, 199–201.

rary religious belief, the verse epigraphy of the Christian episcopacy was highly formulaic and lacked elegance.[67] The testament of the bishop Bertichramnus of Le Mans (616), for instance, requested that Bishop Cabimoald take responsibility for his dignified burial. The traditional appearance of such a stone ensured that Bertichramnus's name would receive appropriate honors even if the verses on it were less than spontaneous in their expression. With appropriate tributes to Christian virtues added to this inscribed form of *laudatio* for the leaders of the faithful, such tombstones spread word of the deceased's reputation among members of the Christian community both at home and further abroad.[68]

A new set of values related to otherworldly standing rapidly gained the prominent position once occupied by legal status on the pagan epitaphs of Rome. Funerary inscriptions expressed great confidence in the eternal well-being of the soul in the afterlife and reassured readers of the benefits of a pious lifestyle.[69] In some cases, they also sought to protect the tomb from violation.[70] A no-longer-extant stele of a monk who died in 491, for instance, discovered in the seventeenth century in the convent of Saint-André-le-Haut (Vienne), bore an epitaph that proclaimed: "In this tomb is interred Severianus of good memory, who took up the religious life with a devoted mind, whose soul, returning to God its creator, left his terrestrial limbs to the earth. Having completed thirty-two years of life, he died on the day before the ides of August [and] will be resurrected in Christ our

---

67. Sanders, "Les inscriptions," 57–61.

68. "[C]orpusculo meo dignanter sepeliant, ut et de Domini mercedem conquirant, et in populo laus percurrat." G. Busson and A. Ledru, eds., *Le testament de Saint Bertrand,* in *AHM* 2 (Le Mans: Société des Archives historiques du Maine, 1902), 135; Heinzelmann, *Bischofsherrschaft,* 54–56.

69. Pietri, "Grabinschrift II," 580–84; Iiro Kajanto, "The Hereafter in Ancient Christian Epigraphy," *Arctos* 12 (1978): 27 ff.; Iiro Kajanto, "On the Idea of Eternity in Latin Epitaphs," *Arctos* 8 (1984): 59–69.

70. Ernst Diehl, ed., *ILCV* 2,3863, new ed. (Dublin: Weidmann, 1970), 295; Münz, "Anathema und Verwünschungen auf altchristlichen Monumenten," *Annalen des Vereins für nassauische Alterthumskunde und Geschichtsforschung* 14 (1875): 169–81, esp. 172–73.

Lord."[71] Having fulfilled his religious duties, Severianus was prepared for resurrection following the Last Judgment. As was stated unequivocally on other contemporary epitaphs, his soul thus obtained in the afterlife the reward he had earned in his lifetime.[72] The inscription and its location *ad sanctos* effectively laid claim to and publicized this success to his religious community and a broader audience.[73]

In spite of evidence of the popularity of epigraphy in elite circles in late antique Gaul, workmanship of burial monuments continued to decline during this period. Southwestern Gaul, the only region in which the quarrying of marble continued until the sixth century, was exceptional in its production of sarcophagi. Tombs of the "Aquitainian School," such as that found in the crypt of Saint-Seurin, Bordeaux, were skillfully decorated with vines, acanthus leaves, grapes, and in some instances the *Chi-Rho* insignia.[74] By the fifth century elsewhere in Gaul, however, the main source of marble for tombs and epitaphs was recycled stone from former pagan or, on occasion, Christian monuments. The tomb of Syragia, located at La Gayolle (Provence) during the medieval period and in the

---

71.   In hoc tumulo conditur bonae
                 memoriae Seuerianus, qui religionem
                 deuota mente suscepit [*sic*], quem
                 anima ad authorem D(eu)m
                 remeante, terrena membra
                 terris reliquit; exactis uitae
                 annis XXXII, obiit pridie idus
                 augustas, resurgit in Chr(ist)o D(o)m(in)o
                 nostro . . .

Descombes, *RICG* 15,152, 500–502. Edmond Le Blant, ed., *Inscriptions chrétiennes de la Gaule antérieures au VIIIe siècle* 2,436 (Paris: A l'Imprimerie impériale, 1865), 109–10.

72. "oravit semper quod obtenere meruit." Descombes, *RICG* 15,41, 275–77; 15,172, 527–30; Le Blant, *Inscriptions chrétiennes* 2,450, 122–24; 2,407, 59.

73. Duval, "Sanctorum," 343–46.

74. Raymond Duru, Paul-Albert Février, and Noël Duval, "Bordeaux: Saint-Seurin: Nécropoles et édifices cultuels (?)," in *Les premiers monuments chrétiens de la France* 2 (Paris: Picard, 1996), 40–45.

library of the Séminaire de Brignolles during the nineteenth century, is one example. This wealthy Christian woman's epitaph was inscribed sometime in the sixth century on the border of an elaborately carved Christian sarcophagus dating from the late second century.[75] In the extraordinary case of Saint-Maximin (Provence), which was rediscovered in the thirteenth century, the mausoleum's walls were carved with simple line drawings of Old and New Testament figures, as well as subjects inspired by the liturgy. White-marble slabs, whose date has not been confirmed, adorned the walls of a narrow chamber that contained imported and Arlesian marble sarcophagi of no earlier than the late fourth century. The somewhat crudely carved stones depicted a number of figures with their arms upraised in prayer, including Mary, the virgin and servant of the temple in Jerusalem, Daniel flanked by two lions, and an anonymous female figure (lacking its head but retaining the ends of long hair) in flowing vestments. The binding of Isaac was the subject of a fourth marble in the same location.[76]

Even in long-established stonecutting centers, fifth-century workshops began to opt for less costly and more easily accessible materials for their clients. By the mid-sixth century, for example, three of five extant milestone markers between Poitiers and Saintes were appropriated and transformed into sarcophagi.[77] The same type of reuse was true of markers along the old Roman road between Poitiers and Tours, contributing to the general difficulty of travel along the networks established by the Romans.[78] Elsewhere

75. Edmond Le Blant, *Les sarcophages chrétiens de la Gaule,* Collection de documents inédits sur l'histoire de France, troisième série archéologie (Paris: Imprimerie nationale, 1886), no. 215, pl. LIX,1, p. 157.

76. Paul-Albert Février, "Saint-Maximin: Mausolée antique," in *Les premiers monuments chrétiens de la France* 1 (Paris: Picard, 1995), 175–80; Le Blant, *Les sarcophages,* pls. LVII,1–2, LVIII,1–2, pp. 147–78; Le Blant, "Les bas-reliefs," 223–33, 280–92.

77. Heidrich, "Südgallische Inschriften," 169.

78. Dietrich Claude, *Topographie und Verfassung der Städte Bourges und Poitiers bis in das 11. Jahrhundert* (Lübeck: Matthiesen Verlag, 1960), 63.

in Poitou, limestone for fifth- and sixth-century carved tombs was quarried just a few kilometers from the cemeteries in which it was to be used. Stone sarcophagi in places such as Civaux and Antigny, by contrast, were sometimes employed multiple times despite legislation against such practices. The shape of these tombs was trapezoidal, and, if decorated at all, they depicted geometric shapes or a cross with three arms.[79] Written sources, however, such as the hagiographical works of Gregory of Tours, also describe lavishly adorned tombs in churches. Some were augmented with precious metals or cloth.[80] The surviving physical evidence is thus not representative of all of the types of tombs that once existed in sixth-century Gaul, especially those fashioned from or with costly or organic materials.

In cemeteries in which epitaphs were prevalent, stonecutters often relied upon informal models for funerary inscriptions, since the services of fully literate individuals capable of composing original verse or prose were difficult to procure. Sidonius Apollinaris, for instance, referred to two separate responsibilities in the production of an epitaph: his own work as the composer and that of the engraver (*quadratarius*). He had little positive to say about the latter and noted their tendency to make multiple errors.[81] The frequency with which existing stones were copied is reflected in the propensity of epitaphs from particular geographical regions to contain similar or identical phrases. This trend was likely magnified by workshops' development of "house styles" characteristic of a particular cemetery.[82] After the fourth century, the increasingly common use of formulae brought even greater conservatism to Christian epigraphic expression.[83] Chosen

79. James, *The Merovingian Archaeology* 1, 68–77.
80. Ian Wood, "Sépultures ecclésiastiques et sénatoriales dans la vallée du Rhône (400–600)," *Médiévales* 31 (1996): 13–27.
81. Anderson, *Sidonius* 3,12, 44–45. Edmond Le Blant has noted that in the Roman catacombs the gravediggers (*fossores*) were also responsible for carving inscriptions and burying the dead. Le Blant, *Inscriptions chrétiennes* 2, 192–93.
82. Handley, *The Early Medieval Inscriptions*, 253–55.
83. Pietri, "Grabinschrift II," 563–66.

not only from professional manuals, verses or formulae might easily be copied from pagan and Christian stones in the same or another cemetery.[84] On occasion, entire gravestones were appropriated for creating new epitaphs. Such was the case for two fifth-century Christian inscriptions found on opposite sides of one stone near the church of St. Matthias, Trier. The longer and more evenly engraved epitaph occupied the back side of a marble plaque containing an earlier commemoration on its front. The more recent engraver, who was presumably responsible for scratching out the earlier names of the deceased and the person who dedicated the original stone, copied the first inscription with few adaptations. There was little to add beyond chiseling in the names of the recently deceased as well as Concordius and Concordialis as commemorators.[85] Widespread plagiarism in epigraphy, however, contributed to numerous grammatical errors; the seventh-century epitaph of Riculfus and Guntello incorrectly modified its model, an inscription composed in the singular.[86] Such practices were indicative of the deteriorating Latin skills of those who sponsored and composed funerary inscriptions produced in Gaul. This evolution was not linked to a decline in the status or resources of individuals who commissioned gravestones, but reflected instead a shift in the training and priorities of those responsible for the commemoration of the deceased.

---

84. See Le Blant's categorization of phrases common to particular regions of Gaul. Le Blant, *Inscriptions chrétiennes* 2, 152–58, 178–85; Sanders, "Les chrétiens," 288–89.

85. Gauthier, *RICG* 1,13, 136–39; Edmond Le Blant, ed., *Inscriptions chrétiennes de la Gaule antérieures au VIIIᵉ siècle* 1,239 and 1,239A (Paris: A l'Imprimerie impériale, 1856), 344.

86. According to an eighteenth-century transcription, the seventh-century inscription at the château de Saint-André, Briord (canton Lhuis, Ain), read:

    IN HOC TVMVLO RIQVIISCVNT BENE MEMORIE
    RICVLFVS ET IVGALIS SVA GVNTELLO QVI FVERVNT
    INSIGNIS MERITIS IN AMVRE SEMPIR AMICI OMNEVOS ABSTVTI
    PASSIINS DVLCISSIMI APTI . . .

Descombes, *RICG* 15,269, 698–701; Le Blant, *Inscriptions chrétiennes* 2,380, 18.

Due to increasing difficulty in locating accomplished stonecutters and changes in commemorative customs, epigraphy was sometimes reduced to the barest identification of the Christian by name. The sixth-century rural cemetery of Neuvicq-Montguyon (Charente-Maritime), in which sarcophagus burial appears to have been the norm rather than the exception, constituted an unusual site. In the Merovingian necropolis, numerous inscriptions on the sarcophagus covers consisted of just a cross followed by the name of the deceased. It was clearly not a shortage of stone but more likely literacy levels or local tradition that led to this brevity. The population, to the extent to which it is possible to rely on names for an indication of ethnicity, probably represented a mixture of persons of Germanic and Gallo-Roman identity.[87] In this particular community, a cross and a single name was deemed sufficient to commemorate the deceased as a faithful Christian.

The early medieval Christian reuse and adaptation of previously pagan burial facilities was also quite common in the fifth and sixth centuries. Appropriating an older pagan sarcophagus decorated with a sculpture of a reclining figure upon a couch, one early-sixth-century Christian stonecutter apparently defaced what he perceived to be an unacceptable image. In its place, he created a smooth surface for a new inscription that boldly commemorated the transition of the nobleman Ennodius from the height of secular power to the otherworldly glory of Christian solitude.[88] Although

87. Louis Maurin, "Le cimetière mérovingien de Neuvicq-Montguyon (Charente-Maritime)," *Gallia* 29 (1971): 151–89.

88.   ✝ stemmate precipuum, trabeatis fascibus ortum
              Innodium leti hic sopor altus habet.
          qui post patricia preclarus cingola rectur
              subiecit X̄p̄i colla subacta iogo,
          post pones ultra mundi protendere ponpas
              et potius domeno soluere uota malens.
          sic gemeno felix perfunctus munere gaudet,
              egregius mundo placetus et domeno.
          hoc tomolo cuius tantum nam membra quiescunt,
              letatur patria mens, paradise, tua.

the antique marble sarcophagus may have already been damaged in events unrelated to its reuse, its further destruction and the addition of an epitaph reflected early medieval Christians' ambivalence toward secular Roman statuary.[89] Sometimes older Christian tombs were reused without the mutilation of their sculpture exhibiting more acceptable scenes. An antique tomb depicting Jonas and Moses, among others, remained untouched until its appropriation for the burial of the nun Eusebia of Marseilles, who was commemorated with the addition of a late-sixth-century epitaph.[90] Charlemagne (d. 814) is thought to have been interred in a second-century Roman marble sarcophagus depicting the rape of Proserpina.[91] The reuse of ancient tombs was thus not always viewed negatively in the early Middle Ages, especially considering the shortage of comparable examples of funerary sculpture, since they were no longer being produced in workshops in Gaul.[92] The abandonment of this medium reflected not only lack of demand for skilled stonecutters and carvers but also changes in the expression of religious belief, social competition, and artistic vision.

The tomb is located at La Gayolle, Provence. Diehl, *ILCV* 1,149, 39; Le Blant, *Inscriptions chrétiennes* 2,628, 494–97.

89. Reactions to classical tombs varied significantly. In Anglo-Saxon England, Bede described as miraculous the discovery in 695 of an ancient sarcophagus thereafter used for the burial of the saint and former queen Aethelthryth at her monastic foundation of Ely. Bertram Colgrave and R. A. B. Mynors, eds., *Bede's Ecclesiastical History of the English People* 4,19 (Oxford: Clarendon Press, 1969), 392–99.

90. Following the *Chi-Rho* insignia, the inscription stated: "hic requiescet in pa/ce Eusebia, religiosa, / magna ancella d̄ī. qui / in seculo ab heneunte / etate sua uixit / secolares annus XIIII / et, ubi a d̄o. electa est, / in monasterio s̄c̄s. Cyrici / seruiuet annus quinqua/genta. recesset sub die / prid. kal. Octobr. ind. sest." Diehl, *ILCV* 1,1670, 324; Atsma, "Die christliche Inschriften," 36; Le Blant, *Inscriptions chrétiennes* 2,545, 300–302.

91. Janet L. Nelson, "Women at the Court of Charlemagne: A Case of Monstrous Regiment?" in *Medieval Queenship*, ed. John Carmi Parsons (New York: St. Martin's Press, 1993), 43–44.

92. For a general discussion of the use of restraint in the adornment of funerary memorials as an articulation of status, see Aubrey Cannon, "The Historical Dimension in Mortuary Expressions of Status and Sentiment," *Current Anthropology* 30 (1989): 437–49.

The aesthetic evolution in sarcophagi over the course of the Merovingian period was not limited to their decoration but also affected their overall conception. The standard shape of tombs, which had been rectangular in the late Roman period, became trapezoidal, with a wide head and a narrow foot, in the early Middle Ages. Locally produced sarcophagi in southwestern Gaul, for instance, were generally slightly trapezoidal with sloping or roof-shaped lids. Their decoration usually consisted of low-relief vegetal patterns or chrisms carved in Pyrenean marble and may have reflected a return in the sixth century to indigenous pre-Christian sculptural styles and linguistic traditions.[93] The sixth-century marble tomb of Saint-Béat, for instance, was adorned with a repeating pattern of chevrons in two registers. A *Chi-Rho* monogram surrounded by a triple ring of laurels was placed between two columns at the center of the long decorated side.[94] Stone tombs manufactured in southern Gaul, as at Arles, were comparatively slower to change from classical Roman styles.[95] Some rectilinear sarcophagi were supplied with domed covers scavenged from locally quarried columns of the Roman period split in half along their diameters.[96]

The few tomb reliefs in Gaul that date from the early Middle Ages reveal that their decoration had undergone transformation, despite the fact that biblical themes remained appropriate subjects for portrayal. At Charenton-sur-Cher (Cher), a seventh-century depiction of Daniel and the lions adorned one side of a white marble tomb discovered at the probable site of a Columbanian monastic house for women.[97] The Toulouse-Rodez group of

93. James, *The Merovingian Archaeology* 1, 29, 41–43.

94. It later served as a baptismal font. Jean Boube, "Martres-Tolosane: Église et cimetière paléochrétiens," in *Les premiers monuments chrétiens de la France* 2, 170–76.

95. Patrick Périn and Alain Dierkens, *L'art mérovingien: Permanences et innovations*, Feuillets de la cathédrale de Liège 25–26 (Liège: Trésor de la cathédrale de Liège, 1996), 13.

96. Jean-Claude Papinot, *Notices sur les vestiges archéologiques de Civaux* (Poitiers: Société des amis du pays de Civaux, 1971), 9–12.

97. The sarcophagus is now in the collection of the Musées de Bourges. Alain Ferdière and Françoise Prévot, "Centre: Cher, Eure-et-Loir, Indre, Indre-et-Loire, Loir-et-Cher, Loiret," in *Les premiers monuments chrétiens de la France* 2, 82; Le Blant, *Les sarcophages* 73, 55–58, pls. 15,1–2.

sarcophagi likewise included human figures and biblical scenes.[98] Most ornamented sarcophagi of the Merovingian period, regional productions with distinctive styles primarily from south of the Loire, were nonetheless more simply decorated. Single or multiple crosses at the head of tombs were common in the Bordelais and Nivernais, whereas geometric patterns were more typically produced in Burgundy and Champagne.[99] Some tombs may also have been adorned in a more temporary fashion than with stone carving. Written evidence attests that the sarcophagi of saints might have been decorated with paint or cloth coverings. In his hagiographical descriptions of miracles performed at tombs, Gregory of Tours, for instance, made reference to drapery covering the holy graves.[100] This factor may help explain why the vast majority of surviving stone sarcophagi from the Merovingian period were not embellished with designs of any sort.

Aside from their decorative functions, carved tombs with crosses served a purpose similar to that of epitaphs.[101] Because the dead were believed to be resurrected *in situ,* crosses on or in tombs signaled first and foremost the presence of the mortal remains of Christians. In the Paris region, stone and plaster tombs were adorned with a variety of crosses, crosses and palms, or sometimes geometric designs.[102] Three stone sarcophagi discovered in 1974 in the apse of Saint-Étienne, Nevers, for instance, had multiple crosses carved on the surface of the head end of the tomb's base.[103] Similar patterns have been observed on the covers and sides

98. James, *The Merovingian Archaeology* 1, 49–51.

99. Luce Pietri, "Les sépultures privilégiées en Gaule d'après les sources littéraires," in *L'inhumation privilégiée,* 139; Le Blant, *Les sarcophages,* xv.

100. See Gregory of Tours's *Libri historiarum* X 5,48; *Vitae patrum* 15,4 and 19,4; *Liber in gloria confessorum* 21; *Virtutibus sancti Martini episcopi* 2,10, 2,54, 2,60, and 4,43.

101. Périn and Dierkens, *L'art mérovingien,* 13.

102. Denise Fossard, "Les anciennes églises suburbaines de Paris IVᵉ–Xᵉ siècles: Le cimetière Saint-Marcel," *Paris et Île-de-France: Mémoires* 11 (1960): 230ff.

103. May Vieillard-Troïekouroff, "Trois sarcophages mérovingiens découverts à Saint-Étienne de Nevers en janvier 1974," *BM* 138 (1980): 221–27.

of stone sepulchers of the Merovingian period at Saint-Denis and in the region of Trier.[104] Such a tomb represented a source of pride for the family that commissioned it, particularly if it was displayed above ground in a local church. While crosses did not express an individual's identity precisely, they indicated general concern that the deceased be recognized in perpetuity as one of the faithful. In the short term, too, we may surmise that this factor proved critical, since non-Christian graves probably received less respectful handling. Although not especially influential in Merovingian Gaul, legislation under Justinian had differentiated between treatment of a group's own dead and those of its enemies.[105]

Whereas marble tombs were quarried in the region of Burgundy and Arles, and limestone sarcophagi in Poitou,[106] plaster sarcophagi were more typical of the Paris region due to the availability of gypsum. Their ornamentation nonetheless resembled the carved tombs of Poitiers.[107] Found in great numbers, plaster tombs were not imported but produced at or near the burial site. They were apparently too heavy and fragile to have been transported any distance. The visibility of the decoration of such sarcophagi was therefore short-lived; unlike stone tombs, they did not receive attention on their way from the quarry to their cemeterial destinations. Plaster tombs were seen by the living just before and at the time of the funeral.

Molded crosses, chrisms, geometric shapes, and occasionally human figures embellished the exteriors or even interiors of plaster sarcophagi, the latter of which may have been visible to guests peering into an open grave during the funeral. In rare examples, biblical scenes, such as Daniel

104. E. Viollet-le-Duc, "L'église impériale de Saint-Denis," *RA* n.s. 2,3 (1861): 348–50. For sixth- and seventh-century examples with a provenance of the region of Trier, see Wilhelm Reusch, ed., *Frühchristliche Zeugnisse im Einzugsgebiet von Rhein und Mosel 67–72, 74–78* (Trier: Unitas-Buchhandlung, 1965), 97–103, pls. 67–72, 74–78.

105. Jill Harries, "Death and the Dead in the Late Roman Empire," in *Death in Towns*, 56–67.

106. Denise Fossard, "Répartition des sarcophages mérovingiens à décor en France," in *Études mérovingiennes*, 117–26.

107. James, *The Merovingian Archaeology* 1, 68, 85.

in the lions' den, were also depicted.[108] In Paris and Saint-Denis cemeteries alone, more than two hundred cast types have been identified by their patterns.[109] The technique was not always entirely mastered; at Villemomble (Seine-Saint-Denis), tombs 218 and 181 had "PAX TECVM" inscribed on a cross backward, presumably due to a lack of refinement in the making of the molds.[110] Although the simplicity of this type of adornment makes the exact dating of individual monuments very difficult, the practice of decorating plaster tombs likely began in the second half of the sixth century and continued until at least the mid-eighth century.[111]

Noting affinities between the designs appearing on plaster sarcophagi and Merovingian brooches, however, Denise Fossard has proposed that the molds employed constituted direct imitations of the jewelry placed in contemporary graves. In response, Michel Fleury has countered that the artisans of the two art forms were not identical but merely instituted similar designs due to their common dependence on compasses.[112] In either case, the likenesses between cast tomb ornamentation and the more intricate designs characteristic of Merovingian jewelry indicate that the individuals who employed them had similar taste in decoration. Whether or not the artists were the same, their designs must have been conceived for the

108. Denise Fossard, May Vieillard-Troïekouroff, and Élisabeth Chatel, eds., *Recueil général des monuments sculptés en France pendant le haut moyen âge (iv*ᵉ*–x*ᵉ *siècles)* 1,102, Mémoires de la section d'archéologie 2 (Paris: Bibliothèque nationale, 1978), 61–62, pl. 31.

109. M. Durand-Lefebvre, "Les sarcophages mérovingiens de Paris," *CA* 6 (1952): 168–71; Périn and Dierkens, *L'art mérovingien,* 12.

110. Gilbert-Robert Delehaye, "Les sarcophages mérovingiens en plâtre de Villemomble: Fabrication, décor," *CA* 35 (1987): 41–49.

111. Patrick Périn and Laurent Renou, "Les sarcophages mérovingiens de plâtre moulé trouvés à Paris: Technologie, ornementation, chronologie," *Bulletin de liaison: Association française d'archéologie mérovingienne* 5 (1981): 49–52.

112. Fossard, "Les anciennes églises," 250–54; Michel Fleury, "L'origine du décor des sarcophages de plâtre mérovingiens de la région parisienne," in *Problèmes de chronologie relative et absolue concernant les cimetières mérovingiens d'entre Loire et Rhin: Actes du II*ᵉ *colloque archéologique de la IV*ᵉ *section de l'École pratique des hautes études (Paris, 1973),* ed. Michel Fleury and Patrick Périn (Paris: Librairie Honoré Champion, 1978), 111–25.

funerary ceremony as well as to identify the interred Christian in perpetuity. Like some artifacts placed on or near the corpse at burial, decorated sarcophagi may have also fulfilled amuletic functions.

The Demise of Funerary Epitaphs?

What was the fate of funerary epigraphy in the late Merovingian period? The nineteenth-century epigrapher Edmond Le Blant argued that the production of epitaphs in Gaul steadily decreased during the sixth and seventh centuries and ceased altogether during the last decades of the 600s.[113] Describing this evolution as evidence of the demise of Roman towns as centers of cultural, political, and economic interaction, Brent Shaw has linked the alleged abandonment of epigraphy to the transition to the predominantly rural landscape of the early medieval West. For Shaw, the end of funerary inscriptions signaled the profound gulf between Roman imperial settlements and cultural achievements and those of the early Middle Ages.[114]

Yet late Merovingian epigraphy, while scarce, did not drop off as dramatically as has often been portrayed. Although new discoveries from the late seventh century and the early to mid-eighth century are rare, scholars such as Nancy Gauthier, Françoise Descombes, and Françoise Prévot have reevaluated some of the monumental evidence assessed by Le Blant and have reassigned a significant number of epitaphs to the later part of the Merovingian period. Gauthier, in particular, has challenged Le Blant's general assumption that there was a noticeable break between Merovingian and Carolingian epigraphy in Gaul; she suggests that this attitude caused

---

113. Edmond Le Blant, *L'épigraphie chrétienne en Gaule et dans l'Afrique romaine* (Paris: Ernest Leroux, Éditeur, 1890), 26–27.
114. Shaw, "Latin Funerary," 483.

him to date some epitaphs earlier than appropriate.[115] Although Gauthier herself may have mistakenly assigned some of these inscriptions a late date solely on the basis of their inclusion of Germanic names, the situation is not as clear-cut as once assumed by Le Blant.[116] Gravestones were continuously produced not only in Gaul but also in northern Italy, as evidenced, for example, in Pavia during the 730s and 740s.[117]

Although the Carolingians greatly refined the art of composing and engraving funerary inscriptions—above all, those in verse[118]—they did not reinvent epigraphy, since the tradition did not cease completely in the late Merovingian period.[119] Albeit somewhat faltering in their production during the early eighth century, epitaphs remained an effective mode of burial expression among elite Christians in the seventh and eighth centuries. Particularly in the context of ecclesiastical and monastic centers, funerary inscriptions were never completely abandoned in Gaul. To draw a neat line between Merovingian and Carolingian epigraphical traditions corresponding to the rise of the Pippinid family is to presuppose an artificial gap between the two periods' cultural traditions. This premise rests primarily on traditional historiographical assumptions contrasting Merovingian

115. An example is the epitaph of Hlodericus, discovered at the church of St. Maximus, Trier, in 1817. Whereas Le Blant attributed the inscription to the late sixth or early seventh century, Gauthier notes that it cannot be earlier than the eighth century. Gauthier, *RICG* 1,135, 352–55, 102–4; Le Blant, *Inscriptions chrétiennes* 1,261, 369–70.

116. Handley, "The Early Medieval Inscriptions," 9.

117. Paul Deschamps, "Étude sur la paléographie des inscriptions lapidaires de la fin de l'époque mérovingienne aux dernières années du XIIᵉ siècle," *BM* 88 (1929): 11–18; Nicolette Gray, "The Paleography of Latin Inscriptions in the Eighth, Ninth, and Tenth Centuries in Italy," *Papers of the British School at Rome* 16 (1948): 44 ff.; Nick Everett, "Liutprandic Letters in Lombard Epigraphy," in *Roman, Runes, and Ogham: Medieval Inscriptions in the Insular World and on the Continent,* ed. Katherine Forsyth, John Higgitt, and D. Parsons (Stamford, Lincolnshire: Shaun Tyas, forthcoming).

118. Deschamps, "Étude sur la paléographie," 13; Luitpold Wallach, "The Epitaph of Alcuin: A Model of Carolingian Epigraphy," *Speculum* 30 (1955): 367–73.

119. I thank Peter Brown, Mark Handley, and Jean Michaud for sharing with me their expertise in this subject.

barbarity with Carolingian innovation. Carolingian epigraphical renewal was in fact largely dependent upon the antique and early medieval traditions described above.

Of great import, too, are the consequences that the proposed demise of epigraphy would have had for funerary rites of the elite. Although long-term anonymity was already the norm for burial by the seventh century, short-term means of identifying graves likely existed: for example, wood markers, dirt mounds, or even plants, flowers, or cloth banners. For the powerful groups who employed funerary inscriptions in Gaul, however, their alleged abandonment of epigraphy in the late seventh century would have coincided with their rejection of grave goods.[120] If mortuary deposits and funerary inscriptions truly disappeared from common use at roughly the same time, then historians and archaeologists are proposing a radical change in commemorative ideology over a relatively short period. The physical expression of identity intrinsic to both customs would have become obsolete. Ian Morris has interpreted the decline in epigraphy and grave goods as resulting from new definitions of status based upon a hierarchy of spatial symbolism rather than decorative monuments.[121]

Dramatic shifts in early medieval burial practice were indeed possible under certain circumstances, since the rites were dynamic and reflective of the individuals who performed them. Chronic political or economic instability, wars, epidemics, or increased prosperity could bring about considerable alterations to funerary customs over short periods of time.[122] Yet these do not appear to have been the case in the late seventh century. Unlike the steady decrease in the use of grave goods across the population, those who commissioned epigraphy had long constituted an exclusive and limited

120. Günther P. Fehring, *The Archaeology of Medieval Germany: An Introduction*, trans. Ross Samson (London: Routledge, 1991), 76.

121. Morris, *Death-Ritual*, 169–71.

122. Halsall, *Settlement and Social Organization*, 279–80.

circle. For this reason, as well as the essential conservatism of its contents, the custom was by definition less susceptible to drastic change. Likewise, the benefits of identifying the location of the deceased remained important to contemporaries, since they reflected the ability of future generations to care for graves. The growing prestige of burial *ad sanctos* actually promoted the use of epigraphy, since it helped identify the resting places of the dead who were thus honored.[123] Clerics' continued promulgation of ecclesiastical and secular measures protecting markers and resting places of the faithful belied the anonymity of at least elite grave sites.[124] Another century would pass before liturgical recognition of high-status Christians in the *libri memoriales* (addressed in Chapter V) emerged as a possible substitute for epigraphical expression.[125]

A more complete discussion of the provenance, content, and other qualities of the small quantity of surviving late-seventh- and eighth-century epigraphical evidence in Gaul is therefore warranted.[126] A thorough assessment of funerary inscriptions and tomb decoration prior to and contemporary with their alleged demise demonstrates that epigraphy retained a limited but influential role in privileged Christian burial places in the late Merovingian period. Elite families and religious communities continued to express concern with the placement, identification, and protection of the physical remains and tombs of the deceased; they indicated the importance of their burial places in some cases with funerary inscriptions and tomb decoration.

123. Duval, *Auprès des saints*, 6–11; Frederick S. Paxton, *Christianizing Death: The Creation of a Ritual Process in Early Medieval Europe* (Ithaca: Cornell University Press, 1990), 52 ff.

124. E. A. Lowe, "The Vatican MS. of the Gelasian Sacramentary and Its Supplement at Paris," *JTS* 27 (1926): fol. 504, 365–66; Franz Beyerle and Rudolf Buchner, eds., *Lex ribuaria* 55(54),2, *MGH: Leges* 3,2 (Hannover: Impensis bibliopolii Hahniani, 1954), 104.

125. Karl Schmid and Otto Gerhard Oexle, "Voraussetzungen und Wirkung des Gebetsbundes von Attigny," *Francia* 2 (1974): 80–89.

126. My discussion will not present a complete catalogue of these inscriptions. This vast task is currently in capable hands at the Centre national de la recherche scientifique (CNRS), Paris, and the Centre d'études supérieures de civilisation médiévale (CESCM), Poitiers.

Although evidence is lacking for inhabitants of Gaul of lesser financial means, it may be assumed that the visible features of burial display retained their significance for them as well, albeit in less permanent media. No abrupt break in attitudes or behavior toward the dead was communicated through epigraphy in the late Merovingian or early Carolingian periods.

Seventh- and Eighth-Century Funerary Epigraphy and Tomb Imagery

Although increasingly limited in geographical distribution and quantity, seventh-century epitaphs extolled many of the same values as those praised during the preceding centuries. An inscription of the second half of the seventh century found in an early church in Lyons conveyed familial commitment to the appropriate burial of the deceased kin. Incised on a marble plaque, the epitaph of a twenty-eight-year-old woman dated 24 April 653 began: "✝ In this tomb rests Optata of fond memory. Her husband, Arnulfus, on account of his love [for her], interred her in this sepulcher."[127] Another expression of familial piety was the epitaph of the *infacia* Maurolenus, age twenty-three in 660, which was found in 1888 in the church dedicated to Saint-Pierre in Vienne.[128]

Seventh-century inscriptions commemorating clerics and members of monastic houses, by contrast, often commended the deceased for their contributions to the churches in which the bodily remains of the deceased were now housed. The priest Carusus of Briord, Burgundy, buried on 18

127.   ✝ IN HOC TOMOLO REQVIESCIT BONE MEMORI
         AE OPTATA PRO CVIVS AMORE VIR SVVS ARNVL
         FVS CONDEDIT SEPVLTVRA . . .

Pierre Wuilleumier, ed., *Inscriptions latines des Trois Gaules (France)* 292, 17th supplement to *Gallia* (Paris: CNRS, 1963), 115; Michel Colardelle, ed., *Des burgondes à Bayard: Mille ans de moyen âge* 103 (Grenoble: Imprimerie Dardelet, 1981), 62–63.

128. Descombes, *RICG* 15,104, 433–36; Edmond Le Blant, ed., *Nouveau recueil* 107 (Paris: Imprimerie nationale, 1892), 126.

October 629, was remembered on his epitaph as a man vigilant in performing the religious services. Described as a Christian of great compas-
sion, he was alleged to have been the friend of all.[129] A much briefer
epitaph, now lost, commemorated the deacon Saturninus in the year 694.
The stone was found at Toulaud (canton de Saint-Péray, Ardèche), but
according to Françoise Descombes, its style, date, and paleography suggest an origin at the nearby Christian cemetery of Crussol.[130] Likewise, the
epitaph of Amatus (d. circa 633/634), composed by his brother, commemorated him as one "who, due to his distinguished merits, was the first priest
at Vézeronce (and), appointed to the holy altars, participated in this duty."[131]
Religious communities happily preserved such inscriptions because they
considered these esteemed clerics part of the clerical *familia*. Present and
future members of a church benefited from knowing that they were part
of a long and venerable tradition. In the case of Amatus's inscription and
a very similar one at the same location dedicated circa 18 August 630 by

---

129. Descombes reconstructs the now lost inscription from a manuscript of de Veyle as:

> Hic requiiscit bone me-
> moreae in Chr(ist)i no(mine) Carusus,
> pr(e)sb(yter), qui fuit ad Dei officio
> paratus. Vmanetas in eo sa-
> tes laudanda, amicus omne-
> bus . . .

Descombes, *RICG* 15,263, 675–79; Le Blant, *Inscriptions chrétiennes* 2,375, 9–10.
130. Descombes, *RICG* 15,17, 230–32; Le Blant, *Inscriptions chrétiennes* 2,477, 195–97, pl. 400.
131. As reconstructed by Descombes, the first part of the epitaph reads:

> ✟ Hic tua, uenerabilis Amate, requicunt membra
> sepulcro qui fuit insignis meritis Veseroncia prior
> pr(es)b(yte)r officio altarebus sacris prelictus adesit. Ver mag-
> nus ac mente benignus, abstutus, passiins, dulcissemus, aptus,
> non te nouilior criscit ex mure parentum. . . .

This inscription was once preserved at the château of Saint-André, Briord, along with the epitaphs of
Carusus and Felix. Descombes, *RICG* 15,265, 688–92; Le Blant, *Inscriptions chrétiennes* 2,373a, 4–5.

him to his brother, the priest Felix, attention to high status was very prominent in the epitaphs.[132]

An innovative feature of seventh-century epigraphy was the expression of concern not only that the dead be recognized as buried *ad sanctos* but also that they receive the prayers of priests and faithful Christians. Funerary inscriptions might be used to demand assistance in the commemoration of the deceased from those who passed by their graves. Such epitaphs were most effective when placed in a frequently traversed location in a church. Far from signaling a trend toward elite interment with no vested interest in epigraphy, funerary inscriptions of elite lay and religious figures became more aggressive in their approach toward what must have been a predominantly clerical audience. For instance, the gravestone of the presbyter Agapius, who died in 607 or 608 at the age of eighty-five, asked those who recited prayers to include him in them.[133] These individuals could best intone the Psalms and were the only ones who could perform the Masses desired by Christians fearful of purgatorial punishment for their sins. This evidence, discussed in the next two chapters, was symptomatic of growing fears from the late sixth century onward for the fate of Christian souls prior to resurrection.

An example of this increasingly popular genre was the proposed late-seventh-century epitaph of Trasemirus. The stone, which was decorated with two doves and three large standing crosses symbolic of the crucifixion, was discovered at Mandourel, near Durban (Aude). The inscription acted as a call to prayer: "✝ In the name of Christ pray, you men, for the soul of Trasemirus, who retired from this age . . . whose body lies in this grave. He lives with Christ in eternity. Amen."[134] A comparable seventh-

---

132. Descombes, *RICG* 15,264, 679–88; Le Blant, *Inscriptions chrétiennes* 2,377, 12–13.

133. "[Qui]squis deuertis ad ora[ndum] / ora pro Agapio pr(es)b(yte)ro. . . ." Descombes, *RICG* 15,252, 650–53.

134. The epitaph proclaimed: "✝ IN X̄P̄I N̄Ē ORATE HOM̄S PRO ANIMA TRASEMIRI QVIEVIT DE OC saeculo . . . CVIVS CORPVS i?ACEt IN HOC TVMVLO VIBAT C̄V X̄P̄O IN ETERN̄V AM̄Ē." Le Blant,

or eighth-century epitaph dedicated to Hermensen directly addressed those who passed by at Saint-Outrille-du-Château at Bourges (Cher).[135] The clerics who viewed such an inscription might thereby be encouraged to assist the deceased with their devotions, as the early-seventh-century inscription carved into an anonymous stone found at Bourges before 1870 clearly enjoined: "I ask of whoever comes here: pray." This admonishment was followed by a petition to God that the deceased's soul be spared the gates of hell.[136] The desire for prayers of the faithful may also be implicit in gravestones in and outside of Gaul that recounted acts of charity by the deceased, a practice also attested to in contemporary Merovingian wills. Alms to widows, orphans, and the poor, for instance, were enumerated on an early-seventh-century stone commemorating a twenty-year-old woman named Bertichildis found in Kempten (near Bingen).[137]

Inscriptions chrétiennes 2,621B, 482, pl. 85; Gisela Ripoll López and Isabel Velázquez Soriano, "El epitafio de Trasemirus (Mandourle, Villesèque de Corbières, Aude)," *Espacio, tiempo y forma,* ser. 1: *Prehistoria y arqueología* 3 (1990): 273–87.

135. Found in 1874, the inscription on top of the tomb read (as reconstructed by Françoise Jenn):

QVI NEMVS H[O]C PENETRAS ET EO[. . .]
HERMENSEN DISCE HOC POSIT[VM . . .]
HAEC FVLSIT ORBI CARNIS DES[. . .]
EXORTA PROAVVM GERM[. . . .]
OBIIT ENIM VI ID[VS] FEB[RVARIAS]

Françoise Jenn, "Les plates-tombes inscrites de Saint-Outrille-du-Château à Bourges (Cher)," *CA* 34 (1986): #19, 65.

136. As amended by Jenn, the inscription states:

✝ IC REQVIESCIT . . . ONVS BONE MEMOR[IE]
ROGO QVISQ[VIS VE]NIETIS HIC: ORATE
REQVIEM AET(ER)N[AM DO]NA EI D(OMI)NE ET LU[X]
P(ER)PETVA LVCEA[T EI. A] PORTA INFERI ERVE
D(OMI)NE ANIMA(M) EVIS. [REQVIES]CAT IN PACE
AMEN. OBIIT . . . K(A)L(ENDAS) A(V)G(V)S(TI).

Jenn, "Les plates-tombes inscrites," #22, 66–67.

137.   . . . VIDVIS O[RPHA]NIS VEL PAVPEREBVS
ELEMOSIN[A] A SE PRO PEC
CAT[O] L[. . .]

The disputed epitaph of Ursinianus, dated by Edmond Le Blant to as early as the fourth or fifth century, and then reattributed by Nancy Gauthier to the eighth century, has most recently been assigned by Walter Koch to no later than the seventh century on the basis of insular paleographical features.[138] The uneven inscription, engraved between double lines and adorned with the images of two doves on each side of a vessel, stated in faulty hexameter:

Under this grave rest the bones of Ursinianus, subdeacon,
who deserves to be associated with the sepulchers of the saints
(and) whom neither raging Tartarus nor harsh punishment will harm.
Ludula, his dearest wife, has erected this epitaph.
He died the fifth day before the kalends of December. He lived thirty-three years.[139]

Recalling a passage of the twelfth sermon of Maximus of Turin, the epitaph emphasized the importance of the location of the tomb near the saints who might protect the deceased against the horrors of hell.[140] While burial *ad sanctos* played a predominant part in the conception of Ursinianus's resting

---

Gustav Behrens, "Der Bertichildis-Grabstein von Kempten bei Bingen," *Germania* 21 (1937): 113–17.

138. Walter Koch, "Insular Influences in Inscriptions on the Continent," in *Roman, Runes, and Ogham.*

139. As published and annotated by Gauthier, the inscription from Trier states:

> Vrsiniano subdiacono sub hoc tumulo ossa
> quiescunt, qui merui/t/ sanctorum sociari sepulcra
> quem nec Tartarus furens nec poena saeua nocebi[t].
> Hunc titulum posuit /Ludu/la dulcissima coniux.
> R(ecessit) V k(alendas) D(ecembres). Vixit annis XXXIII.

Gauthier, *RICG* 1,170, 426–30; Le Blant, *Inscriptions chrétiennes* 1,293, 396–99.

140. Gauthier, *RICG* 1,170, 429; Almut Mutzenbecher, ed., *Maximus episcopus Taurinensis, Sermones* 12, *CCSL* 23 (Turnhout: Typographi Brepols editores, Pontificii, 1962), 40–42.

place, his wife Ludula was also concerned that the epitaph identify the occupant of the grave as a prestigious Christian. What might otherwise have been an anonymous burial for the subdeacon became an inscribed *memoria* that publicly acknowledged his presence to the congregation.

At the close of the seventh century, burial inscriptions thus facilitated the long-term involvement of the living in the fate of the souls of the deceased in the afterlife. They included identification of Christians by name, a confirmation of their link to the saints, and petitions for prayers. Some epitaphs even expressed confidently that the deceased had already achieved holy peace. An inscription commemorating a seventy-five-year-old woman named Margarita, whose epitaph at Crussol (Ardèche) was dated 1 July 691, revealed the positive influence of funerary liturgy regarding the rewards awaiting the faithful on epigraphy. Margarita's epitaph resembled prayers describing heavenly repose for the worthy dead later recorded in the Gelasian Sacramentary.[141] Other tombstones made reference to the fact that burial *ad sanctos* was deserved by the deceased; such a privileged resting place in turn ensured the well-being of the soul of the Christian thereby commemorated. Discovered in Lyons in 1947, Osildus's epitaph of October 656 noted that he would enjoy resurrection with his patron saint Laurence, to whom the church in which he was buried was dedicated.[142]

Sculpted tombs also communicated the prestige of burial *ad sanctos,* and represented a continued feature of elite burial custom during the seventh and

141. The epitaph concluded: "et sancta reque LE D(eu)s dedit." Descombes, *RICG* 15,19, 234–36; Le Blant, *Inscriptions chrétiennes* 2,476, 178–94, pl. 376. The specific prayer in this case stated: "[D]igneris, Domine, dare ei locum lucidum, locum refrigerii et quietis. Liceat ei transire portas infernorum et vias tenebrarum maneatque in mansionibus sanctorum et in luce sancta." Leo Cunibert Mohlberg, Leo Eizenhöfer, and Petrus Siffrin, eds., *Liber sacramentorum romanae aeclesiae ordinis annis circuli (Cod.Vat.Reg.lat 316/Paris B.N. 7193, 41/56) (Sacramentarium Gelasianum)* 91,1617, Rerum ecclesiasticarum documenta, series maior, fontes 4, 3d ed. (Rome: Casa Editrice Herder, 1981), 236.

142. Wuilleumier, *Inscriptions latines* 297, 117.

eighth centuries. Although some sarcophagi were engraved with funerary images on secular themes, such as depictions of the hunt at Saint-Samson-de-la-Roque (Normandy), Nanteuil (Vienne), and Chelles (Oise),[143] tombs with religious imagery far outnumbered them and were likely viewed as more appropriate for a place in which the faithful would await resurrection. The presence of Christian iconography in a large variety of settings in Gaul suggests that such themes must have been more common than surviving examples reveal. In the late sixth and seventh centuries, Poitiers, for one, appears to have been the location of a small workshop producing sarcophagi in a style highly influenced by Coptic traditions.[144]

An unusual burial monument is the Hypogeum of Dunes, discovered in Poitiers by the Belgian Jesuit Camille de la Croix in the course of excavations near a military depot in 1878. Constructed at the northwest end of a Gallo-Roman cemetery and completed by the late seventh or early eighth century, the once brightly painted semi-subterranean chamber contained an altar and at least fourteen graves, some with multiple remains. The mausoleum was surrounded by additional graves, many protected by stone sarcophagi. Altogether, the Hypogeum of Dunes housed the remains of five women, seven adults of undetermined sex, twenty-two children, and one man of about seventy years of age. All of the skeletons were in disarray except the last, whose corpse de la Croix linked to the inscription and anathema of Mellebaudis.[145]

---

143. Discovered in 1922, a sarcophagus at Saint-Samson, with a *terminus post quem* of the early eighth century based on accompanying grave goods, portrayed eleven dogs and three wild boars on one side, and dogs chasing a boar on the other. May Vieillard-Troïekouroff, "Le sarcophage décoré d'une châsse gravée, provenant de Saint-Samson-de-la-Roque, au Musée de Saint-Germain-en-Laye," in *Actes du 105ᵉ Congrès national des Sociétés savantes, Caen 1980: La Normandie: Études archéologiques*, Section archéologie et histoire de l'art (Paris: Comité des travaux historiques et scientifiques, 1983), 267–73.

144. James, *The Merovingian Archaeology* 1, 75–83.

145. Camille de la Croix, *Monographie de l'Hypogée-Martyrium de Poitiers* (Paris: Librairie de Firmin Didot, 1883), 3–30. His discussion of the *martyrium* was far less reliable than would have been desired for this monument. James, *The Merovingian Archaeology* 1, 278–89.

Lit by a window and probably candles or oil lamps, the interior of the
Hypogeum of Dunes was decorated with dedicatory plaques indicating
the presence of relics and a number of stones carved with interlace. A relief
depicted the two thieves beneath the cross. The chamber's function and
layout have been likened to those of Gallo-Roman Christian mausolea in
the southernmost parts of Gaul.[146] The burial chamber also contained an
epitaph of a previously unknown cleric, Mellebaudis. Composed in the
first person, the cleric's epitaph proclaimed his faith in the eternal glory of
God. The inscription also declared that anyone who dared to destroy the
sepulcher would be cursed for all time.[147] The Hypogeum of Dunes thus

---

146. Camille de la Croix, *La découverte du Martyrium de Poitiers*, Société centrale des architectes,
Conférences 2ᵉᵐᵉ série, vol. 1,4 (Paris: Imprimerie Chaix, 1885), 3–15; Xavier Barral I Altet, Noël
Duval, and Jean-Claude Papinot, "Poitiers: Chapelle funéraire dite 'Hypogée des Dunes,'" in *Les
premiers monuments chrétiens de la France* 2, 302–9.

147. As reconstructed by Carol Heitz, the inscription reads:

✣ IN D(e)I NOMINI. EGO.
(chrism) HIC. MELLEBAUDIS
REVS. ET SERVUS. IH(esu)M XP(ist)O
INISTITUI. MIHI. ISPE
LUNCOLA. ISTA. UBI
IACIT. INDIGNI.
SEPULTURA. MEA.
QUEM. FECI. IN NOME
NI. D(omi)NI IH(esu)M. XP(ist)I. QueM
AMAVI. IN QUOD
CREDEDI. vere digNUM
EST. CONFETIri d(eu)m
vIvum cujus
GLORIA. MAGNA. EST
UBI. PAX. FEDIS. CARI
TAS. EST. IPSE D(eu)S ET HO
MO. EST. ET D(eu)S IN ILLO.
SI QUIS. QUI. NON. HIC.
AMAT. ADORARE. D(omi)N(u)M IH(eus)M
XP(istu)M. ET DISTRUIT. OPERA
ISTA SIT. ANATHEMA
MARANTHA
USQUID. IN SEMPITERNUM.

represented a suitable and exclusive location for burial *ad sanctos* for Mellebaudis and his companions. Another sarcophagus in the chamber was decorated with reliefs depicting the evangelists Matthew and John and the archangels Raphael and Raguel; its imagery expressed similar optimism regarding the afterlife. The mausoleum, which also served as a place of worship, provided the few privileged Christians buried there an optimal setting in which to await their resurrection.[148]

In Poitiers and elsewhere in the Merovingian kingdoms, sarcophagi decorated to improve the prospects for salvation demonstrate that the Hypogeum of Dunes was an unusual but not entirely unique phenomenon. The late-sixth-century Lunes sarcophagus, associated with the last years of the "Narbonne" school of sculptural tombs, may have represented part of an earlier but similar tradition. Now at the Musée lapidaire in Narbonne, it was decorated with acanthus leaves and an interlace knot in addition to images of Adam and Eve.[149] Carved or inscribed tombs or even lead plaques, such as an eighth-century one dedicated to the fifth-century abbot Lupicinus,[150] were especially suited to the needs of saints' cults. Their decoration identified the holy remains in a larger-than-life manner and provided a meaningful focal point for pilgrims.

At Amay, a trapezoidal tomb carved from a chalk monolith and inscribed with the name Chrodoara (d. before 634) was the locus of power for the saint's cult. Discovered in Belgium in 1977, the sarcophagus depicted the noblewoman wearing canonical dress and carrying a staff, the meaning of which is disputed, since she is not known to have held the position of

---

Carol Heitz, "L'Hypogée de Mellebaude à Poitiers," in *L'inhumation privilégiée*, 91–96.

148. Georges Gaillard, "La représentation des évangélistes à l'Hypogée des Dunes," in *Études mérovingiennes*, 135–36.

149. James, *The Merovingian Archaeology* 1, 57–59.

150. The plaque aided in the verification and promotion of Lupicinus's cult at Saint-Lupicin (Jura): "HIC REQUIES/CIT BEATUS LU/PICINUS ABBAS." Robert Favreau, Jean Michaud, and Bernadette Mora, eds., *CIFM* 19,15 (Paris: Éditions du CNRS, 1997), 21.

abbess during her lifetime. Remnants of a staff were also found in the reliquary of Saint Ode, thought to be the same person. Besides bearing her name on its cover, an epitaph at the tomb's head praised Chrodoara.[151] Regarding the date of this monument, Alain Dierkens has proposed that it was probably carved on the occasion of the saint's *elevatio* in the course of the 730s.[152] The decoration of Chrodoara's sarcophagus, which was intended for above-ground display at Amay, was linked very closely to the promotion and expansion of her local cult. Attracting the attention of the faithful participating in her veneration, the image reinforced the benefit of the physical presence of her relics in the church.

The best-known group of decorated tombs of the late Merovingian period in Gaul, however, is that which remains to this day *in situ* in the late-seventh- or early-eighth-century crypt of Jouarre, located near the Marne northeast of Paris. The sarcophagus honoring Theodechild, abbess of the double monastery (d. circa 667), described the virtues of the holy woman of noble birth. While there is much dispute over the date of Theodechild's translation and reburial, her tomb must date from the Merovingian period due to its erection contemporary with a wall of the crypt decorated with *opus reticulatum*.[153] Produced likely on the occasion of

151. "Chrodoara nubelis magna et inclitis ex sua substantia dictavit sanctoaria." Heli Roosens, "Überlegungen zum Sarkophag von Amay," *AK* 8 (1978): 237–41; E. Thirion, "Le sarcophage de Sancta Chrodoara dans l'église Saint-Georges d'Amay," *Bulletin du Cercle archéologique Hesbaye-Condroz* 15 (1977–78): 51–54; T. Delarue and E. Thirion, "Amay (Liège): Le sarcophage de Chrodoara," in *L'archéologie en Wallonie: Découvertes récentes des cercles d'archéologie* (Nivelles: Fédération des archéologues de Wallonie, 1980), no. 58, pp. 133–34.

152. Alain Dierkens, "A propos du sarcophage de Sancta Chrodoara découvert en 1977 à Amay," *Art et Fact: Revue des historiens de l'art, des archéologues, des musicologues et des orientalistes de l'Université de Liège* 15 (1996): 30–32. His conclusions differ considerably from those of Jacques Stiennon, "Le sarcophage de Sancta Chrodoara à Saint-Georges d'Amay: Essai d'interprétation d'une découverte exceptionnelle," *Bulletin du Cercle archéologique Hesbaye-Condroz* 15 (1977–78): 78–87.

153. Patrick Périn, "A propos des cryptes de Jouarre," *Document archeologia (Paris: Foyer d'art au moyen âge)* 3 (1973): 123. Patrick Périn's dating of the tomb is earlier than the Carolingian attribution proposed by Jean Coquet and Victor Elbern. Jean Coquet, *Pour une nouvelle date de la*

her translation to the crypt of St. Paul, the stone sarcophagus was decorated with shells and palm leaves. Its inscription conveyed the congregation's great confidence that her spirit had safely reached its heavenly destination. Resting in its tomb at Jouarre, her body was attended to with appropriate honors by the virgins of the monastic house.[154]

Later traditions at the monastery of Jouarre recounted that Agilbert, the bishop of Paris (d. circa 680/691), directed that his tomb be placed alongside that of his sister Theodechild. The nuns of Jouarre therefore believe that Agilbert is buried in the sculpted stone sarcophagus with a relief on its end of Christ in a mandorla surrounded by the four symbols of the Evangelists.[155] Located *ad sanctos* in the small crypt, this sarcophagus is also adorned along its length with images of orants standing with upraised arms, awaiting the Last Judgment or possibly the Second Coming.[156] The identification of this sarcophagus with the remains of Agilbert was nonetheless not made in contemporary written sources.[157] The prestigious

---

crypte Saint-Paul de Jouarre (Ligugé: Abbaye Saint-Martin, 1970); Victor H. Elbern, "Neue Aspekte frühmittelalterlicher Skulptur in Gallien," in *Kolloquium über spätantike und frühmittelalterliche Skulptur* 2 (Mainz: Verlag Philipp von Zabern, 1970), 13–21.

154. Her epitaph, as reconstructed by Bernhard Bischoff, proclaimed:

✝ HOC MEMBRA POST VLTIMA TEGVNTVR FATA SEPVLCHRO
BEATAE THEODLECHILDIS INTEMERATAE VIRGINIS GENERE NOBILIS ME-
RETIS FVLGENS STRINVA MORIBVS FLAGRAVIT IN DOGMATE ALMO. CENV-
BII HVIVS MATER SACRATAS DEO VIRgines accipienTES OLEVM CVM LAMPADIBVS
PRVDENTES docuit sponsum fILIAS OCCVRRIRE CHRISTVM
HAEC DEMVM EXVLTAT PARADiS.

Bernhard Bischoff, "Epitaphienformeln für Äbtissinnen (achtes Jahrhundert)," in *Anecdota novissima: Texte des vierten bis sechzehnten Jahrhunderts* (Stuttgart: Anton Hiersemann Verlag, 1984), III, 152–53.

155. Beat Brenk, "Marginalien zum sog. Sarkophag des Agilberts in Jouarre," *CA* 14 (1964): 95–107; Jean Hubert, *Les cryptes de Jouarre*, IVᵉ Congrès de l'art du haut moyen âge (Melun: Imprimerie de la préfecture de Seine-et-Marne, 1952), 3–8.

156. Yvan Christ, *Les cryptes mérovingiennes de l'abbaye de Jouarre* (Paris: Éditions d'histoire et d'art, 1966), 16–23.

157. Otto Gerhard Oexle, "Agilbert," in *Lexikon des Mittelalters* 1 (Munich: Artemis Verlag, 1980), 207.

occupant of the sarcophagus, whoever was originally buried there, was confident that burial in close proximity to the holy remains of Theodechild would ensure her intercession. No doubt such a location also gained for the deceased the perpetual prayers of the nuns who frequented the funerary church.

As noted earlier, inscriptions of the late seventh and early eighth centuries were quite rare and for the most part limited in distribution to sites at which funerary inscriptions had long been used. As modern editions are published, however, increasing numbers of epitaphs have been attributed to the late Merovingian or early Carolingian periods.[158] The marble epitaph of the sixteen-year-old youth Modoaldus, discovered in the church of St. Maximus, Trier, in 1936, represents an important example of the survival of this tradition. Gauthier has dated the gravestone, adorned with two doves flanking a *Chi-Rho* monogram from which an alpha and an omega were suspended, to the late seventh or eighth century. Dedicated to the deceased by his parents, the inscription listed not only his age but also the day and month of his death. By providing this information, the stele provided the most relevant data to the performance of annual liturgical commemorations in honor of Modoaldus. Despite omitting the year of his death, his parents supplied the means by which to deliver him from purgatorial suffering. They wished their noble son peace until his resurrection.[159]

---

158. Le Blant, on the other hand, identified no eighth-century epitaphs. Le Blant, *L'épigraphie chrétienne,* 26–27.

159. As transcribed and corrected by Gauthier, the epitaph reads:

> ✝ Hic requiescit uir uenera-
> belis adoliscens nu(mine) Modoal(dus)
> qui uixit plus mi(nu)s an(nos) XVI; obiet
> in pace quod ficit m(e)ns(is)
> F(e)br(uariu)s dies VIII, cuius pater et mat(er)
> in amure ipsius titul(um) posui-
> runt; in pace!

Gauthier, *RICG* 1,147, 381–83.

A characteristic of inscriptions from the late Merovingian and early Carolingian periods was thus their concern for the well-being of the deceased in the afterlife. An inscription dated to 24 April 637 found at Volvic (Canton de Riom-Est, Puy-de-Dôme), for instance, referred to the anonymous Christian as a sinner (*pecca[tor]*) but nonetheless wished him eternal rest.[160] The late-eighth-century epitaph of Mumlenau found *ad sanctos* in the crypt of the church of Sainte-Radegonde of Poitiers asked that the deceased's soul rest in peace.[161] A very similar burial inscription commemorating a cleric named Madalfredus (d. 802/808) was possibly found in the vicinity of Saint-Hilaire-le-Grand, Poitiers.[162] The now lost seventh- or eighth-century epitaph of a consecrated woman named Adata, discovered in 1874 at Saint-Outrille-du-Château, Bourges, similarly expressed the desire that her soul rest in peace.[163]

Surviving seventh- and eighth-century epigraphy east and west of the Rhine attests to the role of liturgy as a driving force behind their creation. The brief epitaph of the deacon and monk Amulricus, which Bernhard Bischoff has attributed to the eighth century, provided the information

---

160. Françoise Prévot, ed., *RICG* 8,47 (Paris: CNRS Éditions, 1997), 175–78; Le Blant, *Nouveau recueil* 230, 228.

161. The remains of the inscription, now in fragments and scarcely legible, are at the Musée Sainte-Croix in Poitiers. As corrected by the editors, it reads:

        ✝ [I]N : AN : NO : XX [. . .] RE[G]NAN : TE
        K : [R]O : LO : RE : GE [FRANCO]R[VM] : VIIII : KALENDAS : IVNIAS:
        SIC : FVID MUMLE : NAV DEO : DEVOTA
        DE : FUNCT[A] : CV : IVS : [COR]P[VS]CVLVS : IC
        [QV]IES : CIT : REQVIES[CAT ANIMA EI]VS : IN P[ACE].

The colons in the text indicate where there were three vertical dots carved in the stone of circa 790, the purpose of which Robert Favreau and Jean Michaud have described as decorative. Robert Favreau and Jean Michaud, eds., *CIFM* 1,91 (Poitiers: CESCM, 1974), 115–16, pl. xxxiv, fig. 67; Abbé Auber, *L'anneau de Sainte Radegonde et ses reliques à Poitiers* (Arras: Rousseau-Leroy, 1864), 24–25.

162. Favreau and Michaud, *CIFM* 1,82, 99, pl. xviii, fig. 36.

163. Jenn, "Les plates-tombes inscrites," #15, 63.

critical to his commemoration.[164] The eighth-century grave inscription of Aldualuhus at Worms noted that the deceased's soul celebrated in heaven while his body remained in the tomb.[165] The eighth-century epitaph of Bernard from the region of Toulouse focused foremost upon the fate of the soul of the deceased. The erection of this tombstone must have conferred significant prestige upon his family or religious community. Decorated with a *Chi-Rho* monogram, the inscription humbly petitioned God to be merciful and pardon Bernard's sins.[166]

Eighth-century funerary inscriptions, like those of earlier periods, expressed confidence in the liturgy and conveyed the hope that Christians' remains would rest undisturbed until resurrection. Some epitaphs thus emphasized the immediacy of the body's presence in the grave, since both flesh and spirit were to be preserved until the end of days. One eighth-century epitaph preserved only in manuscript form referred to the corpse as lying under the stone of the sarcophagus.[167] Similarly, the late-eighth-century epitaph of the bishop Arricius of Toulouse, now at the Musée de Foix (Ariège), asked that the deceased not be disturbed while he awaited

164. The inscription, for which the provenance is unknown, is now at the Rheinisches Landesmuseum in Trier. Reusch, *Frühchristliche Zeugnisse* 73, 100–101, pl. 73.

165. "HIC*PAV/SAT*COR/PUS*ALD/VALVHI* CV/IVS*ANIMA GAVDET*IN/CAELO." This inscription was found embedded in an eighteenth-century wall of the Bergkloster of Worms. Rüdiger Fuchs, ed., *Die Inschriften der Stadt Worms 4, Die deutschen Inschriften* 29 (Wiesbaden: Dr. Ludwig-Reichert-Verlag, 1991), 5–6.

166.   (*Chi-Rho*) VI KALENDAS IVNI
            CLAVDITVR HOC TVMVLO
            BERNARDI CORPVS IN ATRO
            IPSIVS ET ANIMAM DEERAT SVPERNA RESERAT
            PARCAT PARCENDA QVI PARCIT CRI
            MINA DIRA OMNIPOTENS
            PASTOR NE RAPIAT TORTOR.

Robert Favreau, Jean Michaud, and Bernadette LePlant, eds., *CIFM* 7,40 (Paris: Éditions du CNRS, 1982), 76–77, pl. xxi, fig. 43.

167. "hic athletae Christi teguntur membra humata sub saxo." Bischoff, "Epitaphienformeln," I, 151.

resurrection.[168] In the meantime, epigraphical inscriptions encouraged the faithful to engage in liturgical devotions at the burial site.[169] The epitaph of Witbertus at Bourges, dated to the second half of the eighth century, petitioned readers for prayers on his behalf.[170]

In the case of an anonymous early-eighth-century abbess, her epitaph, preserved in Bern MS 611, believed by Bernhard Bischoff to have been copied from a once extant stone, described her noteworthy achievements. It then concluded as follows: "To all of the orthodox and all who are faithful to God praying in this place, we ask that they deign to plead for the mercy of the Lord for this [holy abbess], so that she may be worthy to fly to the lofty heavens and, borne to the upper vaults of the eternal kingdom, she may also enjoy everlasting refreshment. Amen."[171] Urging the nuns of the unidentified monastery and others who had contact with the burial place to pray for the abbess, the epitaph thereby emphasized the effectiveness of devotions in helping the deceased to gain the coveted reward of salvation. The burial inscriptions of the nuns Lea and Hilaritas, extant only in manuscript copy, fulfilled a similar function in eighth-century Trier.[172]

Besides epigraphy, a few rare examples of stone reliefs surviving from the late seventh and early eighth centuries both in Gaul and on its frontiers

---

168. Robert Favreau, Jean Michaud, and Bernadette LePlant, eds., *CIFM* 8,3 (Paris: Éditions du CNRS, 1982), 10, pl. ii, fig. 3.

169. Paxton, *Christianizing Death*, 67–69.

170.   IC REQUIESCIT WITBERTUS NOMINE
                 AC MORIENDO PECIIT CORPUS EJUS UMO
                 PRO CUJUS ANIMA OMNES NOS PRE
                 CEMUR DEUM. OBIIT
                 VI IDUS FEBRUARIAS.

Jenn, "Les plates-tombes inscrites," #5, 52–54. Pertinent commentary is also to be found in a yet unpublished file of the *CIFM* at the CESCM, Poitiers. I thank Jean Michaud for putting this material at my disposal.

171. "Rogamus omnibus hortodoxis vel cunctis Dei fidelibus in hoc loco orantibus, ut pro ipsa Domini dignentur deprecare misericordiam, ut ad alta poli evolare valeat et aethera vehens regni perennis et sempiterna fruatur refrigeria. Amen." Bischoff, "Epitaphienformeln," II, 151.

172. Gauthier, *RICG* 1,219–20, 518–23.

indicate that there was continued interest in the appearance and location of
elite Christian graves. Some were very simple, such as the small standing-
stone cross excavated at the seventh-century necropolis of Audun-le-Tiche
(Moselle).[173] A seventh- or eighth-century stone decorated with a female
orant and dedicated to the memory of Artula was found at Deneuvre
(Meurthe-et-Moselle).[174] A possibly eighth-century example of a ceramic
epitaph was a brick measuring 21 cm × 14 cm discovered at Rochepinard
near Saint-Étienne in 1854. Now displayed at the Musée de la Société
archéologique de Touraine, the piece depicts a cross over the head of a
bearded orant with his hands raised.[175]

The funerary stele of Niederdollendorf ascribed to the end of the seventh century was more elaborate than most of the above. Adorned with
the image of an armed warrior combing his hair, the stone's symbolic
motif must have been more comprehensible to contemporaries than it is
today.[176] The stele communicated the presence of a powerful individual,
and its function may have been analogous to that of the combs decorated
with amuletic imagery that were often placed in graves of the Merovingian
period. On its opposite face, the stone displayed a Christlike figure in a
mandorla, wielding what appears to have been a spear.[177] The artisan who
created the monument demonstrated the fluidity with which pagan and

173. Simmer, "La nécropole mérovingienne," 38–39.
174. Measuring 50 cm × 57 cm, the carved stone was of local provenance. Found in 1883, it is
now preserved at the Musée lorrain de Nancy. Gauthier, *RICG* 1,259, 588–89.
175. Patrick Périn and Laure-Charlotte Feffer, eds., *La Neustrie: Les pays au nord de la Loire de
Dagobert à Charles le Chauve (VIIᵉ–IXᵉ siècles)* 69 (Rouen: Musées et monuments départementaux de
Seine-Maritime, 1985), 207.
176. Averil Cameron, "How Did the Merovingians Wear Their Hair?" *Revue belge de philologie
et d'histoire* 43 (1965): 1203–16; Walter Pohl, "Telling the Difference: Signs of Ethnic Identity," in
Strategies of Distinction: The Construction of Ethnic Communities, 300–700, TRW 2, ed. Walter Pohl
and Helmut Reimitz (Leiden: E. J. Brill, 1998), 51–59.
177. Waldemar Haberey, "Grabstein aus Niederdollendorf," in *Aus rheinischer Kunst und Kultur:
Auswahlkatalog des Rheinischen Landesmuseums Bonn 1963* (Düsseldorf: Rheinland-Verlag, 1963),
no. 9,68, p. 115, pls. 68–69.

Christian motifs might be melded into a single cosmology among local inhabitants. A priest's eighth-century gravestone found in Gondorf (Mosel), by contrast, exhibited a somewhat more traditional Christian image: a cleric in a tunic and pallium with a dove on each shoulder. Surrounded by a mandorla and four eagles, the priest held a book in his right hand.[178] As such, the funerary stele conveyed information similar to that in an epitaph or inscribed cross;[179] the stone likeness, perhaps erected by the ecclesiastical *familia* of the deceased, conveyed an ideal of religious achievement and social prestige to visitors to the grave site.

Like late inscriptions of the previous century, early-ninth-century epitaphs sought to maintain the integrity of the resting places of faithful Christians. Alcuin, for instance, noted the measures taken by Ado, bishop of Poitiers, to protect the graves of his predecessors John II and Aper (d. circa 799) from violation. A low wall around their sepulchers in the church and a monument marked with a cross were intended to prevent the crowds at the site from treading on their remains. Later an altar was also established in the vicinity.[180] Not only did the structures protect the deceased,

178. Waldemar Haberey, "Grabstein eines Priesters," in *Aus rheinischer Kunst*, no. 9,69, p. 115–16, pl. 69.

179. Two early-eighth-century gravestones carved with crosses have been uncovered in the Moselle valley and in Gondorf itself. Haberey, in *Aus rheinischer Kunst*, nos. 9,67 and 9,70, pp. 114–16, pls. 67, 70.

180.   HUJUS HIC PAUSAT PRAECLARUS EPISCOPUS URBIS
          NOMINE JOHANNES VIR PIUS ATQUE BONUS
          HIC REQUIESCIT APER HUJUS VENERABILIS ABBAS
          ECCLESIAE PASTOR PROMPTUS IN OMNE BONUM
          SED PEDIBUS POPULI FUERANT CALCATA SEPULCHRA
          NEC PARIES CINXIT UT DECUIT PATRIBUS
          HOC ATO NON SUFFERT APERI SUCCESSOR HONORIS
          CORPORA CALCARI SACRA PATRUM PEDIBUS
          SED MONUMENTA BREVI PLACUIT CONCINGERE MURO
          PER VIA NE POPULI BUSTA FORENT PEDIBUS
          ADDIDIT ET NOSTRAE STATIM PIA SIGNA SALUTIS
          IN QUO SALVATOR VICTOR AB HOSTE REDIT
          INSUPER ALTARE STATUIT VENERABILE CHRISTO . . .

but they gave the graves of the bishops greater visibility *ad sanctos,* where the Mass was celebrated.[181] An impressive ninth-century stele of over a meter in height likewise honored the virgin Frodeberta (d. 26 December 814) at Éstoublon (Alpes-de-Haute-Provence). The prominent stone drew attention to the mortal remains of the presumably well-born figure.[182] Just as in the time of Sidonius Apollinaris, however, a grave marker was by no means an automatic or necessary feature of the interment of even the most prestigious Christians. Some were only erected by family or followers in response to damage or fear of potential harm to the resting places of the deceased.

In rare instances, locations have been found with multiple funerary inscriptions dating from the late Merovingian and early Carolingian periods. They give hope that additional epitaphs from this transitional period await discovery. One exceptional site is Saint-Outrille-du-Château (Cher), which was excavated during campaigns in 1874, 1934, and 1981. The graves with intact epitaphs were probably associated with the monastic complex dedicated to Austregisillus, bishop of Bourges (d. circa 620). They span in date from the Merovingian period to the fourteenth century. At least ten inscriptions of men, women, and children, many of which have already been described above, were carved in the ninth century or earlier. The stones on which they were carved served as covers for the otherwise

---

Favreau and Michaud, *CIFM* 1,44, 46–47; Ernst Dümmler, ed., *Alcuinus (Albinus), Carmina,* in *MGH: Poetae* 1,1,99,13 (Berlin: Apud Weidmannos, 1880), 325–26.

    181. See also the epigraphical poems commemorating various women of the Carolingian dynasty buried at Saint-Arnoul, Metz. Ernst Dümmler, ed., *Laudes Mediolanensis civitatis,* in *MGH: Poetae* 1,1,20–24, 57–60.

    182. As completed by Favreau, Michaud, and Mora, its inscription stated: "HIC REQUIS / CIT*IN PA / CE*BONE / MEMORIE / FRODEBER / TA*DEI VIR / GO*FIL[I]A / AGHILBER / TO*OBIIT VII / KALENDAS IHANUARIAS*ANNO / PRIMO IMPERAN / [TE] DOMNO LODO / [VIC]O*INDICTI / ONE PRIMMA / ✠." The asterisks here replace triangular markings in the original epitaph. Robert Favreau, Jean Michaud, and Bernadette Mora, eds., *CIFM* 16,5 (Paris: Éditions du CNRS, 1992), 7, pl. 1, figs. 2–3.

unprotected graves beneath. Each measured an average of a meter and a half in length. The epitaphs' contents were very similar to one another in tone and theme, highlighting the piety of the deceased and expressing hope for the afterlife.[183]

Such finds reflect the local idiosyncrasies characteristic of early medieval burial rites. In this particular community, inhabitants had a preference for monumental commemoration of their dead. Individual early Carolingian communities, kin groups, or monastic *familiae* thus chose in certain circumstances to continue employing epigraphy to express their identity and beliefs. Despite a general decrease in the employment of decorated stone sarcophagi and inscribed gravestones across Gaul in the second half of the eighth century, where they were used, their function differed little from that of previous centuries. Rather than attribute the small number of inscribed monuments to economic downturn,[184] an explanation that overlooks the ritual significance of funerary commemoration, this evolution should be recognized as reflecting changes in what families believed was the most effective means to remember their ancestors.[185] Kin groups and religious communities, for as long as they retained some degree of control over funerary arrangements, favored rituals that also conveyed to contemporaries an ideal image of their own beliefs and identity. For some groups well into the Carolingian period, burial inscriptions and decorated tombs best satisfied these needs.

183. Jenn, "Les plates-tombes inscrites," 33–74; Olivier Ruffier, "Notes sur les fouilles de Saint-Outrille-du-Château," *CA* 34 (1986): 42–43.

184. René Louis and Gilbert-Robert Delehaye, "Le sarcophage mérovingien considéré sous ses aspects économiques et sociaux," in *Actes du 105e congrès national des Sociétés savantes, Caen, 1980,* 294–95.

185. Patrick Périn, "Le problème des sarcophages-cénotaphes du haut moyen âge: A propos de la nécropole de Quarré-les-Tombes, site d'une bataille légendaire," in *La chanson de geste et le mythe carolingien: Mélanges René Louis* 2 (Saint-Père-sous-Vézelay: Musée archéologique régional, 1982), 824.

External Identification of Sepulchers in the Transition to the Carolingian Era

As we have seen in this discussion of epigraphy, spatial features of burial constituted a central element of early medieval funerary rites. Families and religious houses therefore directed significant energy not only toward erecting tombstones but also toward maintaining the visibility and integrity of their group's sepulchers. Unlike grave goods, the visible features and location of tombs could be effective in shaping memory of ancestors for generations; they communicated collective images of what close relations or monastic brethren wished or could afford to recall before fellow members of their community.[186] Because epigraphy usually identified the deceased by name, moreover, it added incentive for descendants to contribute to the maintenance and protection of the grave over many years, since they too might wish to be buried there. Until DNA evidence from early medieval cemeterial remains is systematically assessed, however, archaeologists will only be able to hypothesize the intergenerational use of burial plots by persons related by blood. Even then, the identification of other sorts of social bonds, such as those formed through adoption, economic or legal dependence, or childless marriages, will remain elusive. It is nonetheless clear that once successive generations could no longer distinguish the tombs of their ancestors, they lost much of the impetus for commemorating them or for caring for their burial plots.

While some of the concerns for the appearance of sepulchers related to what contemporaries might think, they also grew from the belief that the

186. Lynne Goldstein, "One-Dimensional Archaeology and Multi-Dimensional People: Spatial Organisation and Mortuary Analysis," in *The Archaeology of Death,* ed. Robert Chapman, Ian Kinnes, and Klavs Randsborg (Cambridge: Cambridge University Press, 1981), 57–61, 67; Lewis R. Binford, "Mortuary Practices: Their Study and Potential," in *Approaches to the Social Dimensions of Mortuary Practices,* Memoirs of the Society for American Archaeology 25, ed. James A. Brown (Washington, D.C.: Society for American Archaeology, 1971), 21–23.

grave represented the final resting place of the body until its reunion with the soul at the time of the Resurrection.[187] Its importance was thus paramount for the well-being of the faithful in the afterlife, and as we have seen in Chapter II, a number of attempts were made in both secular and ecclesiastical law to protect the graves of Christians from violation. Adornment of the tomb, whether by means of epitaph or engraved images, was thus frequently directed at showing that the interred was a Christian, and emphasized the role of the sepulcher as the eternal home (*domus aeterna*) of the deceased. The orientation of the sepulcher, whether through burial *ad sanctos* or a churchyard grave, also highlighted the relationship of deceased Christians to God and the saints. As we have seen, Christian funerary inscriptions therefore referred not only to the ranking of the deceased in the temporal hierarchy but to the state of his or her soul in the afterlife. The location of the tomb and pleas for assistance from the faithful in the form of inscribed prayers helped deceased Christians to overcome purgatorial punishment for their sins.

Although the epigraphical vocabulary of status changed during the transition from the Roman to the early medieval period, it continued to favor those of higher social status by highlighting their worldly or spiritual achievements and aspirations.[188] The external appearance of sepulchers thus remained an important component of early medieval funerary rites of the elite. While the evidence suggests that stone inscriptions during the late seventh and early eighth centuries diminished in quantity, the epitaphs and carved imagery that were used stayed fairly consistent. They promoted the reputation of the deceased among contemporaries and brought the attention of future generations to bear on his or her resting place. While the custom of commemorating the dead through funerary inscriptions remained a possibility for some lay elites and members of clerical

187. Duval, *Auprès des saints*, 35 ff.; Duval, "Sanctorum," 338 ff.
188. Effros, "Beyond Cemetery Walls," 8–11.

communities, however, among the majority of the inhabitants of Gaul, graves of Christians may have become increasingly anonymous. This trend was marked by increased spatial disorder in many Christian cemeteries at the end of the seventh century.[189] Such factors make it exceedingly challenging to identify graves dating from the poorly documented period of the late Merovingian and the early Carolingian era. Funerary ceremonies appear to have left far fewer traces than in previous centuries.

Although the thoughts and actions of the general population in late Merovingian Gaul remain elusive, the reluctance of elite Christians to abandon the use of epigraphy without an alternative means to commemorate the dead is somewhat easier to document. The epitaph of Amatus of Remiremont (d. 627/628) is a fitting example of the dramatic changes taking place during the seventh century. According to his *vita,* the humble abbot was laid to rest below a grave inscription that expressed great concerns regarding the destiny of his soul in the afterlife. Positioned at the doorway of the burial church of his monastery at his own request, Amatus's tombstone asked the clerics who regularly entered the building for their assistance through prayers. Although the monks of his house were disturbed that this resting place was less prestigious than what they believed the abbot deserved, Amatus had chosen it because he was confident that the monks' prayers for his soul would aid him in earning God's mercy. Despite performing penance prior to his death, he evidently feared the consequences of his transgressions, however small.[190]

189. Bailey K. Young, "Paganisme, christianisation et rites funéraires mérovingiens," *AM* 7 (1977): 56 ff.; Périn, "Le problème des sarcophages-cénotaphes," 824; Jean Hubert, *L'art pré-roman* (Paris: Les éditions d'art et d'histoire, 1938), 154–57.

190. "Omnis homo Dei qui in hunc locum sanctum ad orandum introieris, si obtinere mereraris que postulas, pro anima Amati penitentis hic sepulti Domini misericordiam deprecari digneris, et si quid mea parvitas de meis multis peccatis obtinere non potuit tepide penitendo, obtineat vestra tantorum caritas sedule Domini misericordiam deprecando." Bruno Krusch, ed., *Vita Amati abbatis Habendensis* 13, in *MGH: SRM* 4 (Hannover: Impensis bibliopolii Hahniani, 1902), 220; Gauthier, *L'évangélisation des pays,* 274–80.

The theology of Gregory I (d. 604) on the Gallic liturgy must have exerted a strong pull on Amatus's humble and self-conscious plea for the devotions of his brothers at Remiremont.[191] Amatus's biographer recognized that the monks' performance of the Mass had become essential to the abbot's escape from the purgatorial fires that awaited all sinners' souls.[192] The monks, by contrast, were slow to appreciate the significance of the abbot's request; they feared only the implications of what they considered to be an inappropriately humble burial place. When one of the brethren had a vision a few days after Amatus's death that confirmed his entry into heaven, the monks used this portent as a timely excuse to celebrate by elevating and translating his remains one year later.[193] The monks' considerations of the abbot's emerging status as a saint outweighed his fears of purgatorial suffering for any sins not fully repented.

It is therefore time to turn to an assessment of the impact of theology and the liturgy on the ways in which Christians perceived the afterlife in the Merovingian period. With clerical encroachment on customs pertaining to the burial of the dead, the responsibilities of families in funerals steadily grew more tenuous.[194] At the same time that familial control in dictating the terms of the funeral decreased, so did the effectiveness of the expression of identity and belief through personal artifacts deposited in the sepulchers. As Masses became the primary means of exchange between the living and the dead, liturgical acknowledgment of the religious and

191. Adalbert de Vogüé, ed., *Grégoire le Grand, Dialogues* 4,57, SC 265 (Paris: Éditions du CERF, 1980), 184–97.

192. Joseph Ntedika, *L'évocation de l'Au-delà dans la prière pour les morts: Étude de patristique et de liturgie latines (IVe–VIIIe siècle)*, Recherches africaines de théologie 2 (Louvain: Éditions Nauwelaerts, 1971), 93 ff.; Aaron J. Gurevich, "Au moyen âge: Conscience individuelle et image de l'Au-delà," *Annales ESC* 37 (1982): 255–75; Duval, *Auprès des saints*, 165–66; Paxton, *Christianizing Death*, 66–68.

193. Krusch, *Vita Amati abbatis Habendensis* 15–17, 220–21; Effros, "Beyond Cemetery Walls," 22–23.

194. Patrick J. Geary, "Exchange and Interaction Between the Living and the Dead in Early Medieval Society," in *Living with the Dead in the Middle Ages* (Ithaca: Cornell University Press, 1994), 79–82, 90–92; Effros, "Beyond Cemetery Walls," 1–23.

profane achievements of the deceased eventually replaced the functions of both grave goods and the external appearance of graves among all but the most elite Christians.[195] These developments ultimately led to widespread disregard for the integrity of graves.[196] With more effective means of expressing religious affiliation and other sorts of identity, liturgical commemoration of the dead far removed from their resting places largely supplanted the need for physical *memoria*.[197]

195. Otto Gerhard Oexle, "Die Gegenwart der Toten," in *Death in the Middle Ages*, Mediaevalia Louvaniensia ser. 1, studia 9, ed. Hermann Braet and Werner Verbeke (Louvain: Leuven University Press, 1983), 29–57.
196. Young, "Paganisme, christianisation," 56ff.; Périn, "Le problème des sarcophages-cénotaphes," 824.
197. Otto Gerhard Oexle, "Memoria und Memorialüberlieferung im früheren Mittelalter," *FS* 10 (1976): 82–94.

CHAPTER IV

⇥ • ⇤

Membership in the Kingdom of the Elect

The Diversity of Early Medieval Funerary Ritual

For the Christian faithful in early medieval Gaul, clerics passed little legislation affecting burial practices, including the widespread custom of grave goods. In the sixth and seventh centuries, ecclesiastical councils only forbade activities with a detrimental impact on the clerical monopoly of liturgical vessels and the eucharistic wafer.[1] Over time, as discussed in Chapter II, they even came to accept in certain circumstances the once forbidden practices of burial *intra muros*. Nor did the clergy make any apparent effort to regularize the content of funerary epigraphy. Certain customs long discouraged by the Church Fathers, such as offerings for the dead, were widely tolerated, despite the fact that such traditions were not scripturally based. Many clerics in Gaul, as elsewhere, were not concerned that Christian belief was thereby adversely affected.[2] Burial was primarily a familial and community affair largely outside of the purview of church authorities.

---

1. Charles de Clercq, ed., *Conc. Claremontanum*, c.3 and 7, and *Syn. Diocesana Autissiodorensis*, c.12, in *Concilia Galliae A.511–A.695*, *CCSL* 148a (Turnhout: Typographi Brepols editores Pontificii, 1963), 106–7, 267; Bailey K. Young, "Merovingian Funeral Rites and the Evolution of Christianity: A Study in the Historical Interpretation of Archaeological Material" (Ph.D. diss., University of Pennsylvania, 1975), 52; 76–80.

2. Theological precedents included Tertullian's defense of Christian offerings for the dead as an expression of funerary ritual and not belief. Jacques Fontaine, ed., *Q. Septimius Florentus Tertullianus, De corona* 3,4–4,1, in *Érasme* 18 (Paris: Presses universitaires de France, 1966), 67–70; Salomon Reinach, "L'origine des prières pour les morts," *Revue des études juives* 41 (1900): 163.

Since a funeral represented the final display of an individual's identity as envisioned by kin, followers, or religious brethren, it afforded powerful opportunities to underline solidarity or emphasize differences among members of a community. Often entailing a common meal that included the deceased symbolically, derived from the rite practiced by the Gallo-Romans, or rituals involving fire, funerary customs must have made a lasting impression upon Christian faithful. Such experiences may have overshadowed anything experienced at Mass or at the shrines of the saints.[3] Since the earliest surviving texts with Christian liturgical ceremonies for the dead in Gaul date from the sixth century, many features of burial custom not addressed by the sacramentaries were apparently tolerated by religious authorities. Until at least the eighth century, funerary rites practiced by Christians in rural and church settings included many pre-Christian elements.[4] Christian liturgical rituals for the dead were simply not as fully developed in the early Middle Ages as many scholars have assumed them to have been.

Some Christians, especially the elite inhabitants of the cosmopolitan centers in southern Gaul and members of monastic houses and ecclesiastical communities, may well have been buried with a variant of the liturgical ceremonies documented in other Roman cities in the West.[5] Given the virtual absence of texts testifying to the fourth- and fifth-century Christian liturgy for the dead, however, the exact contents of this rite are uncertain. One may

3. Burkhard Gladigow, "*Naturae deus humanae mortalis:* Zur sozialen Konstruktion des Todes im römischer Zeit," in *Leben und Tod in den Religionen: Symbol und Wirklichkeit,* ed. Gunther Stephenson (Darmstadt: Wissenschaftliche Buchgesellschaft, 1980), 119–20; Bonnie Effros, *Creating Community with Food and Drink in Merovingian Gaul* (New York: Palgrave, forthcoming).

4. Patrick Périn, "Remarques sur la topographie funéraire en Gaule mérovingienne et à sa périphérie: Des nécropoles romaines tardives aux nécropoles du haut–moyen âge," *CA* 35 (1987): 21–22.

5. Frederick S. Paxton, *Christianizing Death: The Creation of a Ritual Process in Early Medieval Europe* (Ithaca: Cornell University Press, 1990), 2–5; Megan McLaughlin, *Consorting with Saints: Prayer for the Dead in Early Medieval France* (Ithaca: Cornell University Press, 1994), 26–33.

therefore not assume that Christian liturgical rites were performed at the majority of Christian funerals in Gaul.[6] Evidence for sufficient numbers of local churches, clerics, and manuscripts to have fulfilled these functions is lacking even for the sixth and seventh centuries. Especially in regions north of the Loire, it is difficult to conceive of the celebration of liturgical rites on a broad basis. Almost all features of a specifically Christian ritual preceding and subsequent to death were first documented in Gaul in the seventh and eighth centuries, and it is unknown how widespread they were. Although Yitzhak Hen has suggested that the small number of surviving texts related to burial services resulted from the poor likelihood of the retention of outdated liturgical manuscripts rather than the extent to which particular liturgical practices had circulated,[7] his argument exudes great confidence in very little evidence. It is more easily argued that the laity effected their relationships with the dead without the spiritual intervention of clerics during much of the Merovingian period. Priests' roles as intermediaries only became widely accepted in the seventh and eighth centuries.[8] Centuries passed, however, before their contributions became essential to fulfillment of the burial rites.[9]

Nor were prayers for the dead uniform throughout Gaul; in the early-eighth-century Gelasian Sacramentary, for instance, clerics adapted the liturgy to the needs of the communities to which they ministered.[10] These

---

6. Éric Rebillard, *"In hora mortis"*: *Évolution de la pastorale chrétienne de la mort au* IVe *et* V^e *siècles dans l'Occident latin,* Bibliothèque des Écoles françaises d'Athènes et de Rome 283 (Palais Farnèse: École française de Rome, 1994), 63–70.

7. Yitzhak Hen, *Culture and Religion in Merovingian Gaul, A.D. 481–751* (Leiden: E. J. Brill, 1994), 143–60; Yitzhak Hen, "Priests and Books in the Merovingian Period," in *Priests in the Early Middle Ages,* ed. Rob Meens and Yitzhak Hen (forthcoming).

8. Patrick Geary, "Exchange and Interaction Between the Living and the Dead in Early Medieval Society," in *Living with the Dead in the Middle Ages* (Ithaca: Cornell University Press, 1994), 89–92.

9. But see Megan McLaughlin's earlier dating of this transformation to late antiquity: McLaughlin, *Consorting with Saints,* 29–33.

10. Yitzhak Hen, "The Liturgy of St Willibrord," *Anglo-Saxon England* 26 (1997): 48–53.

services perpetuated concerns voiced in theological and hagiographical texts circulating from the late sixth century, which advocated the importance of liturgical provisions for the well-being of the deceased in the afterlife and placed greater emphasis on the recitation of psalms and Masses.[11] Alms and church donations also constituted means of expiating lesser sins that stained the deceased souls; the diversion of wealth to these ends likely contributed to, but nonetheless cannot be seen as primary cause of, the abandonment of the deposition of grave goods or the increasing rarity of epigraphy in the seventh and eighth centuries.[12]

Very little evidence exists for clerical control of cemeterial burial (*ius tumulandi*) from late antiquity; privileged interment was normally a matter of social standing rather than religious merit, a practice Augustine of Hippo sought to combat.[13] Likewise, it is unclear to what extent clerics in the fourth and fifth centuries regulated burial of the poor, although private donations to churches might have been directed toward the interment of those who could not otherwise afford it.[14] As church cemeteries became more common in the late Merovingian period, however, Christian clerics

11. Arnold Angenendt, "Theologie und Liturgie der mittelalterlichen Toten-Memoria," in *Memoria: Der geschichtliche Zeugniswert des liturgischen Gedenkens im Mittelalter*, MMS 48, ed. Karl Schmid und Joachim Wollasch (Munich: Wilhelm Fink Verlag, 1984), 174ff.; Cécile Treffort, *L'église carolingienne et la mort: Christianisme, rites funéraires et pratiques commémoratives*, Collection d'histoire et d'archéologie médiévales 3 (Lyons: Presses universitaires de Lyon, 1996), 27–29.

12. Paul Reinecke, "Reihengräber und Friedhöfe der Kirchen," *Germania* 9 (1925): 103–5; W. A. Van Es, "Grabsitten und Christianisierung in den Niederlanden," *Probleme der Küstenforschung im südlichen Nordseegebiet* 9 (1970): 89–90; Donald A. Bullough, "Burial, Community, and Belief in the Early Medieval West," in *Ideal and Reality in Frankish and Anglo-Saxon Society: Studies Presented to J. M. Wallace-Hadrill*, ed. Patrick Wormald (Oxford: Basil Blackwell, 1983), 197.

13. Éric Rebillard, "La figure du catéchumène et le problème du délai du baptême dans la pastorale d'Augustine: A propos du *post-tractatum* Dolbeau 7: *De sepultura catechumenorum*," in *Augustin prédicateur (395–411): Actes du colloque international de Chantilly (5–7 septembre 1996)*, Collection des études augustiniennes, série antiquité 159, ed. Goulven Madec (Paris: Institut d'études augustiniennes, 1998), 286–87.

14. Éric Rebillard, "Les formes de l'assistance funéraire dans l'Empire romain et leur évolution dans l'antiquité tardive," *AnTard* 7 (1999): 273–82.

acquired greater influence over funerary topography. Far more vocally than they had expressed themselves in preceding generations, the clergy claimed the right to determine which Christians had the right to such interment, and could exclude those excommunicated from the Christian community.[15] Their new powers necessitated appropriation of a tradition that had been under the control of kin groups when burial still took place in row-grave or other rural cemeteries, and it is unclear how successful they were in meeting their goals. Only during Charlemagne's reign was legislation passed to enforce greater uniformity in Christian burial rites.[16] Then, too, the evidence for the application of these new measures is sketchy at best.

Written evidence for liturgical ritual in conjunction with somewhat enigmatic archaeological evidence therefore serves to identify a broader variety of funerary practices than those documented in clerical accounts of noble, royal, and, above all, holy burials. Merovingian graves have revealed traces of ceremonial rites, including funerary meals, votive food offerings for the dead, ritual fires of various types, the deposition of snails, and animal sacrifices, not all of which were likely sanctioned by Christian clerics.[17] Despite their unorthodox appearance for modern historians, however, these widespread practices cannot accurately be termed "pagan," since they were followed by a significant number of Christians. Many of these rites were not prohibited by law prior to the formulation of the *Indiculus superstitionum et paganiarum* (744–45), which contained measures defining

15. Bonnie Effros, "Beyond Cemetery Walls: Early Medieval Funerary Topography and Christian Salvation," *EME* 6 (1997): 1–23.

16. Bonnie Effros, "*De partibus Saxoniae* and the Regulation of Mortuary Custom: A Carolingian Campaign of Christianization or the Suppression of Saxon Identity?" *Revue belge de philologie et d'histoire* 75 (1997): 269–87.

17. Bailey K. Young, *Quatre cimetières mérovingiens de l'Est de la France: Lavoye, Dieue-sur-Meuse, Mézieres-Manchester et Mazerny*, BAR International Series 208 (Oxford: BAR, 1984), 123–25, 148, 153–54, 173; Valerie I. J. Flint, *The Rise of Magic in Early Medieval Europe* (Princeton: Princeton University Press, 1991), 213–16.

and forbidding a variety of "superstitious" or pagan customs. Some of the illegal practices included in this legislation were associated with burial, including funerary meals or libations (*dadsisas*), sacrifices, phylacteries, certain fires (*nodfyr*), and possibly the ritual deposition of snail shells in graves (*cocleae*).[18] Burial ritual in early medieval Gaul and surrounding regions thus represented an incredibly diverse tradition, one left largely unregulated by either lay or religious authorities. A juxtaposition of written and archaeological sources demonstrates some of the challenges inherent to untangling the events that transpired following the deaths of Christians.

Triumphant Burials of the Saints

Since the written sources focused most frequently on the saints, it is useful to begin with an assessment of contemporary depictions of their deaths and funerals. In late antiquity and the early Middle Ages, the passing of exemplary Christians constituted occasions for joy. In death saints achieved not only the release of their souls from the prison of their bodies[19] but also triumph over the fragmentation of the flesh that normally occurred with death.[20] Sulpicius Severus, in a letter to his mother, Bassula, therefore depicted the funeral procession of Martin of Tours as that of a triumphant

18. Alfred Boretius, ed., *Indiculus superstitionum et paganiarum* c.1, 2, 10, 15, 22, in *MGH: Leges* 2, *Capitularia* 1,108 (Hannover: Impensis bibliopolii Hahniani, 1883), 222–23; Alain Dierkens, "Superstitions, christianisme et paganisme à la fin de l'époque mérovingienne: A propos de l'*Indiculus superstitionum et paganiarum*," in *Magie, sorcellerie, parapsychologie*, Laïcité série recherches 5, ed. Hervé Hasquin (Brussels: Éditions de l'Université de Bruxelles, 1984), 18 ff.

19. The Bobbio Missal began its Mass for the dead: "Omnipotentem deum fratres karissimi deprecimur, ut animam famoli tui *ill.* quam de corpore carceris absoluta, in illo sempiterno et inviolabilem saeculum migrare precepisti." E. A. Lowe, ed., *The Bobbio Missal: A Gallican Mass-Book (Ms.Paris.Lat. 13246)* 2,530 (London: Harrison & Sons, 1920), 162; Werner Goez, "Die Einstellung zum Tode im Mittelalter," in *Der Grenzbereich zwischen Leben und Tod* (Göttingen: Vandenhoeck & Ruprecht, 1976), 116–17.

20. Caroline Walker Bynum, *The Resurrection of the Body in Western Christianity, 200–1336* (New York: Columbia University Press, 1995), 48–51.

conqueror.[21] The late-fourth-century *adventus* ceremony of Victricius of Rouen similarly celebrated the entry of relics into the city, comparing the virtues of the saints to celestial gems and their dress to senatorial counterparts: "[I]nstead of regal dress, the clothing of eternal light is present. The togas of the saints have drunk this purple. Here are the diadems adorned with the diverse lights of gems of wisdom, intellect, knowledge, truth, counsel, courage, tolerance, temperance, justice, prudence, patience, chastity. Those virtues are individually expressed and written on individual stones. Herein the Savior, an Artist, ornamented the crowns of the martyrs with spiritual gems."[22] Reinforced by wording borrowed from imperial liturgy, Christian ceremonial likened the saint to a bountiful spiritual defender of the city.[23] The Carolingians, in turn, easily adapted the litany of saints for use in the *laudes regiae*.[24]

A mixture of imagery of earthly riches and praise for pious accomplishments characterized burial and translation ceremonies of the saints.[25]

21. "[H]aec igitur beati viri corpus usque ad locum sepulchri hymnis canora caelestibus turba prosequitur. conparetur, si placet, saecularis illa pompa non dicam funeris, sed triumphi: quid simile Martini exequiis aestimabitur?" Karl Halm, ed., *Sulpicius Severus, Libri qui supersunt* Ep. 3, in *CSEL* I (Vienna: Apud C. Geroldi Filium, 1866), 150–51.

22. "[P]ro regali amictu praesto est aeterni luminis indumentum. Hanc purpuram togae bibere sanctorum. Sunt hic diademata variis gemmarum distincta luminibus sapientiae, intellectus, scientiae, veritatis, consilii, fortitudinis, tolerantiae, temperantiae, iustitiae, prudentiae, patientiae, castitatis. Istae in lapidibus singulis sunt singulae expressae scriptaeque virtutes. Hic spiritalibus gemmis coronas Martyrum artifex Salvator ornavit." René Herval, ed. and trans., *Sanctus Victricius Rothomagensis episcopus: De laude sanctorum* 12, in *Origines chrétiennes: De la IIe Lyonnaise gallo-romaine à la Normandie ducale (IVe–XIe siècles)* (Rouen: Saul H. Maugard & Cie., 1966), 145; Nikolaus Gussone, "Cérémonial d'*adventus* et translation des reliques: Victrice de Rouen—*De laude sanctorum*," in *Actes du colloque international d'archéologie: Centenaire de l'abbé Cochet* (Rouen: Le Musée départemental des antiquités de Seine-Maritime, 1978), 287–89.

23. Sabine G. MacCormack, *Art and Ceremony in Late Antiquity* (Berkeley and Los Angeles: University of California Press, 1981), 64–65.

24. Ernst H. Kantorowicz, *Laudes regiae: A Study in Liturgical Acclamations and Medieval Ruler Worship*, University of California Publications in History 33 (Berkeley and Los Angeles: University of California Press, 1946), 56 ff.

25. "[A]c Deo ex mente gratias agens & velut hospes novus alienum habitaculum reliquens & ad propria vadens cum ipsarum actione gratiarum beatum exhalavit [Eustadiola] spiritum; qui

Derived from imperial precedent, the sanctoral liturgy transmitted the glorious merits of holy relics and saints to their audience. Such language reinforced current uses of precious grave goods and the ornamentation of liturgical objects, such as the chalice of Chelles (no longer extant) and the "paten of Charles the Bald," now held at the Gallérie d'Apollon of the Louvre. Possibly crafted by Eligius, bishop of Noyon, both works of solid gold date to the seventh century.[26] As noted by the anonymous author of the *vita* of Gertrude of Nivelles (d. 659), such physical signs paralleled imagery of the saint's spiritual accomplishments. In describing Gertrude's tonsure, the cleric stated: "And the holy Gertrude, giving thanks to God, rejoiced because she had merited in this short life, by virtue of Christ, to receive the crown on her head, so that she had purity of the body and the soul, there in heaven, the perpetual crown."[27] Her entry into the cloister foreshadowed eternal splendor and a heavenly diadem. Similarly, in Sulpicius Severus's and Venantius Fortunatus's accounts of a vision of Martin of Tours on the day of his death, the saint's white toga signaled his membership among God's chosen.[28]

In the early Middle Ages, visions at the time of saints' deaths often confirmed that the dying holy person had been granted special spiritual

Angelorum sociatus choris coelestia regna petivit, ubi inter ignitos lapides in coelestis Regis ornamento coruscat." Philippe Labbé, ed., *Vita sanctae Eustadiolae abbatissae*, in *Novae bibliothecae manuscriptorum librorum* 2 (Paris: Apud Sebastianum Cramoisy, 1657), 378; Martin Heinzelmann, *Translationsberichte und andere Quellen des Reliquienkultes*, Typologie des sources du moyen âge Occidental 33 (Turnhout: Brepols, 1979), 35–40.

26. Hayo Vierck, "Werke des Eligius," in *Studien zur vor- und frühgeschichtlichen Archäologie: Festschrift für Joachim Werner zum 65. Geburtstag* 2, Münchner Beiträge zur Vor- und Frühgeschichte, suppl. vol. 1/II, ed. Georg Kossack and Günther Ulbert (Munich: Verlag C. H. Beck, 1974), 312–14, 337, 352–57.

27. "Beata autem Geretrudis Deo gratias agens, gaudebat, eo quod meruisset in brevi hac vita pro Christo in capite coronam accipere, ut perpetuam illic coronam corporis et animae integritatem haberet in caelis." Bruno Krusch, ed., *Vita sanctae Geretrudis* B.2, in *MGH: SRM* 2, new ed. (Hannover: Impensis bibliopolii Hahniani, 1956), 456.

28. Isabel Moreira, *Dreams, Visions, and Spiritual Authority in Merovingian Gaul* (Ithaca: Cornell University Press, 2000), 53.

status by God. The eagerness with which visions were welcomed in the Merovingian period differed from the outlook of Augustine of Hippo, who was more cautious in accepting the veracity of visions except as concerning Christian martyrs; in a letter to Paulinus of Nola, the bishop had argued that the ordinary dead did not have the power to interfere in the affairs of the living.[29] Augustine attributed revelations regarding the fate of the dead to a process similar to dreaming, aided by the angels. The souls of most deceased Christians were confined to a place where they could not perceive events transpiring on earth.[30]

Gregory I's influential *Dialogues* a century and a half later painted a rather different picture. Unlike Augustine, Gregory rejected the notion that the ability to heal or otherwise intervene among the living was reserved for martyrs.[31] By pointing to the miraculous final moments of saints' mortal existences, Gregory provided Christians greater incentive for repenting of their evil habits. Each would receive his or her just reward in the next world, even if it was not yet evident during his or her lifetime.[32] The pope nevertheless cautioned that most individuals who claimed to have experienced visions of the afterlife were likely subject

29. "Sed respondendum est non ideo putandum esse mortuos ista sentire, quia haec dicere vel indicare vel petere videntur in somnis. Nam et viventes apparent saepe viventibus dormientibus dum se ipse nesciant apparere et ab eis quae somniaverint audiunt dicentibus quod eos in somnis agentes aliquid vel loquentes viderint." Gustave Combes, ed., *De cura gerenda pro mortuis* 12, in *Oeuvres de Saint Augustin*, 1st ser., pt. 2, Bibliothèque augustinienne (Paris: Desclée de Brouwer et Cie., 1937), 418–19.

30. "Ibi ergo sunt spiritus defunctorum ubi no vident quaecumque aguntur aut eveniunt in ista vita hominibus." Combes, *De cura gerenda pro mortuis* 16, 434–35.

31. "Non ideo igitur putandum est vivorum rebus quoslibet interesse posse defunctos quoniam quibusdam sanandis vel adiuvandis Martyres adsunt; sed potius intelligendum est quod per divinam potentiam Martyres vivorum rebus intersunt quoniam defuncti per naturam propriam vivorum rebus interesse non possunt." Combes, *De cura gerenda pro mortuis* 19, 440–43.

32. Wilhelm Levison, "Die Politik in den Jenseitsvisionen des frühen Mittelalters," in *Aus rheinischer und fränkischer Frühzeit: Ausgewählte Aufsätze von Wilhelm Levison* (Düsseldorf: Verlag L. Schwann, 1948), 231–36. The concept of the measuring scale, however, did not arise until the Carolingian period. Angenendt, "Theologie und Liturgie," 123–27.

not to divine revelation but stomach ailments or hallucinations.[33] Although he acknowledged that laypersons, just like minor clergy and monks, might receive holy dreams,[34] only the elect could distinguish illusions from revelations. He therefore advised faithful Christians to avoid engaging in such matters.[35]

According to Gregory I, holy men were the most frequent recipients of miraculous visions. For instance, Gregory wrote that upon the death of Germanus, bishop of Capua, Benedict of Nursia (d. circa 550) perceived a light that brightened the night with its splendor.[36] Despite the great geographical distance that separated Benedict from Germanus, the former witnessed the bishop's soul in a sphere of fire being carried toward heaven by two angels.[37] Because Benedict's soul had expanded through lengthy divine contemplation, Gregory believed that he was able to discern the work of God with great clarity. The unworthy, by contrast, were denied such visions.[38] At the death of Father Stephen, for instance, some of those

33. "Sciendum . . . est quia sex modis tangunt animam imagines somniorum. Aliquando namque somnia ventris plenitudine vel inanitate, aliquando vero inlusione, aliquando cogitatione simul et inlusione, aliquando revelatione, aliquando autem cogitatione simul et revelatione generantur." Adalbert de Vogüé, ed., *Grégoire le Grand, Dialogues* 4,50,2, *SC* 265 (Paris: Éditions du CERF, 1980), 172–73.

34. Moreira, *Dreams, Visions,* 37–38.

35. "Sancti autem viri inter inlusiones atque revelationes ipsas visionum voces aut imagines quodam intimo sapore discernunt, ut sciant vel quid a bono spiritu percipiant, vel quid ab inlusione patiantur. Nam si erga haec mens cauta non fuerit, per deceptorem spiritum multis se vanitatibus immergit." De Vogüé, *Grégoire le Grand, Dialogues* 4,50,6, *SC* 265, 174–77.

36. "[Benedictus] vidit fusam lucem desuper cunctas noctis tenebras exfugasse, tantoque splendore clarescere, ut diem vinceret lux illa, quae inter tenebras radiasset." Adalbert de Vogüé, ed., *Grégoire le Grand, Dialogues* 2,35,2, *SC* 260 (Paris: Éditions du CERF, 1979), 236–39.

37. "Qui venerabilis pater [Benedictus], dum intentam oculorum aciem in hoc splendore coruscae lucis infigeret, vidit Germani Capuani episcopi animam in spera ignea ab angelis in caelum ferri." De Vogüé, *Grégoire le Grand, Dialogues* 2,35,3, *SC* 260, 238–39.

38. "Fit vero ipsa videntis anima etiam super semetipsam. Cumque in Dei lumine rapitur super se, in interioribus ampliatur, et dum sub se conspicit, exaltata conprehendit quam breve sit, quod conprehendere humiliata non poterat. Vir ergo qui [intueri] globum igneum, angelos quoque ad

present saw angels; they were so deeply struck with fear by the vision that they fled his bedside.[39] With the passing of Spes, the founder and abbot of a monastery at Campi, near Benedict's abbey of Nursia, Gregory reported that the monks present witnessed a dove fly out of his mouth and up toward heaven through an opening in the roof of the oratory.[40]

Gregory I and some of his contemporaries similarly recorded the divine wonders that accompanied the passing of holy nuns. According to Gregory, as the abbess Redempta approached Romula's sickbed with the other members of her Roman house, a celestial light of great splendor filled her cell and frightened the sisters deeply. Although the brightness gradually faded over the next three days, fragrance pervaded the chamber and comforted the nuns as a reminder of the perfume of the heavenly garden.[41] A putrid odor emitted from a tomb, by comparison, revealed the presence of a sinner.[42]

The influence of Gregory's *Dialogues* was felt by clerics across western Europe, especially with regard to his depiction of the afterlife. In Gaul a century later, Queen Balthild had a vision at Chelles, her monastic foundation, to which she had retired following her fall from power. Immediately prior to her death, she saw before the altar of Mary in the monastery's

---

caelum redeuntes videbat, haec procul dubio cernere nonnisi in Dei lumine poterat." De Vogüé, *Grégoire le Grand, Dialogues* 2,35,6, *SC* 260, 240–41.

39. De Vogüé, *Grégoire le Grand, Dialogues* 4,20,4, in *SC* 265, 76–77; Angenendt, "Theologie und Liturgie," 88, 100–101.

40. "Omnes vero fratres, qui aderant, ex ore eius exisse columbam viderunt, quae mox aperto tecto oratorii egressa, aspicientibus fratribus, penetravit caelum." De Vogüé, *Grégoire le Grand, Dialogues* 4,11,4, *SC* 265, 48–49; Angenendt, "Theologie und Liturgie," 105–6.

41. "Cumque noctis medio lectulo iacentis adsisterent subito caelitus lux emissa omne illius cellulae spatium inplevit, et splendor tantae claritatis emicuit, ut corda adsistentium inaestimabili pavore perstringeret, . . . Quam lucem protinus miri est odoris fragrantia subsecuta, ita ut earum animum, quia lux emissa terruerat, odoris suavitas refoueret." De Vogüé, *Grégoire le Grand, Dialogues* 4,16,5–7, *SC* 265, 64–69; Ernst Benz, *Die Vision: Erfahrungsformen und Bilderwelt* (Stuttgart: Ernst Klett Verlag, 1969), 373.

42. Yvette Duval, *Auprès des saints corps et âme: L'inhumation "ad sanctos" dans la chrétienté d'Orient et d'Occident du IIIᵉ au VIIᵉ siècle* (Paris: Études augustiniennes, 1988), 163.

church a ladder on which angels accompanied her as she climbed to heaven.[43] Although she humbly avoided discussing the contents of her revelation too widely, Balthild was heartened by this confirmation of her future status. She therefore forbade the sisters to tend to her too closely or to exhibit great sorrow, since her imminent death was supposed to constitute an occasion for great joy.[44] Such visions were not unique; in Anglo-Saxon England just before the death of Aethelburga, abbess of Barking (founded 665/675), the nun Torhtgyth saw a body wrapped in a brilliant shroud raised up into the heavens by means of golden cords.[45] Whether recounted by male or female witnesses, these visions confirmed the welcome reception of ecclesiastical and monastic leaders, often future saints, into the heavenly domain.[46]

In the late Merovingian and early Carolingian periods, however, these encouraging Continental and Anglo-Saxon vision texts came up against a growing number of horrifying tales of the fates of unrepentant sinners in the afterlife. For instance, Bede recounted that at the death of a layman who refused to confess, angels brought a small book within which his good deeds were inscribed. At the same time, an army of demons arrived, carrying a much larger codex filled with accounts of his evil deeds.[47] The contrast of this vision and those depicting the ease with which saints

---

43. "At vero, iam propinquante glorioso eius obitu, visio praeclara ei fuit ostensa. Scala enim erecta et stans ante altare sanctae Mariae, cuius culmen caelum contingeret, et quasi angelos dei commitantes, ipsa domna Balthildis ascenderet per eam." Bruno Krusch, ed., *Vita sanctae Balthildis* A.13, in *MGH: SRM* 2, 498–99.

44. Krusch, *Vita sanctae Balthildis* A.13–14, 498–501.

45. Bertram Colgrave and R. A. B. Mynors, eds., *Bede's Ecclesiastical History of the English People* 4,9 (Oxford: Clarendon Press, 1969), 360–61.

46. Peter Dinzelbacher, *Vision und Visionsliteratur im Mittelalter*, Monographie zur Geschichte des Mittelalters 23 (Stuttgart: Anton Hiersemann, 1981), 226–27.

47. "Quod vero prius candidum codicem protulerunt angeli, deinde atrum daemones, illi perparuum isti enormem." Colgrave and Mynors, eds., *Bede's Ecclesiastical History* 4,13, 498–503; Aaron J. Gurevich, "Au moyen âge: Conscience individuelle et image de l'Au-delà," *Annales ESC* 37 (1982): 263–64; Leo Koep, *Das himmlische Buch in Antike und Christentum: Eine religionsgeschichtliche Untersuchung zur altchristlichen Bildersprache*, Theophaneia 8 (Bonn: Peter Hanstein Verlag, 1952), 53–54.

entered the heavenly sphere was intended to remind Christians of the importance of good works and humility in the course of their lives. For the majority, who could not hope to achieve such an exemplary existence, prayer, penance, and alms played an increasing role in alleviating purgatorial suffering, a subject to which we will return in the next chapter.

The Privilege of Burial Ad Sanctos

For the edification of the Christian faithful, liturgical and hagiographical texts highlighted the rewards enjoyed by the saints. Although the sanctoral cycle varied among different communities in Gaul, the celebration of feast days represented a major preoccupation of churches by the late sixth century. At Auxerre, the church marked the deaths of as many as thirty saints, whereas at Chelles the nuns commemorated as many as forty-eight.[48] Burial *ad sanctos,* an important component of such veneration, represented a privilege and a means of physically appropriating access to the holy.[49] As noted by Peter Brown, "Contact with the holy [was] used to mark out unambiguously those individual members of the community who enjoyed a permanent status different from the rest."[50] The exclusive space in the close vicinity of the saints was thus reserved for the sepulchers of the religious *familia* in addition to leading members of the lay nobility.[51] At the

48. Hen, *Culture and Religion,* 84–99.

49. Peter Brown, *The Cult of Saints: Its Rise and Function in Latin Christianity* (Chicago: University of Chicago Press, 1981), 33–35; Yvette Duval, "Sanctorum sepulcris sociari," in *Les fonctions des saints dans le monde occidental (IIIᵉ–XIIIᵉ siècle): Actes du colloque organisé par l'École française de Rome, 27–29 octobre 1988,* Collection de l'École française de Rome, 149 (Palais Farnèse: École française de Rome, 1991), 338–45.

50. Peter Brown, "Eastern and Western Christendom in Late Antiquity: A Parting of the Ways," in *Society and the Holy in Late Antiquity* (Berkeley and Los Angeles: University of California Press, 1982), 185 ff.

51. Duval, *Auprès des saints,* 65 ff., 91 ff., 146–47; Ian Wood, "Sépultures ecclésiastiques et sénatoriales dans la vallée du Rhône (400–600)," *Médiévales* 31 (1996): 14–15; Nancy Gauthier, ed., *RICG* 1,170 (Paris: Éditions du CNRS, 1975), 426–30.

house of Caesaria II at Arles, mid-sixth-century legislation on behalf of her charges actually conserved burial space *ad sanctos* for the nuns by prohibiting either priests or laypersons from using it.[52] Such drastic measures, while supportive of individual nuns, were probably not long successful, since such privileges represented a considerable incentive for potential donors.

Early medieval funerary liturgy also emphasized the glory of the company that the righteous would soon enjoy. If received by God, the soul of the faithful Christian could eventually expect to join the martyrs, patriarchs, prophets, apostles, and angels.[53] Following a period of rest that would end with the Final Judgment, the deceased would be surrounded by the saints and the elect for all eternity.[54] Referred to in prayers as the heavenly Jerusalem, the afterlife was filled with the chanting of psalms and brilliant light.[55] From the early sixth century onward, leading royal donors sought to re-create this state on earth through sponsorship of the perpetual recita-

52. The *constitutum* added to the Rule after its initial composition stated: "quia membrum ipsum basilica facta est. devotis virginibus praeparata sepeliendis. non clericis. quibus per alteras basilicas debitus sepulture negari non potest locus; Nam si deserventium occupetur sepulturis orationis ambitus. numquid iustum videbitur. ut nos foris eiciamur quandoque sepeliendae." Germain Morin, "Problèmes relatifs à la règle de S. Césaire d'Arles pour les moniales," *Revue bénédictine* 44 (1932): 19–20.

53. "Suscipe, domine, animam servi tui . . . ut inter gaudentes gaudeat, et inter sapientes sapiat, et inter martires coronatos consedeat, et inter patriarchas et prophetas proficiat, et inter apostolos Christum sequi studeat, et inter angelos et archangelos claritatem dei pervideat." Leo Cunibert Mohlberg, Leo Eizenhöfer, and Petrus Siffrin, eds., *Liber sacramentorum romanae aeclesiae ordinis anni circuli (Cod.Vat.Reg.lat. 316/Paris B.N. 7193, 41/56) (Sacramentarium Gelasianum)* 1611, Rerum ecclesiasticarum documenta, series maior, fontes 4, 3d ed. (Rome: Casa Editrice Herder, 1981), 235.

54. "Rogamus etiam domine pro animam famoli tui, *ill.*, quod in pace dominica adsumere dignatus est, ut locum refrigerii teneat, vitae merita, consequatur, aeterna, ibique eum statuere digneris, ubi est, omnium beatitudo iustorum, et cum dies ille iudicii advenerit inter sanctus et elictus tuos, eum facias suscitare." Lowe, *The Bobbio Missal* 2,532, 162.

55. "[E]t inter cherubin et syraphin claritatem dei inveniat, et inter viginti quattuor seniores cantica canticorum audiat, et inter lavantes stolas in fonte luminis vestem lavet, et inter pulsantes pulsans portas caelestis Hierusalem apertas reppereat." Mohlberg, Eizenhöfer, and Siffrin, *Liber sacramentorum* 1611, 235.

tion of psalms (*laus perennis*) at their burial places. Their uninterrupted performance meant that approximately three Psalters could be read in the course of twenty-four hours.[56] By granting religious houses such as Saint-Maurice (Agaune), Saint-Marcel (Chalon-sur-Saône), and Saint-Denis privileges and immunities for such undertakings, monarchs sought to assure themselves of the salvation of their souls. At Agaune, for instance, the Burgundian king Sigismund sponsored *laus perennis* to ensure his health and the stability of the kingdom.[57] Although this brand of *memoria* was aimed at moving the dead into heavenly bliss as quickly as possible, so that their remembrance would no longer be necessary,[58] the exchange of lands for prayers had the consequence of perpetuating worldly distinctions in the afterlife.[59]

During the offices of worship, clerics had regular contact with holy tombs. Covered with cloths, they often functioned as altars. The level of access to these monuments highlighted differences between the privileges of clerical and monastic authorities and those of the general Christian population. At Nivelles, for instance, the nuns had numerous opportunities for prolonged contact with the tomb of Gertrude.[60] By comparison, common Christians had far fewer chances to visit such sites.[61] Only at special religious events such as translations, feast days, and Easter were holy relics publicly

---

56. Angenendt, "Theologie und Liturgie," 139–40.

57. Karl Heinrich Krüger, *Königsgrabkirchen der Franken, Angelsachsen und Langobarden bis zur Mitte des 8. Jahrhunderts,* MMS 4 (Munich: Wilhelm Fink Verlag, 1971), 439–40, 475–76.

58. Jean-Claude Schmitt, *Les revenants: Les vivants et les morts dans la société médiévale* (Paris: Éditions Gallimard, 1994), 17–19.

59. Annette B. Weiner, *Inalienable Possessions: The Paradox of Keeping-While-Giving* (Berkeley and Los Angeles: University of California Press, 1992), 33–34.

60. "Cum omnia quae circa beatissimum corpus agebant et officia fuissent impleta, in cisterna, quam sibi olim praeparaverat, cum divinis laudibus et sacerdotibus et ancillis Dei corpus beatissimae virginis Christi Geretrudis honorificae traditur sepulturae, ubi cotidie orationum prestantur beneficia per Dominum nostrum Iesu Christum." Krusch, *Vita sanctae Geretrudis* B.7, 464.

61. Luce Pietri, "Les sépultures privilégiées en Gaule d'après les sources littéraires," in *L'inhumation privilégiée,* 139.

displayed. Seventh-century liturgical ceremonies thereby emphasized the exclusive relationships of prestigious groups to the saints.[62] In the case of the two translational processions that took place after the discovery of the remains of Foillan (d. 31 October 655) and his companions, who had been brutally murdered seventy-seven days earlier, each gave attention to particular components of the religious and social hierarchy. At the first, the clergy and laity sang antiphons and psalms and carried the bodies, along with candles and torches, from the forest where they had been found back to Gertrude's foundation of Nivelles. In the second procession, Grimoald, the brother of Gertrude and then mayor of the palace, helped to carry the saint's remains. His gesture not only underlined his status as a member of this noble family but promoted his authority through his special connection to this holy relic housed at his sister's monastery.[63]

Interment churches in possession of saints' relics thus provided numerous opportunities to display Merovingian royal and elite prerogatives.[64] Although not specifically related to the presence of royal graves, the privileges received by most Merovingian monasteries were given in exchange for prayers on behalf of the king and kingdom. Queen Balthild therefore used the cult center that she cultivated at Chelles, as elsewhere, to reinforce dynastic stability, cement her close relationship with Merovingian clerics, and validate the authenticity of her royal prerogative.[65] Monastic houses in

62. Paul Fouracre, "The Work of Audoenus of Rouen and Eligius of Noyon in Extending Episcopal Influence from the Town to the Country in Seventh-Century Neustria," in *The Church in Town and Countryside: Papers Read at the Seventeenth Summer Meeting and Eighteenth Winter Meeting of the Ecclesiastical History Society*, ed. Derek Baker (Oxford: Basil Blackwell, 1979), 83 ff.

63. "Suscepta vero corpora cum cereis ac facellarum luminibus, cum antiphonis et canticis spiritalibus a clero et populo per totam noctem ad monasterium Nivalcham honorifice humeris deportat sunt." Bruno Krusch, ed., *Additamentum Nivialense de Fuilano*, in *MGH: SRM* 4 (Hannover: Impensis bibliopolii Hahniani, 1902), 451.

64. Krüger, *Königsgrabkirchen*, 469 ff.

65. Eugen Ewig, "La prière pour le roi et le royaume dans les privilèges épiscopaux de l'époque mérovingienne," in *Mélanges offerts à Jean Dauvillier* (Toulouse: Université des sciences sociales, 1979), 255–67.

Paris sheltering royal graves similarly acted as administrative centers and the preferred locations of synods and councils. Palaces and royal sanctuaries were often closely linked: Chlothar III's move to Clichy paralleled the early-seventh-century transfer of the royal family's necropolis from the abbey of Saint-Vincent (later Saint-Germain-des-Prés) to Saint-Denis.[66] The creation of saints' cults around royal figures, by contrast, was never a priority for the Merovingian dynasty. Balthild's translation did not take place at Chelles until 833, long after Merovingian ambitions could have played a role.[67] The canonization of the Merovingian kings Dagobert II (d. 679) and Sigibert III (d. 656) began even later.[68] The late emergence of royal saints' cults in Gaul differed significantly from practices in Anglo-Saxon England, where some royal figures were venerated as early as the seventh century.[69]

Not only did church liturgy and burial *ad sanctos* afford members of royal and noble families the opportunity to display publicly their status and Christian orthodoxy, but they promoted the significance of familial burial places as community monuments. Jacques Fontaine has therefore suggested that the Christian faithful were encouraged to be devoted not just to their own deceased kin but also to the spiritual ancestors or forebears of leading families of their region.[70] These distinctions were just as relevant among clerics. The sixth-century adaptation of the Roman custom of

---

66. Eugen Ewig, "Résidence et capitale pendant le haut moyen âge," *Revue historique* 230 (1963): 50–53.

67. *Translatio corporis beatissimae Baltechildis reginae*, in Paris BN MS Latin 18296, fols. 17v–20v.

68. Robert Folz, "Tradition hagiographique et culte de saint Dagobert, roi des Francs," *Le moyen âge* 69 (1963): 17–35; Robert Folz, "Vie posthume et culte de saint Sigisbert roi de Austrasie," in *Festschrift Percy Ernst Schramm zu seinem siebzigsten Geburtstag von Schülern und Freunden zugeeignet* 1 (Wiesbaden: Franz Steiner Verlag, 1964), 7–26.

69. David Rollason, *Saints and Relics in Anglo-Saxon England* (Oxford: Basil Blackwell, 1989), 118–35.

70. Jacques Fontaine, "Le culte des saints et ses implications sociologiques: Réflexions sur un récent essai de Peter Brown," *AB* 100 (1982): 23–24.

funerary orations (*laudatio funebris*) and its inclusion in the funerary liturgy through the recitation of saints' lives perpetuated the memory of clerical elites on the anniversaries of their deaths.[71] The honor of noble saints, such as Rusticula of Arles, was also reinforced through exclusive burial to the right of the altar.[72] Interment in one of the church's entryways, a very prominent location chosen by Amatus of Remiremont, meant that the sepulcher of a saint or a high-status patron might be more easily incorporated into liturgical ceremonies such as processionals.[73] The promotion of holy graves bolstered in turn the status of their secular relations and supporters.[74]

Commemorative Inscriptions on Moveable Possessions in Graves

Beyond burial *ad sanctos* and liturgical commemoration, a number of other media were used by Christians to ease their passage into the afterlife. Some Christians chose inscribed objects such as brooches and buckles, and less frequently amulet cases and swords, to accompany late relations into their graves. Although they were not necessarily fashioned for inclusion in

71. Martin Heinzelmann, "Neue Aspekte der biographischen und hagiographischen Literatur in der lateinischen Welt (1.–6. Jahrhundert)," *Francia* 1 (1973): 40–44; Martin Heinzelmann, *Bischofsherrschaft in Gallien: Zur Kontinuität römischer Führungsschichten vom 4. bis zum 7. Jahrhundert: Soziale, prosopographische und bildungsgeschichtliche Aspekte*, Beihefte der Francia 5 (Munich: Artemis Verlag, 1976), 23 ff. On Venantius Fortunatus's use of a more personal expression of empathy than the *laudatio funebris*, see Judith W. George, *Venantius Fortunatus: A Latin Poet in Merovingian Gaul* (Oxford: Clarendon Press, 1992), 87–105.

72. "Deinde sanctae Mariae basilicae venerandum corpus [Rusticulae] infertur, et sacri altaris misteria celebrantes, cum digno honore sanctum illud corpus, splendore nimio coruscante, ad dexteram partem altaris tumulo conlocatur." Bruno Krusch, ed., *Vita Rusticulae sive Marciae abbatissae Arelatensis* 25, in *MGH: SRM* 4, 350.

73. "Omnis homo Dei, qui in hunc locum sanctum ad orandum introieris, si obtinere mereris que postulas, pro anima Amati penitentis hic sepulti Domini misericordiam deprecari digneris." Bruno Krusch, ed., *Vita Amati abbatis Habendensis* 13, in *MGH: SRM* 4, 220; Michel Fixot, "Les inhumations privilégiées en Provence," in *L'inhumation privilégiée*, 118–19.

74. Friedrich Prinz, "Heiligenkult und Adelsherrschaft im Spiegel merowingischer Hagiographie," *Historische Zeitschrift* 204 (1967): 535–42.

burials, these votive goods warned of imminent dangers for Christian souls in the afterlife. Expressing sentiments similar to those commemorated on contemporary tombstones, artifacts engraved with prayers or epitaphs also might point to the status or religious achievements of the deceased. Unfortunately for modern scholars, only those articles pertaining to the interment ceremony and placed into the grave stood a reasonable chance of survival. Vessels left unprotected on the exterior of graves, such as the mass-produced red ceramic, wick-channel pan lamps common in late antique Gaul and North Africa, were far less likely to leave material traces. Lit at the site of tombs to pay respect to the deceased, they were decorated on occasion with images such as Daniel among the lions, a theme common to tombs and belt buckles in early medieval Gaul.[75]

In cemeteries of the Merovingian period, rare examples survive of artifacts engraved or molded with a cross or a Latin inscription. Contemporaries must have deposited these goods in graves to commemorate the deceased whom they accompanied. Klaus Düwel has compiled a list of Latin as well as runic inscriptions discovered on artifacts in graves in eastern Frankish regions.[76] An object serving a commemorative purpose was found at the cemetery of Krefeld-Gellep. Dated to the third decade of the sixth century, the twenty-two-centimeter-high bronze pitcher excavated from the well-outfitted "Fürstengrab" #1782 bore an inscription indicating that Arpvar, possibly the man with whom it was interred, enjoyed elite status.[77]

75. André van Doorselaer, *Les nécropoles d'époque romaine en Gaule septentrionale*, Dissertationes archaeologicae gandenses 10, trans. Marcel Amand(Brugge: De Tempel, 1967), 120–22. For the iconography of Christian lamps in North Africa, see J. W. Solomonson, *Voluptatem spectandi non perdat sed mutet: Observations sur l'iconographie du martyr en Afrique romaine* (Amsterdam: North-Holland Publishing Company, 1979), 11–19, esp. pls. 1 and 10.

76. Klaus Düwel, "Epigraphische Zeugnisse für die Macht der Schrift im östlichen Frankenreich," in *Die Franken: Wegbereiter Europas* 1 (Mainz: Verlag Philipp von Zabern, 1996), esp. 544–52.

77. The inscription, as reconstructed by Géza Alföldy, reads: "Arpvar erat (f)elex undique pr(a)e(celsus?)." Géza Alföldy, "Die Inschrift der Bronzekanne aus dem fränkischen Fürstengrab von Krefeld-Gellep," *Bonner Jahrbücher* 166 (1966): 446–51. Most recently, see Renate Pirling, "Krefeld-Gellep im Frühmittelalter," in *Die Franken: Wegbereiter Europas* 1, 261–65.

Goldblattkreuʒe, or gold-foil crosses, although more commonly found in Alemannic regions north of the Alps, also constituted votive objects that might be deposited in Christian graves in Gaul up to the seventh century. Composed of a paper-thin layer of gold or gold alloy often imprinted with designs, the fragile crosses could not have been worn on the garments of an active individual for any length of time without being damaged. Instead, they were probably presented by kin and sewn directly onto the clothing of the corpse just prior to burial. The *Goldblattkreuʒe,* as well as less costly cloth crosses that imitated them, mimicked the functions of sarcophagi decorated with crosses: they identified the individual thus marked as a member of the Christian community. They may also have fulfilled amuletic functions.[78] In the region of Trier, sixth- and seventh-century brooches in the shape of crosses (*Kreuʒfibeln*), as well as amulets and rings decorated with crosses, when buried with the dead, achieved similar ends.[79]

Like epitaphs, seventh- and eighth-century inscribed artifacts tended to reflect greater concerns regarding the afterlife than had been the case in the previous period. Relatives may have contributed such gifts on the occasion of the funerary ceremony in order to commemorate the deceased. In the case of a seventh-century engraving on the underside of the lavishly decorated brooch found at Wittislingen along the Danube, a donor dedicated a few lines to Uffila, presumably the deceased woman with whom it

78. Rainer Christlein, "Der soziologische Hintergrund der Goldblattkreuze nördlich der Alpen," in *Die Goldblattkreuʒe des frühen Mittelalters,* Veröffentlichungen des Alemannischen Instituts Freiburg i. Br. 37, ed. Wolfgang Hübener (Bühl: Verlag Konkordia, 1975), 73–83; Ernst Foltz, "Technische Beobachtungen an Goldblattkreuzen," in *Die Goldblattkreuʒe des frühen Mittelalters,* 16–17; Hayo Vierck, "Folienkreuze als Votivgaben," in *Die Goldblattkreuʒe des frühen Mittelalters,* 134–42.

79. Wilhelm Reusch, ed., *Frühchristliche Zeugnisse im Einʒugsgebiet von Rhein und Mosel* 81–90 (Trier: Unitas-Buchhandlung, 1965), 105–9, pls. 81–90; Patrick Périn and Alain Dierkens, *L'art mérovingien: Permanences et innovations,* Feuillets de la cathédrale de Liège 25–26 (Liège: Trésor de la cathédrale de Liège, 1996), 9.

was buried.[80] Aside from imparting great confidence in Uffila's destiny in the next world, the brooch, possibly produced in a Frankish workshop, protected the physical remains of the faithful Christian from harm. Although its inscription was orthodox, recesses in the back of brooch may have been destined for relics, a practice forbidden by clerics as superstitious.[81] Similarly, an eighth-century bone disk brooch found in Trier praised the deceased as the handmaid of God. Professing her faith in the Trinity, the inscription identified the woman as a pious Christian, perhaps a nun.[82] Some brooches also portrayed free-standing crosses resembling those found on contemporary tombs.[83] These artifacts reflected heightened awareness of the obstacles faced by Christian souls in achieving salvation.

Some of the larger belt buckles (*plaque-buckles*) found in elite burials bear images linked to the theme of resurrection. Varying noticeably by the region in which they were produced, they depict scenes such as Daniel in the lion's den, Habakuk, Christ's entry into Jerusalem, and anonymous orants.[84] Like brooches, some also functioned as reliquaries, as was the case of a Burgundian buckle found in Chalon-sur-Saône.[85] On a late-

---

80. Bernhard Bischoff, "Epigraphisches Gutachten II," in *Das alamannische Fürstengrab von Wittislingen*, Münchner Beiträge zur Vor- und Frühgeschichte 2, ed. Joachim Werner (Munich: C. H. Beck'sche Verlagsbuchhandlung, 1950), 68–71.

81. Germain Morin, ed., *Sanctus Caesarius Arelatensis, Sermones* 50, in *CCSL* 103, rev. ed. (Turnhout: Typographi Brepols editores Pontificii, 1953), 225; Audrey L. Meaney, *Anglo-Saxon Amulets and Curing Stones*, BAR British Series 96 (Oxford: BAR, 1981), 10ff., 24–28.

82. The inscription on the Rotsuintda-Scheibe (Rheinisches Landesmuseum, 9,865) reads:

> IN X̄P̄O̅ NOMINE ROTSVINTDA ANCELLA X̄P̄I̅ SVM EGO
> IN NOMINE PATRIS ET FILII S̄P̄V̅.S̄C̅I̅ AMEN ALLELVA.

This artifact was found in the Trier amphitheater. Reusch, *Frühchristliche Zeugnisse* 97, 111–12, pl. 97.

83. Ursula Koch, "Beobachtungen zum frühen Christentum an den fränkischen Gräberfeldern von Bargen und Berghausen in Nordbaden," *AK* 4 (1974): 259–66.

84. Michel Colardelle, *Sépulture et traditions funéraires du Ve au XIIIe siècle après J.-C. dans les campagnes des Alpes françaises du nord (Drôme, Isère, Savoie, Haute-Savoie)* (Grenoble: Publication de la Société alpine de documentation et de recherche en archéologie historique, 1983), 112–16, figs. 55 and 56; Reusch, *Frühchristliche Zeugnisse* 134–41, 136–41, pls.134–41.

85. Helmut Roth, "Kunst der Merowingerzeit," in *Die Franken: Wegbereiter Europas* 2, 637–38, fig. 504.

eighth-century buckle discovered in a sarcophagus buried at the crypt of the Collégiale de Saint-Quentin (Aisne), Christ appeared seated in a mandorla formed of two dragons. The buckle, to which were attached the remains of a belt and possibly an amulet case, probably constituted a Christian phylactery meant to protect the corpse from violation.[86] A bronze buckle now housed at the Musée de Chambéry achieved similar objectives with an image of Daniel in the lions' den.[87]

In very rare instances, particularly in the case of grave remains carefully preserved in reliquaries, artifacts fashioned from luxury cloth with embroidered texts and images survive from the seventh and eighth centuries. Just like more durable goods, fabric protected Christian bodies with images consistent with belief in the final resurrection. This genre of *memoria* was especially suitable when it was anticipated that a tomb would be reopened for inspection during translation ceremonies. While too well preserved to have ever rested in her grave, the chasuble of Balthild (d. 680/681) was decorated with an embroidered pectoral cross and images of a lavish necklace.[88] Retained by the nuns of Chelles long after her death, the blouse effectively symbolized the queen's status as former queen turned holy woman.[89] A fragment of a winding clothing discovered in a reliquary in the cathedral of Sens preserves the earliest known representation of the Assumption.[90]

---

86. Albert France-Lanord, "La plaque-boucle reliquaire mérovingienne de Saint-Quentin: Étude analytique," *Comptes rendus de l'Académie des Inscriptions et Belles-Lettres* (1956): 263–65.

87. Colardelle, *Sépulture et traditions*, 114, fig. 55,4.

88. Hayo Vierck, "La 'chemise de Sainte-Bathilde' à Chelles et l'influence byzantine sur l'art de cour mérovingien au VIIᵉ siècle," in *Actes du colloque international d'archéologie: Centenaire de l'abbé Cochet* (Rouen: Le Musée départemental des antiquités de Seine-Maritime, 1978), 539 ff.

89. Jean-Pierre Laporte and Raymond Boyer, *Trésors de Chelles: Sépultures et reliques de la reine Bathilde (✝ vers 680) et de l'abbesse Bertille (✝ vers 704)*, Catalogue de l'exposition organisée au Musée Alfred Bonno (Chelles: Société archéologique et historique, 1991), 45–46; Bonnie Effros, "Symbolic Expressions of Sanctity: Gertrude of Nivelles in the Context of Merovingian Mortuary Custom," *Viator* 27 (1996): 1–2.

90. Patrick Périn and Laure-Charlotte Feffer, eds., *La Neustrie: Les pays au nord de la Loire de Dagobert à Charles le Chauve (VIIᵉ–IXᵉ siècles)* 27 (Rouen: Musées et monuments départementaux de Seine-Maritime, 1985), 140; unpublished file of the *CIFM*, Département 89, Cathédrale, Trésor, Sens.

The iconography of the white linen, measuring 65 cm × 70 cm, was indeed appropriate for wrapping the remains of a holy Christian destined for heaven.

In a somewhat later example from the mid-ninth century, Hincmar of Reims may have commissioned a cushion for the translation of the archbishop Remigius's (d. 533) relics in 852. Red samite from Iran or Byzantium was fashioned into a cushion to cradle the head of the saint in its reliquary. The donor, who embroidered the cloth with an inscription in gold and silk, identified herself as Alpheidis, the sister of Charles the Bald. She asked for the prayers of the saint on her behalf in exchange for her precious gift.[91] The pillow was made in roughly the same period as two other imported luxury cloths, one of which was decorated with a violet and green embroidered dedication to the saint from Hincmar.[92] To be certain, such luxury artifacts were not representative of contemporary funerary rituals, since they were destined to honor holy relics. Yet, the extremely fragile nature of such goods, particularly if placed in a stone coffin in physical contact with decaying human remains, means that there were few places other than sealed reliquaries where they stood a chance of survival. Hence, embroidered luxury objects may have been used more often than extant fragments indicate.

Changing Perceptions of the Afterlife

For early medieval Christians, an individual's destiny after death was far less certain than that of the saints. Late antique descriptions of the afterlife

---

91. The second half of the inscription reads: "QVAE SVB HONORE NOVO PVLVILLVM CONDIDIT IPSVM QVO SVSTENTETVR DVLCE SACRVMQVE CAPVT REMIGII MERITIS ALPHEIDIS VBIQVE JVVETVR IPSIVSQVE PRECES HANC SVPER ASTRA FERANT." Unpublished file of the *CIFM*, Département 51, Basilique Saint-Rémi, Reims.

92. *Les trésors des églises de France* 154–60, 2d ed. (Paris: Caisse nationale des monuments historiques, 1965), 78–79.

in Gaul had promoted the notion that baptized Christians would experience a relatively innocuous interim period of waiting in the bosom of Abraham (*refrigerium interim*). Sulpicius Severus thus contrasted Martin's welcome in this place with the demise of secular conquerors in Tartarus.[93] From the fifth century onward, however, greater uncertainty overshadowed this intermediate place for even the most devout. Aaron Gurevich has attributed the change to growing concern not just with the general destiny of humanity but also the personal fates of individuals. Each Christian had to undergo judgment at death in addition to facing the universal trial of humanity at the end of time.[94]

Although the Church Fathers had long recognized that fear of death was part of the human condition, Augustine of Hippo was among the first to describe the purgatorial fires of the afterlife through which impure souls had to pass in order to be cleansed of all sin before proceeding to heaven.[95] Significant time passed, however, before theologians defined more precisely the nature of this intermediate stage between death and bliss.[96] Gregory of Tours, for instance, associated fire with hell and not purgatorial cleansing.[97] Gregory I's influence, however, brought about widespread belief in a first judgment immediately subsequent to death. This theological concept rapidly replaced confidence in the *refrigerium interim*. Subsequent to the deceased's trial, the soul experienced celestial

93. Halm, *Sulpicius Severus, Libri qui supersunt* Ep. 3, 151. For a discussion of the *refrigerium interim* and further bibliography, see Jacques Le Goff, *La naissance du purgatoire* (Paris: Éditions Gallimard, 1981), 73 ff.

94. Gurevich, "Au moyen âge," 264–65.

95. Rebillard, *"In hora mortis,"* 63–70, 127–28. Earlier reference to this intermediate phase was made in the third-century *Passion of SS. Perpetua and Felicity* 7–8. Perpetua had a vision of the suffering of her late brother Dinocrates, from which he was released by means her prayers. Moreira, *Dreams, Visions,* 143, n. 30.

96. Le Goff, *La naissance,* 100–105, 114 ff.

97. Giselle de Nie, *Views from a Many-Towered Window: Studies of Imagination in the Work of Gregory of Tours,* Studies in Classical Antiquity 7 (Amsterdam: Rodopi, 1987), 149–53.

beatitude, one of two purgatorial locations, or the burning of hell. Some exceptions to belief in a two-tiered purgatorial realm, however, remained. Transcripts of the vision of the seventh-century monk Barontus depicted an intermediate location between heaven and hell reminiscent of the bosom of Abraham.[98] None of these steps, however, precluded the understanding that at the end of time all souls would go before a final, universal court to be judged prior to the Resurrection.[99]

From the seventh century, descriptions of the intermediate stage between death and the soul's eternal resting place occupied a prominent place in hagiographical and visionary literature. As noted by Isabel Moreira, although these traditions nonetheless bore important resemblance to earlier divinely inspired visions in Gaul, they were often conveyed by ordinary Christians or monastic sinners. What distinguished earlier visionaries such as Abbot Sunniulf of Randan and Bishop Salvius of Albi, described by Gregory of Tours, from their seventh-century successors such as the monks Fursey and Barontus, however, was that the latter Christians' death and revival served the express purpose of warning other Christians of the need for penance in achieving salvation.[100]

While there was not just one understanding of the topography of the otherworld, Christians believed in its spatial and temporal proximity to the living. Austregisillus, bishop of Bourges (612–24), was, according to his biographer, seen in a vision assisting in his own funeral.[101] This conception

---

98. "Ut autem venimus inter paradysum et infernum, vidi ibi virum senum pulcherrimum aspectum, habentem barbam prolixam, in alta sede quietem sedentem." Wilhelm Levison, ed., *Visio Baronti monachi Longoretensis* 16, in *MGH: SRM* 5 (Hannover: Impensis bibliopolii Hahniani, 1910), 390.

99. Cyril Vogel, "Deux conséquences de l'eschatologie grégorienne: La multiplication des messes privées et les moines-prêtres," in *Grégoire le Grand: Chantilly, Centre culturel Les Fontaines, 15–19 septembre 1982*, ed. Jacques Fontaine, Robert Gillet and Stan Pellistrandi, Colloques internationaux du CNRS (Paris: Éditions du CNRS, 1986), 268.

100. Moreira, *Dreams, Visions*, 136–43, 148–55.

101. "& cum corpus ipsius Sancti adpositum in sepulchro fuisset . . . stans praefatus Episcopus Rauracus ad pedes eius, & memoratus Presbyter Ianuarius aspexit, quod quasi saepe fatus S.

of the afterlife thus differed greatly from the astral immortality of the spirit proposed by Plato.[102] Although conceived of as an eternal state, the next world was often regulated according to human time and mores. As recounted by Gregory I, two religious women who had been excommunicated for inappropriate language had nonetheless received church burial. Each time the Mass was celebrated, their bodies were miraculously seen exiting their tombs and leaving the church until the service had been completed.[103] In the late-sixth- or early-seventh-century account of the conversion of Mamertinus to Christianity, the pagan took shelter in a cemetery on a mountain near Auxerre. When he awoke, he saw a Mass miraculously being performed by the deceased predecessors of the bishop Germanus.[104] Belief in the resurrection of the flesh, prevalent in late antiquity and the early medieval period, in addition to expressing confidence in the survival of personality and even friendships in the afterlife, strengthened bonds between this world and the next.[105]

In the purgatorial realm, the treatment of Christians reflected the state of their souls and the number and type of sins they had committed. On the Continent just as in Anglo-Saxon England, good and bad deeds were personified in the afterlife and functioned independently of the individuals who committed them. In Wynfrid's letter to the Anglo-Saxon abbess Eadburg of Thanet in 716, for instance, he wrote about a vision of a monk

---

Austregisillus ad dexteram ipsius Rauraci candidis vestibus, & decoro vulto assistere videtur."
Philippe Labbé, ed., *Vita (liber prima) S. Austregisilli Bituricensis archiep.*, in *Novae bibliothecae manuscriptorum librorum* 2, 354.

102. Franz Cumont, *Lux Perpetua* (Paris: Librairie Orientaliste Paul Geuthner, 1949), 358 ff.

103. De Vogüé, *Grégoire le Grand, Dialogues* 2,23,2–5, *SC* 260, 206–9.

104. Godefridus Henschenius and Danielus Papbrochius, eds., *De sancto Corcodemo diacono Autissiodori in Gallia*, in *Acta sanctorum* Mai 1 (Antwerp: Apud Michaelem Cnobarum, 1658), 453; Wilhelm Levison, "Bischof Germanus von Auxerre und die Quellen zu seiner Geschichte," *Neues Archiv* 29 (1904): 160 ff. I am grateful to Max Diesenberger for this helpful reference.

105. J. G. Davies, "Factors Leading to the Emergence of Belief in the Resurrection of the Flesh," *JTS* n.s. 23 (1972): 448–55; Moreira, *Dreams, Visions*, 144–45.

at the house of Wenlock in which former actions pulled a Christian soul in various directions.[106] Alternatively, an individual's sins might simply be identified from the fact that he or she was attacked by demons in the purgatorial realm. At the monastery now called Saint-Cyran-en-Brenne, the Frankish monk Barontus circa 678–79 described his oppressors as black in color, airborne, and possessing long teeth and talons with which they rendered harsh punishment and tortured their victims.[107] The winged angels or guides with more familiar human visages who escorted visionaries such as Barontus and Dryhthelm to the afterlife were clothed in gleaming white garments and gave off a fragrant odor.[108] These images were fairly consistent with Gregory I's images of the afterlife in the *Dialogues*.[109]

Some depictions of the purgatorial experience, however, were grimmer than others. In Bede's account of the self-exiled Irish monk Fursey (d. circa 649–50), who spent much of the latter part of his life in Neustria, the visionary described a shadowy valley above which burned four fires representing falsehood, greed, discord, and injustice.[110] In adding a later Anglo-Saxon visionary account of Dryhthelm to his *Ecclesiastical History*, Bede elaborated that those who delayed repentance until they found themselves on their deathbeds had to pass through a great valley scorched by fire on one side and beset by hail and snow on the other.[111] The souls in

---

106. Michael Tangl, ed., *Die Briefe des heiligen Bonifatius und Lullus* 10, MGH: *Epistolae selectae* 1 (Berlin: Weidmannsche Verlagsbuchhandlung, 1955), 7–15; Gurevich, "Au moyen âge," 264–65.

107. ". . . daemones nigerrimi nimis, qui me cupiebant dentibus et unguibus lacerare crudeliter." Levison, *Visio Baronti* 7, 382; Vogel, "Deux conséquences," 267; Moreira, *Dreams, Visions*, 158–67.

108. ". . . angeli in alba veste et mirifico odore." Levison, *Visio Baronti* 7, 382. ". . . lucidus . . . aspectu et clarus erat indumento." Colgrave and Mynors, *Bede's Ecclesiastical History* 5,12, 488–89.

109. De Vogüé, *Grégoire le Grand, Dialogues* 4,12,4, SC 265, 50–51.

110. Colgrave and Mynors, *Bede's Ecclesiastical History* 3,19, 272–75. For a discussion of the earliest version of these visions, written circa 656/657 at Péronne, which was excluded by Bruno Krusch from his edition of Fursey's *vita*, see Moreira, *Dreams, Visions*, 155–58.

111. "[D]evenimus ad vallem multae latitudinis ac profunditatis, infinitae autem longitudinis, quae ad levam nobis sita unum latus flammis ferventibus nimium terribile, alterum furenti grandine

this purgatorial region were tossed intermittently from ice to fire and back again, and were thereby purified of their sins prior to the time of the final Judgment.

Although tales of purgatorial suffering must have greatly frightened devout Christians, the eternal damnation awaiting unrepentant sinners must have seemed terrifying in comparison. According to both Gregory I[112] and Barontus, sinners in hell were bound to lead seats and then punished according to their crimes.[113] The mouth of Gehenna consisted of a fiery pit from which there was no return, even with the assistance of the living. The pope, in fact, likened this place to the volcanos of Sicily.[114] Both Barontus and Bede related that flaming spheres spewed the souls of humans to great heights and then retracted with them to profound depths. Burning filled the smoky darkness of hell with a fetid odor and the sound of groaning.[115] These images were impressive enough to remain a signifi-

---

ac frigore nivium omnia perflante atque verrente non minus intolerabile praeferebat. Utrumque autem erat animabus hominum plenum, quae vicissim huc inde videbantur quasi tempestatis impetu iactari." Colgrave and Mynors, *Bede's Ecclesiastical History* 5,12, 488–91.

112. "Unus quidem est gehennae ignis, sed non uno modo omnes cruciat peccatores. Uniuscuiusque etenim quantum exigit culpa, tantum illic sentietur poena." De Vogüé, *Grégoire le Grand, Dialogues* 4,45,2, *SC* 265, 160–61.

113. "Sic daemones animas laqueatas in peccatis ad inferni tormenta trahebant et super plumbeas sedes in giro sedere imperebant. Sed ordines malorum et societates eorum quomodo erant, per singula edisseram. Tenebantur ibi superbi cum superbis, luxoriosi cum luxoriosis." Levison, *Visio Baronti* 17, 391; Michel Aubrun, "Caractères et portée religieuse et sociale des 'visiones' en Occident du VI᷎ au XI᷎ siècle," *CCM* 23 (1980): 119–21.

114. De Vogüé, *Grégoire le Grand, Dialogues* 4,31,2–3 and 4,36,12 *SC* 265, 104–5, 122–23.

115. "[E]cce subito apparent ante nos crebri flammarum tetrarum globi ascendentes quasi de puteo magno rursumque decidentes in eundem. Quo cum perductus essem, repente ductor meus disparuit, ac me solum in medio tenebrarum et horridae visionis reliquit. At cum idem globi ignium sine intermissione modo alta peterent, modo ima baratri repeterent, cerno omnia quae ascendebant fastigia flammarum plena esse spiritibus hominum, qui instar favillarum cum fumo ascendentium nunc ad sublimiora proicerentur, nunc retractis ignium vaporibus relaberentur in profunda." Colgrave and Mynors, *Bede's Ecclesiastical History* 5,12, 490–91; Levison, *Visio Baronti* 17, 390–92.

cant part of Carolingian polemic. The ninth-century *Gesta Dagoberti I* similarly depicted Dagobert's punishment in the afterlife for his sins.[116] As discussed earlier, these images of purgatorial suffering and hell contrasted dramatically with heaven as well as the joyous place that awaited even the good who had not yet achieved a state of perfection but had taken steps to assure their salvation.[117] Gregory I urged his readers to make the effort necessary to arrive at this destination in the East. He warned them that on their approach to purgatory, their souls would have to cross a bridge over an intolerably odorous river.[118] Surrounded by a high wall, however, this near paradise resembled a great field filled with light and flowers. The inhabitants of this place were clothed in white and sat about happily in groups; some lived in mansions built of gold bricks.[119] Although not as splendid as the heavenly kingdom, this intermediate location was recognition that even those who had not been perfect in every word, action, and thought during their lives might earn significant rewards. It nonetheless served as a stern reminder that souls guilty of just minor sins could not enter heaven until the Last Judgment.[120] The triumph of the perfect meant the immediate enjoyment of the place for which the resurrected bodies and souls

116. Bruno Krusch, ed., *Gesta Dagoberti I, regis Francorum* 44, in *MGH: SRM* 2, 421–22.

117. "Locus vero iste florifer, in quo pulcherrimam hanc iuventutem iucundari ac fulgere conspicis, ipse est, in quo recipiuntur animae eorum qui in bonis quidem operibus de corpore exeunt; non tamen sunt tantae perfectionis, ut in regnum caelorum statim mereantur introduci; qui tamen omnes in die iudicii ad visionem Christi et gaudia regni caelestis intrabunt." Colgrave and Mynors, *Bede's Ecclesiastical History* 5,12, 494–95.

118. "Aiebat enim [miles] . . . quia pons erat, sub quo niger atque caligosus foetoris intolerabilis nebulam exhalans fluvius decurrebat." De Vogüé, *Grégoire le Grand, Dialogues* 4,37,8, *SC* 265, 130–31.

119. De Vogüé, *Grégoire le Grand, Dialogues* 4,37,9, *SC* 265, 130–31; Levison, *Visio Baronti* 10, 384–85; Colgrave and Mynors, *Bede's Ecclesiastical History* 5,12, 492–93.

120. De Vogüé, *Grégoire le Grand, Dialogues* 4,26,1, *SC* 265, 84–85; Joseph Ntedika, *L'évocation de l'Au-delà dans la prière pour les morts: Étude de patristique et de liturgie latines (IVe–VIIIe siècle)*, Recherches africaines de théologie 2 (Louvain: Éditions Nauwelaerts, 1971), 159–85.

of the rest of the faithful had to wait until the end of time.[121] Many thus yearned for the overpowering light and fragrance of the celestial abode, where the air was said to carry the sound of fervent singing and praying.[122] Hence we will now turn in the next chapter to a discussion of the rituals that prepared the dying and the dead for their existence in such places.

121. Aubrun, "Caractères et portée religieuse," 117–18; McLaughlin, *Consorting with Saints,* 65–66.

122. Dryhthelm recounted: "[A]spicio ante nos multo maiorem luminis gratiam quam prius, in qua etiam vocem cantantium dulcissimam audivi; sed et odoris flagrantia miri tanta de loco effundebatur." Colgrave and Mynors, *Bede's Ecclesiastical History* 5,12, 494–95.

CHAPTER V

✦ • ✦

Christian Liturgy and the Journey to the Next World

Religious Ceremonies in Advance of Dying

Prior to the seventh century, funerary liturgy in Merovingian Gaul focused on the heavenly joys awaiting Christian souls.[1] Similar to contemporary tomb iconography and epigraphy, discussed in Chapter III above, images of redemption and resurrection predominated in the liturgical services for the dead.[2] Prayers appended to Caesarius of Arles's early-sixth-century *Rule for Virgins*, for instance, devoted few words to the horrors to be faced by sinners. Once over the gates of hell and its paths of darkness (*vias tenebrarum*), the deceased would join the saints and the elect in a place of light and joy until the time of the final resurrection.[3] Such prayers encouraged faithful Christians to celebrate death with positive images of what awaited them in the next world.[4]

1. Joseph Ntedika, *L'évocation de l'Au-delà dans la prière pour les morts: Étude de patristique et de liturgie latines (IVᵉ–VIIIᵉ siècle)*, Recherches africaines de théologie 2 (Louvain: Éditions Nauwelaerts, 1971), 115 ff.
2. Edmond Le Blant, "Les bas-reliefs des sarcophages chrétiens et les liturgies funéraires," *RA* n.s. 38 (1879): 223–33, 280–92.
3. "Te domine sancte pater omnipotens aeterne deus supplices deprecamur pro spiritu famulae tuae . . . ut digneris domine dare ei locum refrigerii et quietis. Liceat ei transire portas infernorum et vias tenebrarum, maneatque in mansionibus sanctorum, et in luce sancta, quam olim Abrahae promisisti et semini eius . . . sed cum magnus dies ille resurrectionis ac regenerationis advenerit, resuscitare eam digneris domine una cum sanctis et electis tuis." Germain Morin, ed., *S. Caesarius Arelatensis episcopus, Regula sanctarum virginum aliaque opuscula ad sanctimoniales directa*, in *Florilegium Patristicum* 34 (Bonn: Sumptibus Petri Hanstein, 1933), 30.
4. Frederick S. Paxton, *Christianizing Death: The Creation of a Ritual Process in Early Medieval Europe* (Ithaca: Cornell University Press, 1990), 54–55.

In response to such cautionary visionary accounts of the afterlife as conveyed by Gregory I, Fursey, and Barontus in the seventh century, however, the funerary liturgy lost its predominantly confident tone and gave increased attention to the chastisement of the dead following interment. Liturgical works such as the mid-eighth-century Gelasian Sacramentary referred, for instance, to the punishment of the darkness (*paenas tenebrarum*).[5] Gates of infernal fire and gloom surrounded the dead and cleansed them so that they might reach the holy light. The liturgy gave comfort, however, to fearful Christians by emphasizing the eternal rest and quiet merited by the deserving faithful.[6] Therefore, although both the Gelasian Sacramentary and the Bobbio Missal warned of the punishments certain to befall the wicked,[7] the former also described a celestial Jerusalem populated by the patriarchs where Christian souls awaited their resurrection.[8] The liturgy also provided efficacious remedies for souls that had to pass through purgatorial regions.

The main difficulty that exists in judging the significance of these changes in prayers for the dead stems from uncertainty as to how widespread such customs were in actuality. The relative dearth of funerary ceremonial in

5. Damien Sicard, *La liturgie de la mort dans l'Église latine des origines à la réforme carolingienne*, Liturgiewissenschaftliche Quellen und Forschungen 63 (Münster: Aschendorffsche Verlagsbuchhandlung, 1978), 268.

6. "[U]t digneris, domine, dare ei locum lucidum, locum refrigerii et quietis. Liceat ei transire portas infernorum et vias tenebrarum maneatque in mansionibus sanctorum et in luce sancta, quam olim Abrahae promisisti et semini eius." Leo Cunibert Mohlberg, Leo Eizenhöfer, and Petrus Siffrin, eds., *Liber sacramentorum romanae aeclesiae ordinis anni circuli (Cod.Vat.Reg.lat. 316/Paris B.N. 7193, 41/56) (Sacramentarium Gelasianum)* 1617, Rerum ecclesiasticarum documenta, series maior, fontes 4, 3d ed. (Rome: Casa Editrice Herder, 1981), 236.

7. "Tu nobis, domine, auxilium praestare digneris, tu opem, tu misericordiam largiaris; spiritum eciam famuli tui *ille* ac cari nostri vinculis corporalibus liberatum in pace sanctorum tuorum recipias, uti locum paenalem et gehenne ignem flammamquae tartari in regione vivencium evadat." Mohlberg, Eizenhöfer, and Siffrin, *Liber sacramentorum* 1609, 234. "Tu nobis domine auxilium prestare digneris, tu per misericordiae largiaris animam quoque famulo tuo *ill.* a vinculis corporalibus, liberato in pace sanctorum tuorum recipias, et gehenne ignis evadat." E. A. Lowe, ed., *The Bobbio Missal: A Gallican Mass-Book (Ms.Paris.Lat. 13246)* 2,536 (London: Harrison & Sons, 1920), 164.

surviving Gallic sacramentaries of the seventh and eighth centuries suggests that priests did not yet play a large role in most Christians' burials. Composed by clerics, both liturgical and hagiographical works concentrated on the funerary ceremonies of fellow clerics and lay elites. Whether prescriptive compilations or rhetorical hagiographical works promoting the glory of a particular saint's resting place, they sought to regale their readers with details of the burials of the most worthy Christians. Such texts, by contrast, did not present an image of what occurred at the deaths and funerals of a broader segment of the population,[9] leaving modern readers to wonder how representative such rites were of the experiences of most baptized Christians in the Merovingian period. Although valuable for determining what was thought desirable at the passing of a monk, nun, or bishop, seldom can these accounts be reconciled with the activities of the general Christian population. Particularly outside the Gallo-Roman cities and monastic centers, in which such ideal accounts were written, clerics' view of the appropriate train of events before and after the death of a baptized Christian must have differed from common practice in the seventh and eighth centuries. We do not know the extent of the presence of clerics in rural parishes in early medieval Gaul.

Keeping the limitations of the sources in mind, we may only piece together the events typical of Christian funerals witnessed by clerics. When a Christian in southern Gaul became gravely ill, his or her family might send for a doctor or a cleric, depending upon the nature of the malady and the preferences of kin. For the sick, Caesarius of Arles (d. 542) recommended the benefits of anointment with blessed oil in conjunction

---

8. "Suscipe, domine, servum tuum *illum* in aeternum habitaculum et da ei requiem et regnum id est Hierusalem caelestem, ut in sinibus patriarcharum nostrorum id est Abraham Isaac et Iacob collocare digneris; et habeat partem in prima resurrectione, et inter surgentes resurgat, et inter suscipientes corpora in die resurrectionis corpus suscipiat." Mohlberg, Eizenhöfer, and Siffrin, *Liber sacramentorum* 1612, 235.

9. Sicard, *La liturgie de la mort*, 304–5.

with communion. In later centuries, the Bobbio Missal and the Gelasian Sacramentary offered prayers to rid healing oil of infernal powers. Once it was exorcised and blessed, holy oil was used to anoint sick individuals in an effort to bring healing, pardon from sin, and celestial health.[10] In Caesarius's eyes, holy oil far outweighed any assistance that the ill could expect from the use of amulets, herbs, or other methods,[11] all of which had become more common than traditional medicine in sixth-century Gaul.[12] Yet, Caesarius also believed that anointing had as its primary objective not the cure of sickness but rather purification and preparation for eternal life. The practice of prayer and the unction of the sick thus shifted ailing individuals' focus from physical healing to their salvation.[13] This theme resonated in later works such as the *vita* of Eligius of Noyon.[14] With the decreasing availability of physicians in Gaul, the sick also grew dependent upon saints' relics for the cure of life-threatening ailments.[15]

10. Lowe, *The Bobbio Missal* 2,574–76, 172–73; Antoine Chavasse, *Étude sur l'onction des infirmes dans l'Église latine du IIIe au XIe siècle* 1, doctoral thesis (Lyons: La Faculté de Théologie de Lyon, 1942), 40–48, 76–78.

11. "Et atque utinam ipsam sanitatem vel de simplici medicorum arte conquirerent. Sed dicunt sibi: Illum ariolum vel divinum, illum sortilegum, illam erbariam consulamus." Germain Morin, ed., *Sanctus Caesarius Arelatensis, Sermones* 52,5, *CCSL* 103, rev. ed. (Turnhout: Typographi Brepols editores Pontificii, 1953), 232. A similar passage is repeated in the *Vita Eligii*. Bruno Krusch, ed., *Vita Eligii episcopi Noviomagensis* 2,16, in *MGH: SRM* 4 (Hannover: Impensis bibliopolii Hahniani, 1902), 707.

12. Morin, *Sanctus Caesarius Arelatensis, Sermones* 50,1, 224–25; Valerie I. J. Flint, *The Rise of Magic in Early Medieval Europe* (Princeton: Princeton University Press, 1991), 252–53; Chavasse, *Étude sur l'onction,* 100–115.

13. Paxton, *Christianizing Death,* 50–51; Chavasse, *Étude sur l'onction,* 114–15.

14. "[S]ed qui aegrotat, in sola Dei misericordia confidat et eucaristiam corporis ac sanguinis Christi cum fide et devotione accipiat oleumque benedictum fideliter ab ecclesia petat, unde corpus suum in nomine Christi ungat, *et* secundum apostolum *oratio fidei salvabit infirmum et allevabit eum Dominus;* et non solum corporis sed etiam animae sanitatem recipiet." Krusch, *Vita Eligii episcopi Noviomagensis* 2,16, 707.

15. A herniary brace in grave 500 of the cemetery of Frénouville (Normandy) provides one small example of the survival of rudimentary medical practices as late as the mid–seventh century. Christian Pilet, *La nécropole de Frénouville: Étude d'une population de la fin du IIIe à la fin du VIIe siècle* 1, BAR International Series 83(i) (Oxford: BAR, 1980), 145–47.

A disdain for traditional physicians characterized hagiographical as well as liturgical texts of the sixth, seventh, and eighth centuries. Gregory of Tours, for instance, associated reliance upon doctors with a lack of faith.[16] Hagiographers likewise highlighted the readiness of faithful saints to embrace illnesses that brought death and the reward of eternal salvation. In the *vita* of Balthild (d. 680/681), her anonymous biographer sought to impress upon apparently skeptical readers her spiritual achievements at Chelles during the last two and a half decades of her life,[17] after the Neustrian mayor of the palace Ebroin banished the former queen to her monastic foundation.[18] She allegedly preferred healing of a spiritual type to the intervention of physicians for a physical cure. Although her *vita* included no mention of holy oil, it emphasized that the former queen "always had greater faith in the celestial healer regarding her health"[19] and desired salvation foremost. This sentiment was likewise expressed by her contemporary, the Frankish monk Barontus,[20] and appeared in the mid-eighth-century Gelasian Sacramentary.[21] A prayer in the Burgundian

---

16. Edward James, "A Sense of Wonder: Gregory of Tours, Medicine and Science," in *The Culture of Christendom: Essays in Medieval History in Commemoration of Denis L. T. Bethell*, ed. Mark Anthony Meyer (London: Hambledon Press, 1993), 52–59.

17. Janet L. Nelson, "Queens as Jezebels: Brunhild and Balthild in Merovingian History," in *Politics and Ritual in Early Medieval Europe* (London: Hambledon Press, 1986), 17–23; Ian Wood, *The Merovingian Kingdoms, 450–751* (London: Longman, 1994), 198–202.

18. Friedrich Prinz, *Frühes Mönchtum im Frankenreich: Kultur und Gesellschaft in Gallien, den Rheinlanden und Bayern am Beispiel der monastischen Entwicklung (4. bis 8. Jahrhundert)*, 2d ed. (Darmstadt: Wissenschaftliche Buchgesellschaft, 1988), 274–75.

19. "Coepit ipsa domna Balthildis corpore infirmari et viscerum incisione, pessimo infirmitatis vitio, graviter laborare, et nisi medicorum studia subvenissent, pene deficere. Sed magis ipsa ad caelestem medicum semper fidem habebat de salute sua." Bruno Krusch, ed., *Vita sanctae Balthildis* A.12, in *MGH: SRM* 2, new ed. (Hannover: Impensis bibliopolii Hahniani, 1956), 497.

20. "[Q]ui [fratres Baronti] psalmodiae cantus recitarent per ordinem, ut caelestis medicus mitteret animam in corpore." Wilhelm Levison, ed., *Visio Baronti monachi Longoretensis* 2, in *MGH: SRM* 5 (Hannover: Impensis bibliopolii Hahniani, 1910), 378.

21. "Deus qui humani generis et salutis remedii vitae aeternae munera contulisti, conserva famulo tuo tuarum dona virtutum et concede ut medellam tuam non solum in corpore sed in anima sentiat." Mohlberg, Eizenhöfer, and Siffrin, *Liber sacramentorum* 1536, 221.

Missale Gothicum (circa 690–710) similarly petitioned the Lord for the gift of celestial medicine for the sick. Focused primarily on the spiritual health of the individual rather than a bodily cure,[22] the prayer emphasized that God's merciful intervention made possible the healing of the infirm.[23]

In Balthild's *vita*, the saint received visitors who wished to pay their final respects prior to her imminent death.[24] The visitors served as witnesses to the saint's appropriately contrite behavior at this time. They might also have sought from a dying abbot or abbess counsel about their future, as some did of Wandrille of Fontanelle in the seventh century.[25] The recitation of the *Credo* and the chanting of psalms and the litany of saints also eased the Christian's transition into the afterlife.[26] Those saints to whom visions had revealed that they did not have long to live used the interval for penitential preparation. According to Sulpicius Severus, Martin of Tours spent his last hours in vigils, lying on a bed of sackcloth and ashes.[27] Jonas of Bobbio similarly described the days leading to the

22. "Universae salutis Deum et universae virtutis Dominum dipraecimor pro fratribus et sororibus nostris, qui secundum carnem diversis aegretudinum generibus insultantur ut his Dominus caeleste medicinae suae munus indulgeat." Leo Cunibert Mohlberg, ed., *Missale Gothicum: Das gallikanische Sakramentar (Cod. Vatican. Regin. lat. 317) des VII.–VIII. Jahrhunderts*, Codices liturgici e Vaticanis praesertim delecti phototypice expressi 1,240 (Augsburg: Dr. Benno Filser Verlag, 1929), 159r; Paxton, *Christianizing Death*, 57–59.

23. "Domine . . . restitue aegrotantibus pristinae sanitati, ne terreni medicaminis remedia desiderent, quicumque medillam caelestis misericordiae tuae dipraecantur." Mohlberg, *Missale Gothicum* 241, 159r; Mohlberg, Eizenhöfer, and Siffrin, *Liber sacramentorum* 1539–42, 222; Paxton, *Christianizing Death*, 57–59.

24. Krusch, *Vita sanctae Balthildis* A.12, 497–98.

25. His disciples asked him: "Quid facturi sumus, ut nobis tam cito relinques, pater? Verba tua audire vellemus, adsueta admonicionem tuam omnes desideramus corregi!" Bruno Krusch, ed., *Vita Wandregiseli abbatis Fontanellensis* 18, in *MGH: SRM* 5, 22–23; Isabel Moreira, *Dreams, Visions, and Spiritual Authority in Merovingian Gaul* (Ithaca: Cornell University Press, 2000), 179.

26. Louis Gougaud, "Étude sur les 'Ordines commendationis animae,'" *Ephemerides liturgicae* 49 (1935): 3–4, 11.

27. Karl Halm, ed., *Sulpicius Severus, Libri qui supersunt* Ep. 3, in *CSEL* 1 (Vienna: Apud C. Geroldi Filium, 1866), 149.

deaths of Sisetrude and Gibitrude at the house of Faremoutiers under the abbess Burgundofara (d. circa 641/655): prayer, almsgiving, contemplation, and self-mortification (e.g., by fasting and wearing hair shirts) purified their souls for the next life.[28]

Religious texts advocated that immediately prior to death final confession be made to a cleric. If time remained, the appropriate penance was to be performed. In fact, the twenty-ninth canon of the Second Council of Arles (442–506) stated that all clerics were obligated to grant penitential duties to any who desired them.[29] Although Merovingian legislation between 511 and 650 gave little guidance,[30] fifth-century councils had earlier indicated that administration of both penance and unction was the responsibility of priests (*sacerdotes*) as well as bishops.[31] The twenty-eighth canon of the Second Council of Arles also permitted penitents too ill to complete reconciliation to receive communion.[32] Two and a half centuries later the Gelasian Sacramentary therefore included special prayers for the reconciliation of dying penitents.[33]

---

28. Bruno Krusch, ed., *Ionas, Vitae Columbani abbatis discipulorumque eius libri II* 2,11–12, in *MGH: SRG* 37 (Hannover: Impensis bibliopolii Hahniani, 1905), 257–62; Gisela Muschiol, *Famula Dei: Zur Liturgie im merowingischen Frauenklöstern*, Beiträge zur Geschichte des alten Mönchtums und des Benediktinertums 41 (Münster: Aschendorff, 1994), 313–21.

29. "Paenitencia desiderantibus etiam clericis non negandam." C. Munier, ed., *Concilia Galliae A.314–A.506, CCSL* 148 (Turnhout: Typographi Brepols editores Pontificii, 1963), 120.

30. Paxton, *Christianizing Death*, 59–61.

31. Antoine Chavasse, *Le sacramentaire gélasien (Vaticanus Reginensis 316)*, Bibliothèque de théologie, ser. 4, vol. 1 (Paris: Desclée et Co., 1958), 141–51.

32. "De his qui in extremis pereclitantur paenitentia accepta placuit sine reconciliaturia manus impositione eis communicare. Quod si accepto hoc viatico supervixerint, stent in ordine paenitentum, ut ostensis necessariis paenitentiae fructibus, legitime reconciliaturia manus impositione recipiant." Munier, *Concilia Galliae*, 120.

33. "Deus misericors, deus clemens, qui indulgentiam tuam nullum temporum lege concludis, sed pulsantis misericordiae tuae ianuam aperis, paenitentis etiam sub ipso vitae huius terminum non relinquis: respice propicius super hunc famulum tuum remissionem sibi omnium peccatorum tota cordis confessione poscentem." Mohlberg, Eizenhöfer, and Siffrin, *Liber sacramentorum* 367, 59.

As early as the time of Paulinus of Nola's *Vita Ambrosii* (circa 411–13), hagiographical works suggested that on rare occasions dying Christians might receive the viaticum.[34] On the Continent and in Anglo-Saxon England, confession, penance, and communion functioned as final reconciliation (*in extremis*).[35] In its fifteenth canon, the Council of Agde (506) reinforced this trend by strenuously prohibiting priests from depriving the dying of the Eucharist.[36] The rituals of penance and viaticum thus came to be perceived as a single act.[37] Reconciliation was symbolized by an informal laying on of hands (*impositio manus*).[38] The death of a monk at Luxeuil, described by Jonas of Bobbio, also merited the kiss of peace.[39] The Synod of Auxerre (561–605) nonetheless forbade priests to give communion or the kiss of peace to those who had already died.[40] The performance of these rituals and the anticipated recitation of prayers on behalf of the deceased (*post mortem eius*) represented preparatory steps for entrance into the afterlife; the dying faithful thereby gained confidence in the remission of their sins.[41] Only during the seventh and eighth centuries was deathbed

34. Éric Rebillard, *"In hora mortis": Évolution de la pastorale chrétienne de la mort au IVe et Ve siècles dans l'Occident latin*, Bibliothèque des Écoles françaises d'Athènes et de Rome 283 (Palais Farnèse: École française de Rome, 1994), 200–202; Muschiol, *Famula Dei*, 323–24.

35. Regarding Cuthbert's death (d. 687), Bede wrote: "Et ubi consuetum nocturnae orationis tempus aderat, acceptis a me [Bedis] sacramentis salutaribus exitum suum quem iam venisse cognovit dominici corporis et sanguinis communione munivit." Bertram Colgrave, ed., *Bede's Life of Cuthbert* 39, in *Two Lives of St. Cuthbert* (Cambridge: Cambridge University Press, 1940), 284–85; Chavasse, *Étude sur l'onction*, 123, 134–37.

36. "Viaticum tamen omnibus in morte positis non negandum." Munier, *Concilia Galliae*, 201.

37. Paxton, *Christianizing Death*, 51–52.

38. Cyril Vogel, *La discipline pénitentielle en Gaule des origines à la fin du VIIe siècle*, doctoral thesis, Strasbourg, 1950 (Paris: Letouzey et Ané, 1952), 25–37.

39. "[C]orpus Christi abeunte de hac vita viaticum praebet hac post externa oscula functionis cantus implevit." Krusch, *Ionas, Vitae Columbani abbatis discipulorumque eius libri II* 1,17, 184.

40. Charles de Clercq, ed., *Concilia Galliae A.511–A.695*, in *CCSL* 148a (Turnhout: Typographi Brepols editores Pontificii, 1963), 267; Megan McLaughlin, *Consorting with Saints: Prayer for the Dead in Early Medieval France* (Ithaca: Cornell University Press, 1994), 31.

41. Cyril Vogel, "La discipline pénitentielle en Gaule des origines au IXe siècle: Le dossier hagiographique," *RSR* 30 (1956): 14–18, 158–62.

penance (*paenitentia in extremis*) replaced by repeated and sacramental confession.[42]

Passage from Death to the Afterlife

Hagiographical sources indicate that following a Christian's death the corpse was washed, groomed, dressed, and in many cases wrapped in a shroud.[43] It is possible that a member of the deceased's family, someone appointed by them, or a member of a religious community fulfilled these duties.[44] If a cleric was present, he accompanied these activities with a prayer, such as the one beginning *Suscipe, domine* in the Gelasian Sacramentary, which urged the Lord to receive the soul of the deceased.[45] Preparation for burial probably lasted as little as a few hours but no longer than a few days except under unusual circumstances, such as an unexpected death far from home. Some elite families chose to transport the bodies of relatives to particular resting places. The remains of the Merovingian queen Chrodechild, for instance, were carried about two hundred kilometers from Tours to Paris after her death in 544.[46]

42. Cyril Vogel, "Une mutation cultuelle inexpliquée: Le passage de l'eucharistie communautaire à la messe privée," *RSR* 54 (1980): 231–32.

43. "[I]ta barba et capilli eius [Eligii], qui tempore abitus sui iuxta morem fuerant abrasi, mirum in modum creverant in tumulo." Krusch, *Vita Eligii episcopi Noviomagensis* 2,48, 728; Nikolaus Kyll, *Tod, Grab, Begräbnisplatz, Totenfeier: Zur Geschichte ihres Brauchtums im Trierer Lande und in Luxemburg unter besonderer Berücksichtigung des Visitationshandbuches des Regino von Prüm (†915),* Rheinisches Archiv 81 (Bonn: Ludwig Röhrscheid, 1972), 20–21; Muschiol, *Famula Dei,* 334–35.

44. "Quadam vero die, dum eius hospitium, quod non longe ab ecclesia aberat, intrasset, cuiusdam pauperculae mulieris maritus iuxta defunctus est. Quem ex more locum, vestimentis indutum et sabano constrictum, superveniente vespere, sepelire nequiverunt. Iuxta defuncti igitur corpus viduata mulier sedit, quae in magnis fletibus noctem ducens, continuis lamentorum vocibus satifaciebat dolori." Adalbert de Vogüé, ed., *Grégoire le Grand, Dialogues* 3,17,2, *SC* 260 (Paris: Éditions du CERF, 1979), 336–39.

45. "Suscipe, domine, animam servi tui . . . vestem caelestem indue eam et lava eam sanctum fontem vitae aeternae." Mohlberg, Eizenhöfer, and Siffrin, eds., *Liber sacramentorum* 1611, 235; Paxton, *Christianizing Death,* 65.

46. Karl Heinrich Krüger, *Königsgrabkirchen der Franken, Angelsachsen und Langobarden bis zur Mitte des 8. Jahrhunderts,* MMS 4 (Munich: Wilhelm Fink Verlag, 1971), 447.

According to contemporary accounts, the needy sometimes received
from lay or religious volunteers and donors charitable assistance in burying
their dead. These activities represented for them a form of penance.[47]
Although just such a topos in the *vita* of Balthild was aimed at heightening
the image of the humility of the future saint, and we do not know how
reliably it reflected the former queen's actions, the passage nonetheless
demonstrated the importance of burial for all Christians. Caesarius of
Arles, for instance, employed penitents to assist in the interment of the
dead.[48] The honorable treatment of the body prior to burial reflected the
desire of surviving family members for the deceased's soul to be warmly
received in the heavenly realm.

Winding cloths were fashioned in certain circumstances from costly
fabrics and elaborately adorned. Although shrouds of lay and religious
leaders may not have been made of cloth of comparable quality to that
used to wrap and protect relics, the only surviving evidence relates to
saints' remains.[49] As noted in the first chapter, textiles covering relics were
often of luxurious quality and distant provenance, such as the silks used in
the mid-eighth century at Chelles and Faremoutiers.[50] In Radegund's
vision of the nun Disciola (d. 583), Gregory of Tours recounted that the
former queen wrapped the nun's corpse in a brilliant white linen shroud

47. "Cum ipse rex pius consulens iuxta fidem et devotionem eius [Balthildis], dedit ei in adiuto-
rium suum fidelem famulum abbatem Genesium, per cuius manus ministrans ipsa sacerdotibus et
pauperibus, pascebat egenos et induebat vestibus nudos studioseque sepelire ordinabat mortuos."
Krusch, *Vita sanctae Balthildis* A.4, 486.

48. Paxton, *Christianizing Death*, 52, n. 20.

49. See the written description of the linen covering of the relics hanging in the bed chamber of
Eligius of Noyon (d. 660): "multorum pignora sanctorum in suppremis dependentia, sub quorum
sacro velamine." Krusch, *Vita Eligii episcopi Noviomagensis* 1,8, 675.

50. Jean-Pierre Laporte, "Tissus médiévaux de Chelles et Faremoutiers," in *Tissu et vêtement: 5000
ans de savoir-faire, 26 avril–30 novembre 1986* (Guiry-en-Vezin: Musée archéologique départemental
du Val-d'Oise, 1986), 153–72.

reflective of the purity of her soul.[51] The eighth-century linen shroud decorated with a scene of the Assumption, now preserved in the treasury of
the cathedral of Sens, must once have been similarly dazzling.[52]
Clerics described the prayers and tears with which members of the
deceased's family or of the monastic *familia*, in the case of individuals in
religious communities, tended to the corpses of deceased Christians until
the funeral. Despite the joy they doubtless felt at the good fortune of their
late brethren, even monks and nuns regularly expressed collective sorrow
at the loss of one of their members, such as Balthild or Vaast of Arras.[53] At
the death of Eligius of Noyon (d. 660), lamentations were universally
voiced while the bishop's body was on processional display.[54] Tears at
funerary ceremonies of the lay elite, most notably royalty, were also
deemed acceptable by clerics so long as expressions of sorrow did not
become too extreme, as they did in the rending of hair.[55] In Italy, at least,
some of these customs also had an impact on laypersons of more modest

51. "[Disciola] induta tamen lenteis mundis, sepulturae mandata est." Bruno Krusch, ed.,
Gregorius episcopus Turonensis, Libri historiarum X 6,29, in *MGH: SRM* 1,1, rev. ed. (Hannover:
Impensis bibliopolii Hahniani, 1951), 268.

52. Jacques Dubois, "Utilisation religieuse du tissu," in *Tissu et vêtement,* 149–50.

53. Krusch, *Vita sanctae Balthildis* A.15, 501–2; Bruno Krusch, ed., *Vita Vedastis episcopi
Atrebatensis duplex* 9, in *MGH: SRM* 3 (Hannover: Impensis bibliopolii Hahniani, 1896), 412–13.

54. "Nam et regina devota [Balthildis], cum esset hiemis tempore palus immensa nullatenus
suaderi potuit, ut vehiculo uteretur equi, sed pedestri et gravi labore sequens feretrum, per paludem
lamenta continua cum omni sociabat familia. O quantus luctus omnium, quantus praecipue mona-
chorum fletus et pauperum, qui eo die ibi confluxerant, plateas omnes perstrepebant! Chori siquidem
psallentum lacrimosas reddebant voces, cantus et agmina flentium lugubres reboabant in aere fletus;
omnem populus urbem quatiebat gemitibus celsumque culmen Olimpi implebatur plangoribus."
Krusch, *Vita Eligii episcopi Noviomagensis* 2,38, 722.

55. At the death of Chlodobert (d. 580), the son of Chilperic, Gregory noted strong public reac-
tion: "Quem [Chlodobertum] in basilica sanctorum Crispini atque Crispiniani martirum sepelierunt.
Magnus quoque hic planctus omni populo fuit; nam viri lugentes, mulieresque lucubribus vestimentis induti, ut solet in coniugum exsequiis fieri, ita hoc funus sunt prosecuti." Krusch, *Gregorius episcopus Turonensis, Libri historiarum X* 5,34, 227; Cécile Treffort, *L'église carolingienne et la mort:
Christianisme, rites funéraires et pratiques commémoratives,* Collection d'histoire et d'archéologie
médiévales 3 (Lyons: Presses universitaires de Lyon, 1996), 81–82.

means. In the *Dialogues,* Gregory I recounted how a poor widow recited lamentations all night by her husband's corpse because it had not been buried before sundown the previous day.[56] Since no formal office of the dead existed yet, her vigil likely consisted of prayers and psalms that she had memorized from the daily office.[57]

There were nonetheless limits to what sort of practices might be accepted in expressing sorrow for the Christian dead. In Ireland, just as on the Continent, the seventh-century *Canones hibernenses* sought to curb some local mourning customs. They prescribed, for instance, penance for wailing after the death of a layman or cleric, the penalty for the former being considerably more severe than for the latter.[58] Circumspection regarding wailing and self-flagellation may have stemmed from association of the rite with the pagan *carmen funebris,* and this concern with the survival of the pre-Christian rites was repeated in the *Indiculus superstitionum* with an admonition against the rending of garments and shoes.[59] In contrast to Ireland, however, most of these restrictive regulations first appeared in Gaul in the late eighth century.

Few individuals likely viewed the corpse lying in state within the restricted space of living quarters, hospice (*hospitium*), or church. The most public opportunity to display the deceased and his or her possessions was thus the procession whereby the body was carried from home to possibly the church and finally to the cemetery on a handheld bier or horse-drawn litter.[60] This rite existed long before the arrival of Christianity in

56. De Vogüé, *Grégoire le Grand, Dialogues* 3,17,2, SC 260, 336–39.
57. McLaughlin, *Consorting with Saints*, 31.
58. Ludwig Bieler, ed., *Canones hibernenses* 1,26–29, in *The Irish Penitentials*, Scriptores latini Hiberniae 5 (Dublin: Dublin Institute for Advanced Studies, 1963), 162–63.
59. "De pagano cursu quem yrias nominant scisis pannis vel calciamentis." Alfred Boretius, ed., *Indiculus superstitionum et paganiarum* c.24, in *MGH: Leges* 2, *Capitularia* 1,108 (Hannover: Impensis bibliopolii Hahniani, 1883), 223; Claude Thiry, *La plainte funèbre*, Typologie des sources du moyen âge Occidental 30 (Turnhout: Brepols, 1978), 76.
60. On Martin of Tours's encounter with a pagan funerary procession, see Jacques Fontaine, ed., *Sulpice Sévère, Vie de saint Martin* 12,1–5, in SC 133 (Paris: Éditions du CERF, 1967), 278–79.

Gaul but was thereafter modified with the addition of chanted psalms and antiphons.[61] For those of high rank, such ceremonies were particularly fitting.[62] The anonymous author of the *Liber historiae Francorum* (circa 727), for instance, drew attention to the ornate robes in which Sigibert (d. 575)[63] and Chilperic (d. 584) were respectively laid to rest at Saint-Medard, Soissons, and Saint-Vincent (later Saint-Germain-de-Prés), Paris.[64] Although some corpses may have been draped with a shroud out of respect for the dead or in an effort to protect grave goods,[65] this practice is difficult to substantiate. Clearly, public display of the dead's appearance was a central objective of the rite[66] and may have motivated attempts to preserve corpses

61. "Obsequiis autem rite celebratis, membris ex feretro depositis, tumulo ex more conposito . . ." Mohlberg, Eizenhöfer, and Siffrin, eds., *Liber sacramentorum* 1625, 237; Paxton, *Christianizing Death*, 66; Krusch, *Vita Eligii episcopi Noviomagensis* 2,38, 722.

62. Krusch, *Gregorius episcopus Turonensis, Libri historiarum X* 8,21, 339; Alain Erlande-Brandenburg, *Le roi est mort: Étude sur les funérailles, les sépultures et les tombeaux des rois de France jusqu'à la fin du XIIIᵉ siècle*, Bibliothèque de la Société française d'archéologie 7 (Geneva: Droz, 1975), 5–7.

63. "Tunc egressus Chilpericus a Turnaco cum uxore sua ac populo, vestitum Sighiberto vestibus ornatis apud Lambrus vicum sepelivit. Unde postea Suessionis in basilica sancti Medardi iuxta patrem suum Chlotharium sepelierunt." Bruno Krusch, ed., *Liber historiae Francorum* 32, in *MGH: SRM* 2 (Hannover: Impensis bibliopolii Hahniani, 1888), 296–97.

64. "Mallulfus itaque Silvanectinsis episcopus, qui in ipso palatio tunc aderat, indutumque eum [Chilpericum] vestibus regalibus, in nave levato, cum hymnis et psallentio cum Fredegunde regina vel reliquo exercitu Parisius civitate in basilica beati Vincenti martyris eum sepelierunt." Krusch, *Liber historiae Francorum* 35, 304.

65. Margarete Weidemann, *Kulturgeschichte der Merowingerzeit nach den Werken Gregor von Tours*, Römisch-Germanisches Zentralmuseum Monographien 3,2 (Mainz: Verlag der Römisch-Germanischen Zentralmuseums, 1982), 233–34; Michel Fleury, "L'origine du décor des sarcophages de plâtre mérovingiens de la région parisienne," in *Problèmes de chronologie relative et absolue concernant les cimetières mérovingiens d'entre Loire et Rhin: Actes du IIᵉ colloque archéologique de la IVᵉ section de l'École pratique des hautes études (Paris, 1973)*, ed. Michel Fleury and Patrick Périn (Paris: Librairie Honoré Champion, 1978), 115; Dubois, "Utilisation religieuse," 148.

66. "Repperimus autem eam [Radegundis] iacentem in feretro, cuius sancta facies ita fulgebat, ut liliorum rosarumque sperneret pulchritudinem." Bruno Krusch, ed., *Gregorius episcopus Turonensis, Liber in gloria confessorum* 104, in *MGH: SRM* 1,2, new ed. (Hannover: Impensis bibliopolii Hahniani, 1969), 364.

by artificial means.[67] Candles or torches were used to light processions if dark had already fallen.[68] After death, the liturgy turned again to the restoration of sound bodies to Christians; this renewal would arise from the resurrection of the flesh.[69] Although no formal office for the dead existed in Francia before the beginning of the ninth century,[70] the service appended to the early-sixth-century monastic Rule written by Caesarius of Arles for his sister Caesaria's house focused on the spiritual well-being of the individual who had just died. The prayer beginning *Pio recordationis affectu* included in this Rule, just as two centuries later in the Gelasian Sacramentary, pleaded forgiveness for any minor sins committed by the deceased.[71] The latter collection also incorporated the prayer *Deus apud quem,* which asked that the sins of the deceased be wiped away.[72] Such prayers sought to compensate prophylactically for any possible lapses in Christians' behavior to ensure their

67. M. E. A. Pigeon, "De l'embaumement des morts à l'époque mérovingienne," *Bulletin archéologique du Comité des travaux historiques et scientifiques* (1894): 140–45.

68. Following the discovery of the remains of the murdered Irish monk Foillan and his companions, their bodies were carried to Nivelles: "Suscepta vero corpora cum cereis ac facellarum luminibus, cum antiphonis et canticis spiritalibus a clero et populo per totam noctem ad monasterium Nivalcham honorifice humeris deportata sunt." Bruno Krusch, ed., *Additamentum Nivialense de Fuilano,* in *MGH: SRM* 4, 451; Camillus Callewaert, "De cereis funalibus," in *Sacris erudiri: Fragmenta liturgica collecta a monachis Sancti Petri de Aldenburgo in Steenbrugge ne pereant* (Steenbrugge: Abbatia S. Petri de Aldenburgo, 1940), 725–26.

69. "Debitum humani corporis sepeliendi officium fidelium more conplentes deum cui omnia vivunt fideliter depraecemur, ut hoc corpus a nobis in infirmitate sepultum in virtute et ordine sanctorum resuscitet et eius animam sanctis et fidelibus iubeat adgregari, cuique in iudicio misericordiam tribuat." Mohlberg, Eizenhöfer, and Siffrin, *Liber sacramentorum* 1623, 327.

70. Gougaud, "Étude sur les 'Ordines,'" 23–24.

71. "[O]bsecrantes misericordiam dei nostri, ut ipse ei tribuere dignetur placitam et quietam mansionem, remittat omnes lubricae temeritatis offensas, ut concessa venia plenae indulgentiae quicquid in hoc saeculo proprius error adtulit." Morin, *S. Caesarius Arelatensis episcopus, Regula sanctarum virginum,* 30; Sicard, *La liturgie de la mort,* 260–64; Mohlberg, Eizenhöfer, and Siffrin, *Liber sacramentorum* 1607, 234; Paxton, *Christianizing Death,* 52–54, 64.

72. "[E]t [si] quid de regione mortali tibi contrarium contraxit fallente diabolo, tua pietate ablue indulgendo." Mohlberg, Eizenhöfer, and Siffrin, *Liber sacramentorum* 1627, 238; Paxton, *Christianizing Death,* 61–62.

smooth passage into heaven. These precautions indicate that even the most righteous individuals were thus perceived as facing insecurity during the transition into the next world.[73]

Written accounts of the Merovingian period suggest that clerics rarely celebrated Masses in commemoration of the dead in their presence or during the funeral (*depositio*) itself. These rites were instead reserved for the various anniversaries of Christians' deaths, as had been customary since late antiquity.[74] In North Africa during the lifetime of Augustine of Hippo, the bishop wrote that clerics might perform the Eucharist at the grave site on the third day following the interment of the deceased.[75] In *De sepultura catechumenorum* (404–6), Augustine therefore upheld the decision of a local bishop not to bury a deceased catechumen in consecrated ground. He had not gained the remission of sin necessary for interment at a site close to the celebration of the Eucharist.[76] Baptism was requisite for late antique Christians desiring such an honored resting place.[77]

In his hagiographical works, Gregory of Tours (d. 594) made multiple references to Masses in conjunction with commemoration of the dead. On the thirtieth day following the death of the abbot Senoch (d. 576), for

---

73. Mohlberg, Eizenhöfer, and Siffrin, *Liber sacramentorum* 1621, 236–37.

74. Arnold Angenendt, "Theologie und Liturgie der mittelalterlichen Toten-Memoria," in *Memoria: Der geschichtliche Zeugniswert des liturgischen Gedenkens im Mittelalter*, MMS 48, ed. Karl Schmid and Joachim Wollasch (Munich: Wilhelm Fink Verlag, 1984), 171–72.

75. "[N]am per triduum hymnis Dominum collaudavimus super sepulcrum ipsius, et redemptionis Sacramenta tertio die obtulimus." Luigi Carrozzi, ed., *Sant'Agostino: Le lettere* 158,2, in *Opera di Sant'Agostino* 22 (Rome: Nuova biblioteca agostiniana, Citta' nuova editrice, 1971), 640–41.

76. "[S]ecundum morem disciplinamque ecclesiae, catachumenorum defunctorum corpora inter fidelium corpora, ubi etiam fidelium sacramenta celebrantur, sepelire non debere nec cuidam posse concedi." François Dolbeau, "Nouveaux sermons de saint Augustin pour la conversion des païens et des donatistes (II)," *Revue des études augustiniennes* 37 (1991): 294.

77. "[I]nvenio non tantum passionem pro nomine Christi id quod ex baptismo deerat posse supplere, sed etiam fidem conversionemque cordis, si forte ad celebrandum mysterium baptismi in angustiis temporum succurri non potest. neque enim latro ille pro homine Christi crucifixus est, sed pro meritis facinorum suorum, nec quia credidit passus est, sed dum patitur credidit." M. Petschenig, ed., *De baptismo libri VII* 4,22,29, in *Sanctus Aurelius Augustinus, Scripta contra Donatistas* 1, CSEL 51 (Vienna: F. Tempsky, 1908), 257.

instance, the Eucharistic celebration was held at his sepulcher.[78] The abbot's outdoor grave was covered with a cloth (palla) and thus was decorated and functioned as an altar.[79] Some more celebrated sepulchers became the focus of local cults, such as that of Julian of Brioude (d. circa 400) or Medard of Soissons (d. 561), and therefore received more solid edifices to protect relics and worshipers from the elements.[80] The Gelasian Sacramentary corroborated these traditions, with Masses specified for cemeteries on the seventh and thirtieth days after Christians' passing.[81] These services eventually gave shape to the office of the dead, and were incorporated into the daily liturgical cycle in the ninth century.[82]

Other obligations to the dead that continued long after the funeral included the taking of meals in cemeteries. Although pagan in inspiration, the custom, in the form of the offering of the Eucharist, was very early adopted by Christians and may have been part of the services performed in cemeteries described above.[83] Other aspects of funerary meals remained firmly rooted in the tradition of Roman Parentalia celebrations,[84] during which a family had gathered on anniversaries of the death of a family

78. "Nam trigesimo ab eius [Senochi] obitu die, cum ad eius tumulum missa celebraretur Chaidulfus quidam contractus, dum stipem postulat, ad eius sepulturam accedit. Qui dum pallam superpositam osculis veneratur, dissolutis membrorum ligaturis, directus est." Bruno Krusch, ed., Gregorius episcopus Turonensis, Liber vitae patrum 15,4, in MGH: SRM 1,2, 274.

79. Kyll, Tod, Grab, 185; Muschiol, Famula Dei, 186–89.

80. Bruno Krusch, ed., Gregorius episcopus Turonensis, Liber de virtutibus S. Juliani 4–5, in MGH: SRM 1,2, 116–17; Krusch, Gregorius episcopus Turonensis, Liber in gloria confessorum 93, in MGH: SRM 1,2, 357–58; Kyll, Tod, Grab, 186.

81. Mohlberg, Eizenhöfer, and Siffrin, Liber sacramentorum 1680–84 and 1690–95, 245–47; Chavasse, Le sacramentaire gélasien, 69–70; Kurt Ranke, Indogermanische Totenverehrung, 1: Der dreissigste und vierzigste Tag im Totenkult der Indogermanen, Folklore Fellows Communications 140 (Helsinki: Suomalainen Tiedeakatemia, 1951), 23–28.

82. Camillus Callewaert, "De officio defunctorum," in Sacris erudiri, 169–77; McLaughlin, Consorting with Saints, 27–33, 40–41.

83. Bernhard Kötting, "Die Tradition der Grabkirche," in Memoria: Der geschichtliche Zeugniswert des liturgischen Gedenkens im Mittelalter, 71–73.

84. Hilda Ellis Davidson, The Lost Beliefs of Northern Europe (London: Routledge, 1993), 90 ff.; Flint, The Rise of Magic, 213–15.

member around a stone table (*mensa*) over or near the grave for food and drink.[85] Some clerics denounced the rites for implying the physicality of the souls of the dead,[86] since participants often included the dead in these rites by pouring libations directly into sarcophagi[87] or depositing with them eating and drinking vessels filled with food and liquids. While clerics such as Ambrose of Milan had long discouraged funerary food offerings by suggesting that the poor would benefit more from such donations than the dead, these efforts did not make a large impact on the general populace.[88]

In early medieval Gaul, too, offerings for the dead as well as saints were viewed as the acts of those ignorant of the mores of Christianity.[89] Although this custom did not attract similar complaints in the Eastern Church, Continental clerics claimed that funerary meals encouraged drunken singing and dancing at funerals.[90] Archaeological evidence nonetheless reveals the continued celebration of funerary meals in Gaul north and south of the Loire well into the sixth century, albeit in an increasingly

85. Homeyer, "Der Dreißigste," in *Abhandlungen der Königlichen Akademie der Wissenschaften zu Berlin, 1864*, philologische und historische Abhandlungen (Berlin: Königliche Akademie der Wissenschaften, 1865), 90 ff.

86. See the pseudo-Augustinian sermon castigating libations and other offerings made at the graves of Christians: "[M]iror cur apud quosdam (in)fideles hodie tam perniciosus error increverit, ut super tumulos defunctorum cibos et vina conferant; quasi egressae de corporibus animae carnales cibos requirant." Jacques-Paul Migne, ed., *S. Aurelius Augustinus, Fragmenta sermonum* 190, in *PL* 39 (Paris: Apud editorem in via dicta d'Amboise, 1847), 2101.

87. Franz Cumont, *Lux Perpetua* (Paris: Librairie Orientaliste Paul Geuthner, 1949), 29–41; Richard Krautheimer, "Mensa-Coemiterium-Martyrium," in *Studies in Early Christian, Medieval, and Renaissance Art* (New York: New York University Press, 1969), 45–46.

88. Lucas Verheijen, ed., *Sanctus Augustinus, Confessionum libri XIII* 6,2,2, *CCSL* 27 (Turnhout: Typographi Brepols editores Pontificii, 1981), 74–75; Jean-Paul Jacob and Jean-Régis Mirbeau Gauvin, "Du don au mort à la rédemption: Évolution du dépôt funéraire du Bas-Empire à l'apparition du don *pro anima*," *Revue d'histoire du droit* 48 (1980): 321–22.

89. Bruno Krusch, ed., *Gregorius episcopus Turonensis, Liber in gloria martyrum* 50, in *MGH: SRM* 1,2, 72–74; Richard Morris, *The Church in British Archaeology*, CBA Research Report 47 (London: CBA, 1983), 26.

90. Otto Gerhard Oexle, "Mahl und Spende im mittelalterlichen Totenkult," *FS* 18 (1984): 404–5, 408 ff.; Flint, *The Rise of Magic*, 269–70.

simplified form.[91] The Carolingian ban on funerary meals, libations, and sacrifices at the tombs of saints and other Christians in the *Indiculus superstitionum et paganiarum* (744–45) suggests that the rites may have survived far longer.[92] Funerary feasting constituted a powerful means of commemorating the dead and preserving familial identity.[93]

Reluctance to accept the practice of funerary meals and offerings did not mean, however, that clerics believed that Christians had no graveside responsibilities to their dead. At the Council of Paris (556–73), clerics urged in canon nine that Christian families not neglect their relations' sepulchers.[94] If no one kept grave sites clear, the identity of the interred might be forgotten before their souls were relieved of purgatorial suffering. In an era when most sepulchers were not marked in any sort of permanent fashion, such observations were fairly accurate not only in rural cemeteries but also in monastic churches. In the *Visio Baronti*, Barontus was expected to care for the sepulcher of a fellow monk. His obligation took the form of sweeping his grave and reciting the prayer *Misere mei, Deus*.[95] Attention to the sep-

91. Caroline Walker Bynum, *The Resurrection of the Body in Western Christianity, 200–1336* (New York: Columbia University Press, 1995), 55–56; Donald Bullough, "Burial, Community, and Belief in the Early Medieval West," in *Ideal and Reality in Frankish and Anglo-Saxon Society: Studies Presented to J. M. Wallace-Hadrill*, ed. Patrick Wormald (Oxford: Basil Blackwell, 1983), 188–89.

92. "[2.] De sacrilegio super defunctos id est dadsisas." "[9.] De sacrificio quod fit alicui sanctorum." Boretius, *Indiculus superstitionum et paganiarum*, 223; Alain Dierkens, "Superstitions, christianisme et paganisme à la fin de l'époque mérovingienne: A propos de l'*Indiculus superstitionum et paganiarum*," in *Magie, sorcellerie, parapsychologie*, Laïcité série recherches 5, ed. Hervé Hasquin (Brussels: Éditions de l'Université de Bruxelles, 1984), 18–19.

93. Bonnie Effros, *Creating Community with Food and Drink in Merovingian Gaul* (New York: Palgrave, forthcoming).

94. "De genere servorum, qui sepulchris defunctorum pro qualitate ipsius ministerii depotantur, hoc placuit observari, ut, sub qua ab auctoribus fuerint conditione dimissi, sive haeredibus sive ecclesie pro defensione fuerint depotati, volutas defuncti circa eos in omnibus debeat conservari. Quod si ecclesia eos de his sanctis functionibus in omni parte defenderit, ecclesiae tam illi quam posteri eorum defensione in omnibus potiantur et occursum impendat." De Clercq, *Concilia Galliae A.511–A.695*, 209.

95. Levison, *Visio Baronti* 14, 389; Luce Pietri, "Les sépultures privilégiées en Gaule d'après les sources littéraires," in *L'inhumation privilégiée*, 135.

ulcher of Richarius likewise spared the saint from a leaking tomb.[96] Burial of family members at a great distance from their home must thus have constituted a significant hardship for surviving kin.

Psalms and Charity on Behalf of the Dead

Aaron Gurevich has underlined the physical nature with which early medieval Christian theological texts endowed the soul.[97] In his widely influential *Dialogues,* Gregory I drew attention to the consequences of souls' corporality. The elect felt no pain at the moment of their deaths, and perceived only the sweetness of celestial prayers as their souls separated from flesh.[98] In the case of Christians who had sinned, however, their souls underwent terrible suffering in the course of purgatorial cleansing. When Theodore, a monk at Gregory's monastery, fell into a semiconscious state, he shouted to his fellow monks of excruciating pain. His torments resulted from a dragon's consumption of his spirit.[99] In Gaul, visions of the afterlife revealed similar conceptions of the souls of the dead. According to the author of the late-seventh-century vision of Barontus, for instance, his soul had all of the senses of a living human being.[100] The exiled Irish monk Fursey, who was revived from death after experiencing a horrifying vision

96. Albert Poncelet, "La plus ancienne vie de S. Riquier," *AB* 22 (1903): 192.

97. Aaron J. Gurevich, "Au moyen âge: Conscience individuelle et image de l'Au-delà," *Annales ESC* 37 (1982): 265–72.

98. "Sed inter haec sciendum est, quia saepe animabus exeuntibus electorum dulcedo solet laudis caelestis erumpere, ut, dum illa libenter audiunt, dissolutionem carnis ab anima sentire minime permittantur." Adalbert de Vogüé, ed., *Grégoire le Grand, Dialogues* 4,15,1, *SC* 265 (Paris: Éditions du CERF, 1980), 58–59.

99. De Vogüé, *Grégoire le Grand, Dialogues* 4,40,2–4, *SC* 265, 140–43.

100. "Sic mihi videbatur, similitudinem de parvitatem haberet ut pullus aviculae, quand de ovo egreditur. Sic et ipsa parva caput, oculis, et cetera membra, visum, auditum, gustum, odoratum et tactum ad integrum secum portavit, sed loqui minime potest." Levison, *Visio Baronti* 4, 380; Michel Aubrun, "Caractères et portée religieuse et sociale des 'visiones' en Occident du vi[e] au xie siècle," *CCM* 23 (1980): 113.

of the afterlife, suffered physical burns in the course of his ordeal. Namely, a demon threw at him the scorching remains of a man from whom he had inappropriately accepted clothing, and he exhibited the scars from this incident on his shoulder and jaw after he returned to consciousness.[101]

Due to the precarious position of the soul promoted in early medieval theological texts, an idea that was likely conveyed to the faithful via sermons from the seventh century onward, many Christians doubted their ability to achieve a place in the celestial sphere unaided. Clerics taught that meritorious deeds performed during their lifetimes were insufficient to ensure them relief from purgatorial suffering. To reassure them, church leaders now adapted for the dead a number of practices originally directed at the living for their own salvation. These actions were viewed as alleviating the pain thought to be experienced by the Christian dead in purgatorial realms. These sorts of rituals thus offered families the possibility of granting late relatives respite from their suffering, even if they could not expect immediate salvation. Bede enunciated such ideas more clearly in the eighth century. Although twelfth-hour deathbed confessions could mitigate some of the horrors of purgatorial cleansing, Christian souls would experience great pain until the Last Judgment unless redeemed by the offering of prayers, fasts, alms, and Masses by the living on their behalf.[102]

There had long been demand for the performance of helpful acts on behalf of deceased Christians, but clerics had initially been somewhat lukewarm about their effectiveness. As early as the fifth century, however,

101. Bertram Colgrave and R. A. B. Mynors, eds., *Bede's Ecclesiastical History of the English People* 3,19 (Oxford: Clarendon Press, 1969), 272–75.

102. "[I]pse est locus in quo examinandae et castigandae sunt animae illorum, qui differentes confiteri et emendare scelera quae fecerunt, in ipso tandem mortis articulo ad paenitentiam confugiunt, et sic de corpore exeunt; qui tamen, quia confessionem et paenitentiam vel in morte habuerunt, omnes in die iudicii ad regnum caelorum perveniunt. Multos autem preces viventium et elimosynae et ieiunia et maxime celebratio missarum, ut etiam ante diem iudicii liberentur, adiuvant." Colgrave and Mynors, *Bede's Ecclesiastical History* 5,12, 494–95; Ntedika, *L'évocation de l'Audelà*, 159–61.

Christian theologians had noted the importance of the contributions made by the living on behalf of the dead. Augustine of Hippo, for example, observed that the fear of judgment lay at the heart of the human condition. Unlike Ambrose, Augustine interpreted this anxiety as evidence not of a guilty conscience but instead of original sin. Devout Christians could not deny this condition. He therefore enumerated the means, such as prayers, the offering of the Mass, and alms, by which Christians might liberate the souls of the dead.[103] In *De cura gerenda pro mortuis*, Augustine observed that the recitation of the liturgy stood above all other deeds that the living could perform for the well-being of the dead. This responsibility ultimately rested with the next of kin. Clerics, however, could perform prayers in a more general fashion for all properly buried Christians, even in the event that the members of the deceased's family chose to neglect their duty.[104] Such rites were to be undertaken with the utmost seriousness of intent and humility, kneeling or lying prostrate upon the ground.[105]

In the early sixth century, clerics also linked the faithful application of prayer to the liberation of tormented souls from their purgatorial state.[106]

103. Rebillard, *"In hora mortis,"* 157–67; Ntedika, *L'évocation de l'Au-delà*, 54–56, 92–101.

104. "[N]on sunt praetermittendae supplicationes pro spiritibus mortuorum. Quas faciendas pro omnibus in christiana et catholica societate defunctis etiam tacitis nominibus eorum sub generali commemoratione suscepti Ecclesia, ut quibus ad ista desunt parentes aut filii aut quicumque cognati vel amici ab una eis exhibeantur pia matre communi. Si autem deessent istae supplicationes quae fiunt recta fide ac pietate pro mortuis, puto quod nihil prodesset spiritibus eorum quamlibet in locis sanctis exanima corpora ponerentur." Gustave Combes, ed., *De cura gerenda pro mortuis* 6, in *Oeuvres de Saint Augustin*, 1st ser., pt. 2, Bibliothèque augustinienne (Paris: Desclée de Brouwer et Cie., 1937), 400–403.

105. "Simul enim et quis et cui commendatus sit non utique infructuose religiosam mentem precantis attingit. Nam et orantes de membris sui corporis faciunt quod supplicantibus congruit cum genua fignunt, cum extendunt manus vel etiam prosternuntur solo et si quid aliud visibiliter quamvis eorum invisibilis voluntas et cordis intentio." Combes, *De cura gerenda pro mortuis* 7, 402–3.

106. Julian of Toledo (d. 690) cited Julian Pomerius's *Dialogue on the Nature of the Soul* in his *Prognosticon:* "Spiritus illi qui nec tam perfectae sanctitatis hinc exeunt, ut ire in paradisum statim post depositionem suorum corporum possint, nec tam criminose ac damnabiliter vivunt, aut ita in suis criminibus perseverant, ut cum diabolo et angelis eius damnari mereantur, ecclesia pro eis hic efficaciter supplicante, ac poenis medicinalibus expiati, corpora sua cum beata immortalitate recipient,

By the close of the century, the relevance of assistance of the living for the
dead grew in response to more widespread concerns for the safety of
Christians in the afterlife. One activity believed to have the power of exor-
cism and other miraculous consequences was psalmody.[107] In his *Dialogues*,
Gregory I recounted that a layman from Todi named Marcellus died on
the evening of Holy Saturday. Prior to dawn on Easter, Fortunatus, the
bishop of the city, arrived with two deacons to pray for the man.
Following their devotions, the bishop called out the name of the deceased.
A witness recounted that Marcellus arose as if from a light sleep and then
gave a description of the manner in which two individuals had taken his
soul from his body. The prayers of Fortunatus had caused a messenger to
instruct Marcellus's two heavenly guides to reunite the layman's soul with
his body.[108] In addition to echoing the timing of the resurrection of Christ,
the account gave credence to the role of prayer, particularly that of a
devout bishop, in reviving an individual from premature death or a more
grievous fate.

A century later in Gaul, the vision of Barontus, a monk of a house now
called Saint-Cyran-en-Brenne (Indre), projected a far more negative
image of the afterlife. In March of 678 or 679, Barontus, who had entered
the community just a few years before, suddenly fell ill while praying the

---

ac regni coelestis facti participes, in eo sine ullo defectu suae beatitudinis permanebunt." J. N
Hillgarth, ed., *Sanctus Iulianus Toletanae sedis episcopus, Prognosticorum futuri saeculi libri tres* 2,10
CCSL 115,1 (Turnhout: Typographi Brepols editores Pontificii, 1976), 49; McLaughlin, *Consorting
with Saints*, 192–93.

107. Ntedika, *L'évocation de l'Au-delà*, 63.

108. "Subsequente autem die dominico ante exurgentis lucis crepusculum, vocatis duobus dia
conibus suis perrexit ad domum defuncti, accessit ad locum ubi iacebat corpus exanime, ibique se in
orationem dedit. Expleta autem prece, surrexit et iuxta corpus defuncti sedit, non autem grandi voce
defunctum per nomen vocavit, dicens: 'Frater Marcelle.' Ille autem ac si leviter dormiens ad vicinam
vocem quamvis modicam fuisset excitatus, statim oculos aperuit, atque ad episcopum respiciens
dixit: 'O quid fecisti? O quid fecisti?' Cui episcopus respondit dicens: 'Quid feci?' At ille ait: 'Duo
hesterno die venerunt, qui me eicientes ex corpore in bonum locum duxerunt. Hodie autem unu
missus est, qui dixit: "Reducite eum, quia Fortunatus episcopus in domum illius venit."'" De Vogüé
Grégoire le Grand, Dialogues 1,10,18, *SC* 260, 108–9.

office of Matins. Stricken with great pain and a high fever, he was confined to his bed, where his condition rapidly deteriorated. One monk observed with fear that Barontus had been set upon by a group of evil spirits. After making the sign of the cross, he started to pray for Barontus, but to no avail.[109] Barontus fell into unconsciousness, and the brothers began to recite continuous psalms for him in order that God restore him to health. Sometime following dawn the next day, after the monks had prayed throughout the night, Barontus opened his eyes and praised God. He then recounted to the brethren what had occurred to him in the interim.[110] After he had entered his sleeplike state, two repulsive demons with enormous teeth tried to strangle him and led him to a lower region. The archangel Raphael came to his defense and thereby saved him from further violence, stating that God would judge whether Barontus's death was yet timely. The demons, who outnumbered the archangel, nevertheless sought to prevent his soul from going to heaven.[111] The psalms of the monks aided Raphael's task, enabling him to fly with Barontus's soul away from the evil spirits.[112] Although more demons would soon return, the monks' psalms had effectively interceded on behalf of the dying member of the community.

109. "Tunc tremefactus frater, ad cottidiana arma conversus, coepit se signare et cum gemitus graves rogabat consparsum in ipsam domum facere, ut turba malignorum spirituum exinde fugaret. Sed ille frater [Barontus], manus suas ad latum suum extensas, oculos clusos, coepit semivivus iacere, ita ut nullum omnino possit videre." Levison, *Visio Baronti* 1, 377–78.

110. "Qui [fratres] ut viderunt nullum membrum agitare, lacrimare prae dolore vehementer nimis coeperunt et pro eius animam turmasque conponere, qui psalmodiae cantus recitarent per ordinem, ut caelestis medicus mitteret animam in corpore. Sicque factum est, ut psallentius fratrum tota die numquam interrumperet." Levison, *Visio Baronti* 2, 378–79.

111. Levison, *Visio Baronti* 3–4, 379–81. In the Gelasian Sacramentary, the archangel Michael accompanied souls to heaven. Mohlberg, Eizenhöfer, and Siffrin, *Liber sacramentorum* 1621, 236–37.

112. "Ista dicendo ut enim ascendimus super monasterii silvam, signum sonavit ad vespera statim super ipsam basilicam. Mox Rafahel sanctus imperavit daemonibus, dicens: 'Recedite, recedite, cruentae bystiae; iam non potestis nocere ad istam animolam, dum signum sonavit super ipsam ecclesiam, quia fratre congregantur, ut orarent pro illam.'" Levison, *Visio Baronti* 5, 381–82.

For those whose grave sins stained their conscience and who had not been redeemed by penance, clerics warned that prayer was of little consequence. According to Gregory I, neither the saints nor the living were to pray for the impious and nonbelievers, since their eternal punishment had already been irrevocably determined.[113] Psalmody, while aiding those who had committed minor infringements, might actually add to the agony of dying mortal sinners. Theodore, a monk whom Gregory described as a member of his house by necessity rather than by choice, was surrounded by his brothers bowed in devotions at the time of his passing. Suddenly he began to cry out to those present, interrupting the prayers the monks recited for his safety. He shouted that he had already been half-devoured by a dragon for his sins; their presence was actually increasing his torture by preventing the beast from completing its task.[114] Although the tears and supplications of the monks eventually caused the dragon to flee, they did not manage to save Theodore from terrible punishment for his numerous sins.[115] Devotions might grant sinners temporary reprieve, but Christians needed to prove their own worth through pious actions during their lifetimes.

Although Gregory I promoted the efficacy of prayer in aiding deceased who had committed minor sins, he recognized the centrality of an individual's own deeds in meriting the rewards of the heavenly abode. Over the

113. "Eadem itaque causa est cur non oretur tunc pro hominibus aeterno igne damnatis, quae nunc etiam causa est ut non oretur pro diabolo angelisque ejus aeterno supplicio deputatis. Quae nunc etiam causa est ut non orent sancti homines pro hominibus infidelibus impiisque defunctis, nisi quia de eis utique, quos aeterno deputatos supplicio iam noverunt, ante illum iudicis iusti conspectum orationis suae meritum cassari refugiunt?" De Vogüé, *Grégoire le Grand, Dialogues* 4,11,4, *SC* 265, 48–49.

114. "Cum repente coepit [Theodorus] eisdem fratribus adsistentibus clamare, atque cum magnis vocibus orationes eorum interrumpere, dicens: 'Recedite. Ecce draconi ad devorandum datus sum, qui propter vestram praesentiam devorare me non potest. Caput meum in suo ore iam absorbuit. Date locum, et non me amplius cruciet, sed faciat quod facturus est. Si ei ad devorandum datus sum, quare propter vos moras patior?'" De Vogüé, *Grégoire le Grand, Dialogues* 4,40,2–4, *SC* 265, 140–43. Improper burial *ad sanctos* had similar consequences. De Vogüé, *Grégoire le Grand, Dialogues* 4,52–56, *SC* 265, 176–85.

115. De Vogüé, *Grégoire le Grand, Dialogues* 4,40,5, *SC* 265, 142–43.

next two centuries, however, clerics attributed ever greater powers to the liturgy. In the Bobbio Missal, for instance, prayers reminded members of monastic communities of the common stain of original sin shared by all humans. Their devotions were thus essential to efforts to secure peace for those who had already passed into the afterlife.[116] A prayer similar to these was also included in the Gelasian Sacramentary.[117] Seventh- and eighth-century liturgical texts emphasized a group's commitment to its individual members and thereby reinforced the bonds between the living and the dead.[118]

Not only prayers but donations to the poor contributed to the well-being of the community and the salvation of Christian souls. Like almsgiving performed throughout a Christian's lifetime, generosity immediately prior to death expressed repentance and humility.[119] Augustine extended this recommendation by suggesting to Christians that they give alms to the poor for the sake of the souls of the deceased,[120] advice repeated by Caesarius of Arles on behalf of his nuns.[121] Radegund, for instance, distributed various

---

116. "Antique memores, cyrographum, fratres dilectissimi, quo primo homenis peccato et cor-rupcione addicta est, humana condicio sub cuius lege id, sibi unusquisque formidat, quod alia investi-gavit, videatque omnipotentis dei, misericordia, deprecimur, pro anima kari nostri *ill.*, cuius hodiae deposicionem celebramus, ut, eam in aeternam requiem suscipiat, et beate resurreccionis represen-tit." Lowe, *The Bobbio Missal* 2,538, 164; Paxton, *Christianizing Death*, 63; Sicard, *La liturgie de la mort*, 286–88.

117. Mohlberg, Eizenhöfer, and Siffrin, *Liber sacramentorum* 1613, 235.

118. Otto Gerhard Oexle, "Memoria und Memorialüberlieferung im früheren Mittelalter," *FS* 10 (1976): 86–87.

119. Cyril Vogel, "La discipline pénitentielle en Gaule des origines au ıxᵉ siècle: Le dossier hagiographique," *RSR* 30 (1956): 176–77.

120. "Neque negandum est defunctorum animas pietate suorum viventium relevari, cum pro illis sacrificum mediatoris offertur vel elemosinae in ecclesia fiunt." Almut Mutzenbecher, ed., *Sanctus Aurelius Augustinus, De octo dulcitii quaestionibus* 2,4, in *CCSL* 44A (Turnhout: Typographi Brepols editores Pontificii, 1975), 273.

121. "Totum vero, quicquid est maius atque utilius, usque in finem saeculi profuturum pau-peribus tribue, ut elemosinae tuae usque ad diem iudicii per refrigeria pauperum transeant ad regna caelorum." Germain Morin, ed., *S. Caesarius, Ad sanctimoniales epistolae* 2,8, in *Sanctus Caesarius Arelatensis, Opera omnia* 2 (Brugge: Jos. van der Meersch, 1942), 141.

garments to the poor or left them on the altars of churches she visited before the time of her enclosure in her monastery at Poitiers.[122] Gregory I also promoted the benefits of caring for the poor, noting that a Christian's generosity on earth would be repaid in the heavenly kingdom.[123] Bede, too, affirmed the efficacy of donations to the poor on behalf of those who had confessed before dying.[124]

In the *Visio Baronti*, too, one of the chief avenues by which to achieve paradise was the offering of charity.[125] Barontus recounted that the apostle Peter himself acknowledged the power of alms in attaining spiritual salvation.[126] In his *Ecclesiastical History* a half century later, Bede wrote of Sebbi of the East Saxons, who took up the religious habit when afflicted with illness toward the end of his life. The former monarch donated a large sum of money to the church, stipulating that it was to be given to the needy so that he might thereby ensure himself a place in the celestial kingdom.[127] Bede also recounted that when Dryhthelm was revived from the dead, he immediately divided his possessions into three portions: a third went to his wife, an equal amount to his sons, and the remainder he distributed to the poor.[128] In later centuries, almsgiving was formally institutionalized as

---

122. Bruno Krusch, ed., *Venantius Fortunatus, Vita sanctae Radegundis* 1,3, 1,9, 1,13, in *MGH: SRM* 2, 366, 368–69.

123. Gregory likened the eternal abode of the elect to a house of gold: "Nam quoniam praemium lucis aeternae elemosinarum largitate promerebitur, nimium constat quia auro aedificat mansionem suam." De Vogüé, *Grégoire le Grand, Dialogues* 4,37,16, *SC* 265, 134–35.

124. Colgrave and Mynors, eds., *Bede's Ecclesiastical History* 5,12, 494–95.

125. "Sed mansiones in caelo ille aedificat, qui esuriente, panem tribuere non cessat." Levison, *Visio Baronti* 10, 385.

126. "'[E]lemosyna enim de morte liberat.'" Levison, *Visio Baronti* 12, 386.

127. "Attulit [Sebbi] autem eidem et summam pecuniae non parvam pauperibus erogandam, nil omnimodis sibi reservans, sed pauper spiritu magis propter regnum caelorum manere desiderans." Colgrave and Mynors, *Bede's Ecclesiastical History* 4,11, 366–67.

128. "[M]ox omnem quam possederat [Drycthelmis] substantiam in tres divisit portiones, e quibus unam coniugi, alteram filiis tradidit, tertiam sibi ipse retentans statim pauperibus distribuit." Colgrave and Mynors, *Bede's Ecclesiastical History* 5,12, 488–89.

dead man's part, a practice by which one-third of an individual's possessions were reserved for the cost of the recitation of prayers for his or her soul as well as for alms for the needy.[129]

One may confirm the importance of almsgiving for the salvation of Christians with contemporary wills in Gaul. Many of the approximately twelve surviving final testaments of the Merovingian period emphasized the uncertainty of human existence and Christians' propensity to fall into evil habits.[130] These documents recorded among other bequests the charitable gifts given on behalf of donors' souls; the distribution of alms just as the freeing of slaves regularly constituted remedies for Christians' shortcomings. These acts helped the faithful to avoid divine retribution for sins.[131] In the last testament of Adalgisel-Grimo of Verdun (634), for instance, the deacon gave donations to feed and shelter the poor as well as to provide for lepers.[132] He used his will to ensure the continued care of sixteen paupers whom he had undertaken to nourish, clothe, and house in

129. Heinrich Brunner, "Der Todtentheil in germanischen Rechten," *Zeitschrift der Savigny-Stiftung für Rechtsgeschichte,* germanistische Abteilung 19 (1898): 120–30.

130. Ulrich Nonn, "Merowingische Testamente: Studien zum Fortleben einer römischen Urkundenform im Frankenreich," *Archiv für Diplomatik* 18 (1972): 25–35, 44–64; Goswin Spreckelmeyer, "Zur rechtlichen Funktion frühmittelalterlicher Testamenta," in *Recht und Schrift im Mittelalter,* Vorträge und Forschungen 23, ed. Peter Classen (Sigmaringen: Jan Thorbecke Verlag, 1977), 91–113.

131. In his will, Bertichramnus, bishop of Le Mans (586–616), explained his motivation for charitable donations: "[E]t pro meis expiandis peccatis, iugiter Domino deprecantur, et pro collata principis coelestis eidem et regnum longevum praestet, et in retributionem aeternam centuplum accipere mereatur." G. Busson and A. Ledru, eds., *Le testament de Saint Bertrand,* in *AHM* 2 (Le Mans: Société des Archives historiques du Maine, 1902), 108.

132. "[Molina]rius tenet vel qui tunc molinarius fuerit, cum familia in mea elemosina consistant et pauperes illos quos in villo Marciaco institui nutriat et gubernet. . . . Villo vero Adtautinna, quantum portio mea continet, cum mancipiis, aedificiis, campis . . . basilica sancti domni Petri et domni Vitoni oppidi Virdunensis, ubi leprosi resident, perpetuo iure percipiat possidendum et ad ipsius actoribus perenniter [defen]da." Wilhelm Levison, "Das Testament des Diakons Adalgisel-Grimo vom Jahre 634," in *Aus rheinischer und fränkischer Frühzeit: Ausgewählte Aufsätze von Wilhelm Levison* (Düsseldorf: Verlag L. Schwann, 1948), 129–30.

a hospice.[133] In the will of Hadoindus of Le Mans dated to 6 February 643, the bishop stipulated that he would free a number of slaves for the sake of his soul. He believed that the act of manumitting his servants in perpetuity would help him to attain eternal salvation.[134]

Beyond almsgiving for the sake of the testator's soul, wills provide evidence of charity being offered on behalf of those already deceased. In the will of Bertichramnus of Le Mans, for example, the bishop instructed his nephew and descendants not only to visit his tomb on anniversaries of his death but also to contribute alms in his memory.[135] The manumission of slaves might similarly be effected on behalf of a deceased Christian's salvation. In her last testament, composed between the years 590 and 630/645,[136] Erminethrudis requested the release of a number of unfree for the cure of her own soul as well as that of her deceased son Deorovaldus. The wealthy widow also directed that her man Gundefredus and his two cows labor to provide wax for candles in the church where her son was buried.[137] In the will of the abbot Aridius and his mother Pelagia (572), the slaves thereby manumitted were obligated to give goods for Masses to commemorate their former owners.[138]

133. "Tu, abba, qui tunc temporis fueris, pauperes XVI, quos in exsenodocio posui ad pascendum et fovendum, ut eos, sicut ego presens alimonia et vestimentum vel reliqua dilectione gubernavi, ita tu et successores tui faciant." Levison, "Das Testament des Diakons," 130.

134. G. Busson and A. Ledru, eds., *Le testament de Saint Hadoind*, in *AHM* 2, 158.

135. "Praecipio tibi, dulcissime nepos meus Sigechelmi, et filiis tuis rogo et adiuvo per Deum omnipotentem, ut quamdiu vos Deus in saeculo suprestitisse voluerit, una cum coniuges vestras vel sobolis vestris, si sanitas permiserit, semper annis singulis, bis aut ter, sepulturola mea visiteris, et pauperes, in quo potueritis reficiatis." Busson and Ledru, *Le testament de Saint Bertrand*, 134.

136. Jean-Pierre Laporte, "Pour une nouvelle datation du testament d'Ermenthrude," *Francia* 14 (1986): 577. This date is significantly earlier than once proposed. Ulrich Nonn, "Erminethrud— Eine vornehme neustrische Dame um 700," *Historisches Jahrbuch* 102 (1982): 135–43.

137. "Gundofredo cum boves duos laborare praecipio unde cera ad baselica domni Sinfuriani conparetur." Hartmut Atsma and Jean Vezin, eds., *Testament d'Erminethrude*, in *ChLA* 14 (Dietikon-Zurich: URS Graf Verlag, 1982), no. 592, pp. 72–75.

138. "[S]ed et aliquos ex ipsis liberos fecimus; hi vero cum campellis eorum et vineolis, vel quidquid habere videntur aut adhuc venire potuerint, habere decernimus, ita ut singulis annis terna pondo carrae inferant nostro, et singulis mensibus Eulogias vicissim ad missas nostras revocent, et inferant in altario quinos argenteos, et donent exenio secundum quod paupertas eorum parare

The emphasis on acts of charity in the small number of extant wills surviving in Merovingian Gaul suggests that alms might have been offered by significant numbers of the faithful. Because there was little motive to preserve in the long term documents recording donations other than land, however, few stood a chance of surviving. The small quantity of highly detailed wills should thus not preclude the existence of more widespread recognition of the perceived benefits of almsgiving for the souls of Christians.

The Growing Use of Masses for Late Christians

In addition to the recitation of the Psalms and the provision of charity, Augustine suggested the efficacy of offering the Mass in procuring divine assistance for the deceased. Unlike psalmody and the litany of saints, the Eucharist had the power to remit minor sins at the same time that it comforted the living. In the *Enchiridion,* Augustine explained that the offering of the Eucharist and the giving of alms were acts of grace for souls of the very good (*valde boni*). They also brought the remission of sins for those Christians who were not very bad (*non valde mali*). Although the Mass could not help unrepentant mortal sinners, it served at least to comfort the living.[139] In *De octo dulcitii quaestionibus,* Augustine therefore noted the beneficial effects of offering the Eucharist and giving alms on behalf of the dead. He did not deny, however, that an individual's destiny was primarily determined by his or her own deeds.[140]

As descriptions of the fate of the deceased in purgatory grew more vivid in the course of the late sixth and seventh centuries, so did the attraction of

potuerit." Jean-Marie Pardessus, ed., *Testamentum Aredii, abbatis Attanensis, et Pelagiae matris eius (Ann 573),* in *Diplomata: Chartae, epistolae, leges aliaque instrumenta ad res Gallo-Francicas spectantia* 1,180, repr. (Aalen: Scientia Verlag, 1969), 139.

    139. E. Evans, ed., *Sanctus Aurelius Augustinus, Enchiridion ad Laurentium de fide et spe et caritate* 29,110, in *CCSL* 46 (Turnhout: Typographi Brepols editores Pontificii, 1969), 108–9.

    140. Mutzenbecher, *Sanctus Aurelius Augustinus, De octo dulcitii quaestionibus* 2,1–4, 271–74; Ntedika, *L'évocation de l'Au-delà,* 93–98.

reciting Masses for the dying and the dead. The receipt of the viaticum by the dying was believed to counter the influence of the devil as the soul passed into eternity. In addressing the horrors of the *ignis purgatorius*, the purifying fires that cleansed Christian souls, Gregory I acknowledged the natural concerns of the faithful arising from this perception of the afterlife. In order to quell their fears, he provided a number of examples in which the living offered daily Masses and thereby successfully interceded for Christians who had repented before dying and whose sins were not very great.[141] Gregory's emphasis on the efficacy of contributions on behalf of the dead in releasing them from purgatorial suffering promoted across western Europe the more frequent celebration of the Eucharist for this purpose.[142]

In the Gallican liturgy directed toward the dead, the objectives of performing the Mass for the dead were not uniform. In the Bobbio Missal, the Mass served to protect vulnerable Christian souls passing into the afterlife.[143] The Gelasian Sacramentary, by contrast, described the transition of Christian souls into the next world with milder language.[144] Both sets of prayers nonetheless included strong pleas for the remission of sins committed by the deceased.[145] The eighth-century Gallican *Missa de defunctis*

141. "Si culpae post mortem insolubiles non sunt, multum solet animas etiam post mortem sacra oblatio hostiae salutaris adiuvare, ita ut hoc nonnumquam ipsae defunctorum animae videantur expetere." De Vogüé, *Grégoire le Grand, Dialogues* 4,57,2, *SC* 265, 184–85; McLaughlin, *Consorting with Saints*, 246–47.

142. Cyril Vogel, "Deux conséquences de l'eschatologie grégorienne: La multiplication des messes privées et les moines-prêtres," in *Grégoire le Grand: Chantilly, Centre culturel Les Fontaines, 15–19 septembre 1982*, ed. Jacques Fontaine, Robert Gillet, and Stan Pellistrandi, Colloques internationaux du CNRS (Paris: Éditions du CNRS, 1986), 267–76; Angenendt, "Theologie und Liturgie," 157 ff.

143. "Quis enim in conspecto tuo iusticie iustus appareat. Non se ei opponat, leo rugiens, et draco devorans, miserorum animas rapere consuetus, non accusacionem exequatur adversus eum." Lowe, *The Bobbio Missal* 2,534, 163; Sicard, *La liturgie de la mort*, 282.

144. "Aperi ei portas iusticiae et repelle ab ea principes tenebrarum." Mohlberg, Eizenhöfer, and Siffrin, *Liber sacramentorum* 1610, 234; Ntedika, *L'évocation de l'Au-delà*, 63–67.

145. "Vere dignum et iustum est, omnipotens deus, tu domine cui omnia adsunt, cui vivunt omnia que vocas, ea que non sunt tamquam ea que sunt aeterne miseratur, qui non secundum iniquitatis

(added to Paris, BN MS Lat. 256) also included prayers to commend the deceased's soul to God.[146] With the spread of the custom of private, as opposed to public, penance and the growing popularity of penitential manuals, the living similarly began to recite or commission Masses to erase particular quantities of penance still owed by the deceased.[147] This system of tariffs for the expiation of sins resulted in a special contract between the individuals requesting Masses and making donations and those who, in exchange, performed the service.[148] The potential for abuse, such as the nobility's payment of exorbitant sums to priests for the commutation of their penance, was great. Consequently, Masses for the dead were periodically criticized as simoniacal.[149]

The result of these developments was that the daily performance of the Mass in monastic houses became more commonplace. Although the Irish were among the earliest to integrate such liturgical duties into their monastic practices, they quickly transmitted these customs to the Continent, as evident from the *Collectio canonum hibernensis* (circa 700).[150] Late Merovingian epitaphs occasionally echoed such concerns with recitation of the Mass. These inscriptions drew directly from the language of the

---

nostras retribuis nobis, adque ideo deprecamus maiestatem tuam omnipotens deus, et remittas famulo tuo *ill.* quos in hac vita abuit carnis erroris." Lowe, *The Bobbio Missal* 2,534, 163. "Libera eam, domine, de princi[pi]bus tenebrarum et de locis poenarum, ne iam ullis primae nativitatis vel ignoranciae confundatur erroribus." Mohlberg, Eizenhöfer, and Siffrin, *Liber sacramentorum* 1621, 236–37.

146. Leo Cunibert Mohlberg, *Missale Gallicanum vetus (Cod.Vat.Palat. lat. 493)*, Rerum ecclesiasticarum documenta, series maior, fontes 3 (Rome: Casa Editrice Herder, 1958), 96–97; Ntedika, *L'évocation de l'Au-delà*, 76–81.

147. Allen J. Frantzen, *The Literature of Penance in Anglo-Saxon England* (New Brunswick, N.J.: Rutgers University Press, 1983), 5–7, 63–68; Aaron J. Gurevich, *Medieval Popular Culture: Problems of Belief and Perception*, Cambridge Studies in Oral and Literate Culture 14, trans. Janos M. Bak and Paul A. Hollingsworth (Cambridge: Cambridge University Press, 1988), 54.

148. Paxton, *Christianizing Death*, 67.

149. Angenendt, "Theologie und Liturgie," 147–68.

150. Hermann Wasserschleben, ed., *Die irische Kanonensammlung* 15, 2d ed. (Leipzig: Verlag von Bernhard Tauchnitz, 1885), 42–45.

funerary liturgy, drawing attention to the sepulchers of the deceased and thereby soliciting the prayers of the faithful.[151] On the eighth-century burial inscription of an anonymous abbess at Bourges, for instance, the author wrote the verses as if in the voice of the community: "To all of the orthodox and all of the faithful of God praying in this place, we ask that they deem it worthy to plead for the mercy of the Lord for this [holy abbess], so that she may deserve to fly to the lofty heavens and, borne to the upper vaults of the eternal kingdom, she may also enjoy everlasting refreshment. Amen."[152] With its form and content resembling the liturgy, the epitaph had become a prayer for the soul of the deceased holy woman.

More frequent recitation of the Mass for Christians' souls nonetheless necessitated the recompense of clerics for their services, fulfilled at least in part by the contribution of moveable property and land to churches.[153] Due to the small number of surviving early medieval testaments, it is impossible to determine either how quickly such donations became customary or what proportion of the population participated in these activities. In exchange for receiving land from Bertichramnus of Le Mans, for instance, the church of Saint-Étienne was asked to inscribe the bishop's name in its book of life (*liber vitae*) for commemoration.[154] The will of Erminethrudis, by contrast, donated to a number of different churches for the sake of her

---

151. Angenendt, "Theologie und Liturgie," 189.

152. "Rogamus omnibus hortodoxis vel cunctis dei fidelibus in hoc loco orantibus, ut pro ipsa Domini dignentur deprecare misericordiam, ut ad alta poli evolare valeat et aethera vehens regni perennis et sempiterna fruatur refrigeria. Amen." Bernhard Bischoff, "Epitaphienformeln für Äbtissinnen (achtes Jahrhundert)," in *Anecdota novissima: Texte des vierten bis sechzehnten Jahrhunderts* (Stuttgart: Anton Hiersemann Verlag, 1984), II, 151.

153. Patrick Geary, "Exchange and Interaction Between the Living and the Dead in Early Medieval Society," in *Living with the Dead in the Middle Ages* (Ithaca: Cornell University Press, 1994), 90–91.

154. "Villa Cresciaco et vallis, sicut per epistolas inter me et domno Arnulfo, episcopo Metensis aecclesiae, convenit: in honore domni Stephani, aecclesiae suae, sicut iam per epistolam nostram prius decrevi . . . et nomen meum in libro vitae, in ibi qui tunc tempore pontifex fuerit, [scribi] iubeat." Busson and Ledru, *Le testament de Saint Bertrand*, 131–32.

soul personal possessions such as clothing and jewelry in addition to land. This document directed that moveable property, such as garnets, a golden brooch, a golden cross, an enameled gold seal ring, and a gold seal ring engraved with her name, along with land, was to be distributed to multiple religious foundations in the region of Paris, including Saint-Denis.[155] In the will of Widerad of Flavigny (18 January 722), the abbot donated to the monastery on behalf of his soul everything from books to liturgical vestments in his possession.[156] From the seventh century, an increasing number of the faithful, including women, engaged in donations in exchange for commemorative Masses. Many must have done so informally on a much smaller scale than suggested by these examples.

With the growing influence of liturgical means by which the living might aid the dead, clerics theoretically gained the ability to determine which individuals merited or would be denied access to such coveted honors. By placing strictures on ceremonies accorded to the dead, the clergy not only emphasized their elevated position in the community, but they also defined the physical boundaries separating the faithful from those excluded from the community. The uneven distribution of services offered to the deceased members of the Christian community itself represented a further sign of this differential treatment. Only members of the ecclesiastical hierarchy and monks, for instance, were privileged with the recitation of the Mass on the day of their interment. The Bobbio Missal therefore contained a Mass specifically for the burial of priests, who

---

155. Atsma and Vezin, *Testament d'Erminethrude*, 72–75.

156. "Et quod superius memorari debueramus, tam aurum quam argentum vel reliquas fabricaturas seu ministeria ecclesiae, vel strumenta cartarum, libros vel vestimenta ecclesiae, vel omne praesidium quod mihi legibus vivens possidere videor, et mihi redebetur, inspecto illo strumento quod antea ad sanctum Praiectum vel ad abbatem Magoaldum et monachos eius fecimus, post nostrum discessum ad ipsum monasterium Sancti Praiecti Flaviniacum revertantur; et ipse abbas Magoaldus, cum monachis suis, pro animae nostrae salute ea recipiat." Jean-Marie Pardessus, ed., *Testamentum Wideradi abbatis (Ann 721)*, in *Diplomata* 2,514, 326.

clearly enjoyed special status.[157] The liturgy of the Gelasian sacramentary contained similar provisions,[158] as did the late-seventh-century penitential attributed to Theodore of Canterbury.[159] In the latter work, lay families were obliged to wait three days for Masses for the dead; deceased penitents only received Masses after their families had fasted and given oblations for a period of seven or thirty days.[160] Frederick Paxton has interpreted this development as the integration of Masses into the timetable of purification characteristic of the penitential process.[161] Masses for the dead thus symbolized forgiveness or reconciliation rather than the reparation invoked later in the Middle Ages. The laity, who most required the aid of the Mass in the eyes of contemporary clerics, received it last.[162]

Otto Gerhard Oexle has therefore proposed that such measures contributed to hierarchical divisions between the clergy and the laity. Since late antiquity, in some churches the names of the patriarchs, prophets, apostles, martyrs, saints, bishops, clerics, and Christian religious had been written on diptychs and placed on the altar. Clerics recited these in order with prayers for the living and the dead. Reading these names audibly caused the person's presence to be felt by the community.[163] During the

157. "Vere dignum et iustum est mistiriorum celestium consecratur, aeterne deus custos, aeclesie: sacerdotum decus, et laus omnium certa ponteficum, aeminenciam maiestatis tue excelsum nomen, orare ut haec sacra mistiria, que pro tuae pietatis, offerimus, pro anima et spiritu sacerdotis tui *ill.* cuius hodie depositionem celebramus inter sanctorum consorcio in libro vitae iubias paginam intimare per christum dominum nostrum." Lowe, *The Bobbio Missal* 2,527, 161.
158. Mohlberg, Eizenhöfer, and Siffrin, *Liber sacramentorum* 1628–42, 238–40.
159. Paul Willem Finsterwalder, ed., *Die Canones Theodori Cantuariensis und ihre Überlieferungsformen* U2,5,1–4 (Weimar: Hermann Böhlaus Nachfolger, Hof-Buchdruckerei, 1929), 318.
160. Finsterwalder, *Die Canones Theodori Cantuariensis* U2,5,5–7, 318–19; Angenendt, "Theologie und Liturgie," 171–72.
161. Paxton, *Christianizing Death*, 67–68.
162. McLaughlin, *Consorting with Saints*, 237–39.
163. Oexle, "Memoria und Memorialüberlieferung," 82–87; McLaughlin, *Consorting with Saints*, 90–91.

service, a priest also intoned a prayer over the diptychs;[164] the names of those who were excommunicated from the community, however, were stricken from the tablet, or book of life (*liber vitae*).[165] Although clerics allowed certain exceptions for those who died untimely deaths,[166] and criminals executed by the king could not be denied offerings made for them after their deaths,[167] those condemned by ecclesiastical authorities or who had committed suicide were excluded from commemoration at Mass. The Synod of Auxerre (561–605) enumerated in canon seventeen the means of committing suicide that disqualified a Christian from commemoration.[168] Suicides and heretics were likewise theoretically denied burial in Christian cemeteries, while those executed by the king could still be interred at these sites.[169]

The Bobbio Missal and the Gelasian Sacramentary honored priests at their deaths with special Masses in addition to possible inclusion on a diptych

---

164. "[Q]uorum animas ad memorandum conscripsemus fidelium catholicorum ortodoxorum qui tibi placuerunt quorum conmemoracionem agemus vel quorum nomina super sanctum altarium scripta adest evidenter remissionem peccatorum indulgenciam." Lowe, *The Bobbio Missal* 2,440, 130–31.

165. Leo Koep, *Das himmlische Buch in Antike und Christentum: Eine religionsgeschichtliche Untersuchung zur altchristlichen Bildersprache*, Theophaneia 8 (Bonn: Peter Hanstein Verlag, 1952), 102–14; Karl Schmid and Otto Gerhard Oexle, "Voraussetzungen und Wirkung des Gebetsbundes von Attigny," *Francia* 2 (1974): 76–78.

166. "[15.] Oblationem defunctorum, qui in aliquo crimine fuerint interempti, recipi debere censuimus, si tamen non sibi ipsi mortem probentur propriis manibus intullisse." De Clercq, ed., *Conc. Aurelianense (533)*, in *Concilia Galliae*, 101.

167. De Clercq, ed., *Conc. Massiliense (533)*, in *Concilia Galliae*, 95; Ntedika, *L'évocation de l'Au-delà*, 33–43.

168. "Quicumque se propria voluntate aut in aqua iactaverit aut collum ligaverit aut de arbore praecipitaverit aut ferrum percusserit aut qualibet occasione voluntate se morte tradiderit, istorum oblata non recipiatur." De Clercq, *Concilia Galliae*, 267.

169. Krusch, *Gregorius episcopus Turonensis, Libri historiarum* X 4,39, 172–73; Krusch, *Gregorius episcopus Turonensis, Liber in gloria martyrum* 79, 541–42; De Clercq, *Conc. Massiliense (533)*, in *Concilia Galliae*, 95; Pietri, "Les sépultures privilégiées," 134; Yvette Duval, *Auprès des saints corps et âme: L'inhumation "ad sanctos" dans la chrétienté d'Orient et d'Occident du IIIᵉ au VIIᵉ siècle* (Paris: Études augustiniennes, 1988), 33–34. On the use of "in cymeterio christianorum" in this last

and burial in a coveted place.[170] Such privileges confirmed their status as indispensable intermediaries between God and the laity.[171] Their successful fulfillment of the duties of baptism and mortuary ritual was believed to have earned them special merit before God.[172] As the boundaries between the faithful and the damned became more impenetrable, the funerary liturgy thus reinforced the status and authority of the clergy as the sole arbitrators of membership in the heavenly kingdom.[173] How widely these practices were recognized, however, is nearly impossible to ascertain from the fragmentary sources.

---

piece of legislation, see Éric Rebillard, "ΚΟΙΜΗΤΗΡΙΟΝ et COEMETERIUM: Tombe, tombe sainte, nécropole," *Mélanges de l'École française de Rome: Antiquité* 105 (1993): 1000–1001.

170. The Bobbio Missal contained a *Missa sacerdotis defuncti* that stated: "Deus qui confitencium te porcio es defunctorum precis nostras quas in sacerdotes tui *ill.* deposicione deferimus, propicius exaudi, ut qui nomine tuo ministerium fideli dependit perpetua sanctorum societate letetur." Lowe, *The Bobbio Missal* 2,525, 161; Mohlberg, Eizenhöfer, and Siffrin, *Liber sacramentorum* 1628–42, 238–40.

171. Oexle, "Memoria und Memorialüberlieferung," 90–91. By the Carolingian period, priests had come to hold the elevated title of *mediator inter Deum et homines.* Angenendt, "Theologie und Liturgie," 143–48.

172. "Omnipotens sempiterne deus, maiestatem tuam supplices exoramus, ut famulo tuo *illo* abbate atque sacerdote, quem in requiem tuam vocare dignatus es, donis sedem honorificatam et fructum beatitudinis sempiternae, ut ea quae in oculis nostris docuit et iessit, non iudicium nobis pareat, sed profectum attribuat." Mohlberg, Eizenhöfer, and Siffrin, *Liber sacramentorum* 1639, 239.

173. Geary, "Exchange and Interaction," 87–89.

++ • ++

Exchanges Between the Living
and the Dead

Late Merovingian Funerary Customs

From the earliest years of Merovingian rule to the end of the seventh century, a significant proportion of the population buried their dead with grave goods. Although the rite steadily declined in lavishness and complexity over the course of two centuries, the changes do not appear to have been directly affected by Christianity. Yet, while this practice was never condemned by clerics, some elites began to include donations to churches among their funerary expenditures from the seventh century onward. These bequests served to mitigate perceived uncertainties faced by Christian souls in attaining salvation. This transition to a church-centered rite, however, cannot be shown to have caused the abandonment of grave goods, which had been decreasing in use since their inception. Although significant economic burdens must have been incurred with the cost of liturgical commemoration,[1] the contents, location, and appearance of sepulchers continued to convey to contemporaries much about the identity of the deceased and their families.[2] Alongside these older customs, however,

---

1. Donald A. Bullough, "Burial, Community, and Belief in the Early Medieval West," in *Ideal and Reality in Frankish and Anglo-Saxon Society: Studies Presented to J. M. Wallace-Hadrill*, ed. Patrick Wormald (Oxford: Basil Blackwell, 1983), 197; Cécile Treffort, *L'église carolingienne et la mort: Christianisme, rites funéraires et pratiques commémoratives*, Collection d'histoire et d'archéologie médiévales 3 (Lyons: Presses universitaires de Lyon, 1996), 182–84.
2. Alain Dierkens, "La tombe privilégiée (IVᵉ–VIIIᵉ siècles) d'après les trouvailles de la Belgique actuelle," in *L'inhumation privilégiée*, 47.

the public recitation at Mass of the names of the deceased in whose memory goods had been donated represented a means of achieving some of the same objectives.[3] Grave goods and donations, sometimes consisting of similar objects, satisfied a need to promote the standing of the deceased among both the living and the dead, in this world and the next. This exchange of material gifts for spiritual service also established powerful economic and religious bonds between lay Christians and clerical communities.[4]

As burial ritual became increasingly focused on church-oriented, liturgical ceremony in the seventh and eighth centuries, clerics claimed the most powerful positions in determining the form that funerals took. While some aspects of Merovingian funerary traditions such as grave goods, epigraphy, and family involvement remained important, the recitation of the names of Christian deceased in conjunction with the Mass became the primary method of preserving their memory. Commemoration in the context of liturgical ceremony, rather than a display of elaborate burial dress or the inscription of names on epitaphs, best highlighted an idealized image of the deceased in public memory and quelled concerns regarding their salvation.[5] At least the wealthiest Christian families now began to express themselves through clerical intermediaries rather than exert themselves directly, as they had done in earlier centuries.

---

3. "Maiestatem tuam clementissime pater exoramus pro fratribus et sororibus nostris seo omnibus benefactoribus nostris vel qui se in nostris oracionibus conmendaverunt tam pro vivos quam et solutis·debitum mortuis quorum elimosinas erogandas suscepemus vel quorum animas ad memorando conscripsemus vel quorum nomina super sanctum altario scripta." E. A. Lowe, ed., *The Bobbio Missal: A Gallican Mass-Book (Ms.Paris.Lat. 13246)* 2,438 (London: Harrison & Sons, 1920), 130; Leo Koep, *Das himmlische Buch in Antike und Christentum: Eine religionsgeschichtliche Untersuchung zur altchristlichen Bildersprache*, Theophaneia 8 (Bonn: Peter Hanstein Verlag, 1952), 116.

4. Otto Gerhard Oexle, "Memoria und Memorialüberlieferung im früheren Mittelalter," *FS* 10 (1976): 87–89.

5. Patrick J. Geary, "Exchange and Interaction Between the Living and the Dead in Early Medieval Society," in *Living with the Dead in the Middle Ages* (Ithaca: Cornell University Press, 1994), 87–89.

Although the transition to new interment sites in and near churches was not as abrupt as once suggested, by the second half of the eighth century growing numbers of Christians engaged in churchyard burial.[6] In some cases these changes may be demonstrated through archaeological evidence for the foundation of new burial grounds. The abandonment of the cemeteries of Colline-du-Tombeau and Tombois, for instance, contributed to the establishment of a new necropolis around the parochial church of Franchimont (Belgium). The two developments were roughly contemporary, transpiring between the end of the sixth century and the beginning of the eighth.[7] Yet our understanding of this process is sketchy at best, and the transformation of burial locations took centuries to complete. In those row-grave cemeteries in Gaul still occupied in the seventh century, however, there is widespread evidence that incoherence grew in the formerly evenly spaced burial sites. Not only was the reuse of previously established sepulchers now commonplace, but the structured placement of graves in the cemetery was noticeably disrupted.[8] Physical display of grave goods and the spatial ordering of burial rituals clearly represented a lower priority than had been the case previously. Disregard for the integrity of existing graves likely stemmed from both decreased familial involvement and the regulation and administration of cemeterial sites by clerical authorities

---

6. Similar developments occurred in Anglo-Saxon England roughly contemporary with those in Gaul. Andy Boddington, "Models of Burial, Settlement, and Worship: The Final Phase Reviewed," in *Anglo-Saxon Cemeteries: A Reappraisal: Proceedings of a Conference Held at Liverpool Museum, 1986*, ed. Edmund Southworth (Phoenix Mill, Gloucestershire: Alan Sutton Publishing, 1990), 196–97.

7. Alain Dierkens, "Un aspect de la christianisation de la Gaule du Nord à l'époque mérovingienne. La 'Vita Hadelini' et les découvertes archéologiques d'Anthée et de Franchimont," *Francia* 8 (1980): 622.

8. Patrick Périn and Laurent Renou, "Les sarcophages mérovingiens de plâtre moulé trouvés à Paris: Technologie, ornementation, chronologie," *Bulletin de liaison: Association française d'archéologie mérovingienne* 5 (1981): 52; Patrick Périn, "Le problème des sarcophages-cénotaphes de haut moyen âge: A propos de la nécropole de Quarré-les-Tombes, site d'une bataille légendaire," in *La chanson de geste et le mythe carolingien: Mélanges René Louis* 2 (Saint-Père-sous-Vézelay: Musée archéologique régional, 1982), 824.

with little personal stake in the status of individual sepulchers. The expression of status and identity now occurred primarily through various sorts of liturgical ritual, Masses for the dead being among the most important of these.

Epilogue: Changes in Burial in the Carolingian World

This study has revealed some of the forces that transformed burial practice in the course of the Merovingian period. Far from unchanging, families' expression of identity through funerals underwent a process of continuous adaptation. The types of artifacts and rituals employed to create and convey an idealized image of the deceased evolved in response to changes in people's lives, the political climate, and the religious hierarchy of Merovingian Gaul and surrounding regions.[9] Burial did not represent an individualistic form of display but instead communicated difference within an accepted range of traditions, some more local and others more regional in their manifestation.[10] Whereas funerary rituals incorporated grave goods to commemorate the deceased early in the Merovingian period, burial customs starting in the sixth century gained a new vocabulary, which grew in strength over the course of the seventh and eighth centuries. With liturgical ceremonies responding to concerns regarding Christian salvation by the early Carolingian period, the recitation of the names of the faithful in conjunction with the Mass theoretically became the most powerful means of asserting temporal and eternal membership in Christian communities.[11]

9. Ellen-Jane Pader, *Symbolism, Social Relations, and the Interpretation of Mortuary Remains*, BAR International Series 130 (Oxford: BAR, 1982), 30–31.

10. Guy Halsall, *Settlement and Social Organization: The Merovingian Region of Metz* (Cambridge: Cambridge University Press, 1995), 245–82.

11. Oexle, "Memoria und Memorialüberlieferung," 87–94; Arnold Angenendt, "Theologie und Liturgie der mittelalterlichen Toten-Memoria," in *Memoria: Der geschichtliche Zeugniswert des liturgischen Gedenkens im Mittelalter*, MMS 48, ed. Karl Schmid and Joachim Wollasch (Munich: Wilhelm Fink Verlag, 1984), 174ff.

These developments were not the logical consequence of the adoption of more "Christian" rites but rather the outcome of older rites' losing their significance over time. When confronted by the institutionalization of the Christian liturgy for the dead and the spread of church burial first among elites and then among the more general population, the age-old traditions could no longer muster any real advocates and certainly no backers as powerful as the clergy. Liturgical customs could furthermore convey status and identity without reference to ethnic affiliations, a benefit particularly important among the early Carolingians, who encouraged unity in burial custom in order to maintain stability in their large and often contentious territories.[12] Just as burial rituals in the Merovingian period had served to create, legitimate, and perpetuate predominating social mores within a set of negotiated and thus evolving parameters,[13] the same was true in the Carolingian kingdoms in much altered circumstances.

Clerical appropriation of many of the responsibilities for burying the dead had significant consequences. Although families continued to make decisions regarding how their late relations were buried and commemorated, their personal involvement was now overshadowed by matters far beyond their control. In establishing the necessity of funerary liturgy to the salvation of Christian souls, members of the clergy promoted their authority as the only persons qualified to perform this duty. They thereby became the primary intermediaries between God and the Christian faithful at the time of death, since the importance of the funerary liturgy came to rival that of baptism.[14]

12. Bonnie Effros, "*De partibus Saxoniae* and the Regulation of Mortuary Custom: A Carolingian Campaign of Christianization or the Suppression of Saxon Identity?" *Revue belge de philologie et d'histoire* 75 (1997): 267–86.
13. Pader, *Symbolism, Social Relations*, 37–40; Sally F. Moore and Barbara G. Myerhoff, "Introduction: Secular Ritual: Forms and Meanings," in *Secular Ritual*, ed. Sally F. Moore and Barbara G. Myerhoff (Assen: Van Gorcum, 1977), 7–17.
14. Geary, "Exchange and Interaction," 89–91; Bailey K. Young, "Merovingian Funeral Rites and the Evolution of Christianity: A Study in the Historical Interpretation of Archaeological

Eighth-century memory books (*libri memoriales*) and the foundation of prayer confraternities responsible for reciting Masses for the dead constituted two of the most notable outcomes of these developments.[15] Karl Schmid and Otto Gerhard Oexle have acknowledged as among the earliest evidence for such institutions Bede's request in the *Vita sancti Cuthberti* to be commemorated in the *album congregationis* of Lindisfarne.[16] The names of the dead were written on rolls of parchment and carried from one house to the next.[17] The practice appears thereafter to have been brought to the Continent by Anglo-Saxon missionaries in an attempt to maintain their connections to home.[18] The formal agreement made at the Frankish Synod of Attigny (762) reveals more clearly what obligations were involved in joining such a confraternity. The five archbishops, twenty-two bishops, and seventeen abbots who signed the document agreed to the singing of one hundred psalms and an equal number of Masses for each deceased member. They also promised personally to recite an additional thirty Masses.[19] In the case of abbots who could not perform the Mass and those who were ill, another bishop would take charge of this responsibility. A similar pledge was made at Dingolfing (Bavaria) in 770. In time, the con-

---

Material" (Ph.D. diss., University of Pennsylvania, 1975), 76–77; Bonnie Effros, "Beyond Cemetery Walls: Early Medieval Funerary Topography and Christian Salvation," *EME* 6 (1997): 1–23.

15. Arnold Angenendt attributes an additional rise in the importance of Masses for the dead to the Carolingian ban on the earlier practice of reciting names in the *post nomina* prayer, and their replacement with the *libri memoriales*. Angenendt, "Theologie und Liturgie," 182–84.

16. "[S]ed et me defuncto pro redemptione animae meae quasi pro familiaris et vernaculi vestri orare et missas facere, et nomen meum inter vestra scribere dignemini." Bertram Colgrave, ed., *Bede's Life of St. Cuthbert*, in *Two Lives of Saint Cuthbert* (Cambridge: Cambridge University Press, 1940), prologue, 146–47; Karl Schmid and Otto Gerhard Oexle, "Voraussetzungen und Wirkung des Gebetsbundes von Attigny," *Francia* 2 (1974): 82.

17. Otto Gerhard Oexle, "Die Gegenwart der Toten," in *Death in the Middle Ages*, Mediaevalia Louvaniensia, ser. 1, studia 9, ed. Hermann Braet and Werner Verbeke (Louvain: Leuven University Press, 1983), 36–38.

18. Jan Gerchow, *Die Gedenküberlieferung der Angelsachsen*, Arbeiten zur Frühmittelalterforschung 20 (Berlin: Walter de Gruyter, 1988), 8–16.

19. Schmid and Oexle, "Voraussetzungen und Wirkung," 85 ff.

fraternities would come to include a broader spectrum of membership, such as devout laymen who donated property to a particular monastic house or group of canons. The names of the living and the dead were thus sometimes arranged in the *libri vitae* according to individual relationships to the monastery rather than in hierarchical order.[20]

The creation of confraternities symbolized clerics' turning away from the physical remains of Christians and toward eternal membership in the celestial kingdom, a development that had a great impact on funerary practices in eighth- and ninth-century Gaul. While the growing role of liturgy did not result in the exclusion of family members from the commemoration of the dead, it meant that the rites enacted to honor the dead and promote Christian families' status could no longer be performed by them independently. Nor did such rites have to center on the resting places of the deceased. Dhuoda, a noblewoman who wrote the *Liber manualis* for her estranged son William between 840 and 843,[21] reminded him specifically of his responsibilities to the dead: "And pray also for all of the deceased faithful, in order that Christ may intervene sooner for them and deem it worthy to gather their souls in the bosom of Abraham, so that they may be worthy of repose and refreshment with the saints in the hereafter."[22] Taking the form of liturgical commemoration, the bonds between the living and the dead were understood by Christians in the Carolingian era, just as their predecessors, as personal and permanent obligations. Far from constituting evidence of true "Christianization" of burial practices in Gaul during the Carolingian period, Dhuoda's manual reveals significant

20. Karl Schmid and Joachim Wollasch, "Die Gemeinschaft der Lebenden und Verstorbenen in Zeugnissen des Mittelalters," *FS* 1 (1967): 366–69.

21. Rosamond McKitterick, *The Carolingians and the Written Word* (Cambridge: Cambridge University Press, 1989), 225–27.

22. "Ora etiam et pro omnibus fidelibus defunctis, ut eis prius subveniat Christus, et in sinu Abrahae animas eorum collocare dignetur, ut requiem et refrigerium in futurum merantur accipere cum sanctis." Pierre Riché, ed., *Dhuoda, Manuel pour mon fils* 8,10, trans. Bernard de Vregille and Claude Mondesert, *SC* 225 (Paris: Éditions du CERF, 1975), 312–13.

continuity with concerns expressed in the seventh and eighth centuries. Although these traditions had not always existed in early medieval Gaul,[23] familial involvement had long been central to the commemoration of the dead. Clerics may now have become engaged in the funerary rites as never before, but families in the Carolingian period, like those in the Merovingian period, had to ensure that these commitments to late relatives were not neglected.

23. Éric Rebillard, *"In hora mortis": Évolution de la pastorale chrétienne de la mort au IVe et Ve siècles dans l'Occident latin*, Bibliothèque des Écoles françaises d'Athènes et de Rome 283 (Palais Farnèse: École française de Rome, 1994), 63–70.

SELECT BIBLIOGRAPHY

Primary Sources

Anderson, Alan Orr, and Marjorie Ogilvie Anderson, eds. *Adomnán's Life of Columba*. Rev. ed. Oxford: Clarendon Press, 1991.

Anderson, W. B., ed. and trans. *Sidonius Apollinaris, Poems and Letters*. Loeb Classical Library 445. Cambridge: Harvard University Press, 1965.

Atsma, Hartmut, Pierre Gasnault, Robert Marichal, and Jean Vezin, eds. *Authentiques de Chelles et Faremoutiers*. In *ChLA* 18, no. 669, pp. 84–108. Dietikon-Zurich: URS Graf Verlag, 1985.

Atsma, Hartmut, and Jean Vezin, eds. *Testament d'Erminethrude*. In *ChLA* 14, no. 592, pp. 72–75. Dietikon-Zurich: URS Graf Verlag, 1982.

Beyerle, Franz, and Rudolf Buchner, eds. *Lex ribuaria*. *MGH: Leges* 3,2. Hannover: Impensis bibliopolii Hahniani, 1954.

Bieler, Ludwig, ed. *Canones hibernenses*. In *The Irish Penitentials*, Scriptores latini Hiberniae 5, 160–75. Dublin: Dublin Institute for Advanced Studies, 1963.

—————, ed. *Muirchú's Vita sancti Patricii*. In *The Patrician Texts in the Book of Armagh*, Scriptores latini Hiberniae 10, 61–123. Dublin: Dublin Institute for Advanced Studies, 1979.

Bischoff, Bernhard. "Epigraphisches Gutachten II." In *Das alamannische Fürstengrab von Wittislingen*, Münchner Beiträge zur Vor- und Frühgeschichte 2, edited by Joachim Werner, 68–71. Munich: C. H. Beck'sche Verlagsbuchhandlung, 1950.

—————. "Epitaphienformeln für Äbtissinnen (achtes Jahrhundert)." In *Anecdota novissima: Texte des vierten bis sechzehnten Jahrhunderts*, 150–53. Stuttgart: Anton Hiersemann Verlag, 1984.

Boretius, Alfred, ed. *Capitulatio de partibus Saxoniae*. In *MGH: Leges* 2, *Capitularia* 1,26, 68–70. Hannover: Impensis bibliopolii Hahniani, 1883.

————, ed. *Indiculus superstitionum et paganiarum.* In *MGH: Leges* 2, *Capitularia* 1,108, 222–23. Hannover: Impensis bibliopolii Hahniani, 1883.

Busson, G., and A. Ledru, eds. *Le testament de Saint Bertrand.* In *AHM* 2, 101–41. Le Mans: Société des Archives historiques du Maine, 1902.

————, eds. *Le testament de Saint Hadoind.* In *AHM* 2, 157–62. Le Mans: Société des Archives historiques du Maine, 1902.

Carrozzi, Luigi, ed. *Sant'Agostino: Le lettere.* In *Opera di Sant'Agostino* 22. Rome: Nuova biblioteca agostiniana, Citta' nuova editrice, 1971.

Colgrave, Bertram, ed. and trans. *Anonymous Life of St. Cuthbert.* In *Two Lives of Saint Cuthbert,* 59–139. Cambridge: Cambridge University Press, 1940.

————, ed. *Bede's Life of Cuthbert.* In *Two Lives of St. Cuthbert,* 141–307. Cambridge: Cambridge University Press, 1940.

Colgrave, Bertram, and R. A. B. Mynors, eds. *Bede's Ecclesiastical History of the English People.* Oxford: Clarendon Press, 1969.

Combes, Gustave, ed. *De cura gerenda pro mortuis.* In *Oeuvres de Saint Augustin,* 1st ser., pt. 2, 377–453. Bibliothèque augustinienne. Paris: Desclée de Brouwer et Cie., 1937.

de Clercq, Charles, ed. *Concilia Galliae A.511–A.695. CCSL* 148A. Turnhout: Typographi Brepols editores Pontificii, 1963.

de Salis, Ludwig Rudolf, ed. *Leges Burgundionum. MGH: Leges* 2,1. Hannover: Impensis bibliopolii Hahniani, 1892.

Descombes, Françoise, ed. *RICG* 15. Paris: Éditions du CNRS, 1985.

de Vogüé, Adalbert, ed. *Grégoire le Grand, Dialogues. SC* 260 and 265. Paris: Éditions du CERF, 1979 and 1980.

Diehl, Ernst, ed. *ILCV* 1 and 2. New ed. Dublin: Weidmann, 1970.

Dümmler, Ernst, ed. *Alcuinus (Albinus), Carmina.* In *MGH: Poetae* 1,1, 160–351. Berlin: Apud Weidmannos, 1880.

————, ed. *Laudes Mediolanensis civitatis.* In *MGH: Poetae* 1,1, 57–60. Berlin: Apud Weidmannos, 1880.

Eckhardt, Karl August, ed. *Pactus legis salicae. MGH: Leges* 4,1, rev. ed. Hannover: Impensis bibliopolii Hahniani, 1962.

Evans, E., ed. *Sanctus Aurelius Augustinus, Enchiridion ad Laurentium de fide et spe et caritate.* In *CCSL* 46, 21–114. Turnhout: Typographi Brepols editores Pontificii, 1969.

Favreau, Robert, and Jean Michaud, eds. *CIFM* 1. Poitiers: CESCM, 1974.

Favreau, Robert, Jean Michaud, and Bernadette LePlant, eds. *CIFM* 7. Paris: Éditions du CNRS, 1982.

――――, eds. *CIFM* 8. Paris: Éditions du CNRS, 1982.

Favreau, Robert, Jean Michaud, and Bernadette Mora, eds. *CIFM* 16. Paris: Éditions du CNRS, 1992.

――――, eds. *CIFM* 19. Paris: Éditions du CNRS, 1997.

Finsterwalder, Paul Willem, ed. *Die Canones Theodori Cantuariensis und ihre Überlieferungsformen*. Weimar: Hermann Böhlaus Nachfolger, Hof-Buchdruckerei, 1929.

Fontaine, Jacques, ed. *Q. Septimus Florentus Tertullianus, De corona*. In *Érasme* 18. Paris: Presses universitaires de France, 1966.

――――, ed. *Sulpice Sévère, Vie de saint Martin*. *SC* 133. Paris: Éditions du CERF, 1967.

Fuchs, Rüdiger, ed. *Die Inschriften der Stadt Worms. Die deutschen Inschriften* 29. Wiesbaden: Dr. Ludwig-Reichert-Verlag, 1991.

Gauthier, Nancy, ed. *RICG* 1. Paris: Éditions du CNRS, 1975.

Gundlach, W., ed. *Epistolae arelatenses genuinae*. In *MGH: Epistolae* 3, 1–83. Berlin: Apud Weidmannos, 1892.

Halm, Karl, ed. *Sulpicius Severus, Libri qui supersunt*. *CSEL* 1. Vienna: Apud C. Geroldi Filium, 1866.

Henschenius, Godefridus, and Danielus Papbrochius, eds. *De sancto Corcodemo diacono Autissiodori in Gallia*. In *Acta sanctorum* Mai 1, 453. Antwerp: Apud Michaelem Cnobarum, 1658.

Herval, René, ed. and trans. *Sanctus Victricius Rothomagensis episcopus, De laude sanctorum*. In *Origines chrétiennes: De la IIe Lyonnaise gallo-romaine à la Normandie ducale (IVe–XIe siècles)*, 108–53. Rouen: Saul H. Maugard & Cie., 1966.

Hillgarth, J. N., ed. *Sanctus Iulianus Toletanae sedis episcopus, Prognosticorum futuri saeculi libri tres*. *CCSL* 115,1. Turnhout: Typographi Brepols editores Pontificii, 1976.

Kottje, Raymund, Ludger Körntgen, and Ulrike Spengler-Reffgen, eds. *Paenitentialia minora: Franciae et Italiae saeculi VIII–IX*. *CCSL* 156. Turnhout: Typographi Brepols editores Pontificii, 1994.

Krusch, Bruno, ed. *Additamentum Nivialense de Fuilano.* In *MGH: SRM* 4, 449–51. Hannover: Impensis bibliopolii Hahniani, 1902.

———, ed. *Gesta Dagoberti I, regis Francorum.* In *MGH: SRM* 2, new ed., 369–425. Hannover: Impensis bibliopolii Hahniani, 1888.

———, ed. *Gregorius episcopus Turonensis, Liber de virtutibus S. Juliani.* In *MGH: SRM* 1,2, new ed., 112–34. Hannover: Impensis bibliopolii Hahniani, 1969.

———, ed. *Gregorius episcopus Turonensis, Liber in gloria confessorum.* In *MGH: SRM* 1,2, new ed., 294–370. Hannover: Impensis bibliopolii Hahniani, 1969.

———, ed. *Gregorius episcopus Turonensis, Liber in gloria martyrum.* In *MGH: SRM* 1,2, new ed., 34–111. Hannover: Impensis bibliopolii Hahniani, 1969.

———, ed. *Gregorius episcopus Turonensis, Liber vitae patrum.* In *MGH: SRM* 1,2, new ed., 211–94. Hannover: Impensis bibliopolii Hahniani, 1969.

———, ed. *Gregorius episcopus Turonensis, Libri historiarum X.* In *MGH: SRM* 1,1, rev. ed. Hannover: Impensis bibliopolii Hahniani, 1951.

———, ed. *Ionas, Vitae Columbani abbatis discipulorumque eius libri II.* In *MGH: SRG* 37, 1–294. Hannover: Impensis bibliopolii Hahniani, 1905.

———, ed. *Liber historiae Francorum.* In *MGH: SRM* 2, 215–328. Hannover: Impensis bibliopolii Hahniani, 1888.

———, ed. *Testamenta sancti Remigii.* In *MGH: SRM* 3, 336–40. Hannover: Impensis bibliopolii Hahniani, 1896.

———, ed. *Venantius Fortunatus, Vita sanctae Radegundis.* In *MGH: SRM* 2, new ed., 364–77. Hannover: Impensis bibliopolii Hahniani, 1956.

———, ed. *Vita Amati abbatis Habendensis.* In *MGH: SRM* 4, 215–21. Hannover: Impensis bibliopolii Hahniani, 1902.

———, ed. *Vita Eligii episcopi Noviomagensis.* In *MGH: SRM* 4, 634–742. Hannover: Impensis bibliopolii Hahniani, 1902.

———, ed. *Vita Gaugerici episcopi Camaracensis.* In *MGH: SRM* 3, 649–58. Hannover: Impensis bibliopolii Hahniani, 1896.

———, ed. *Vita Rusticulae sive Marciae abbatissae Arelatensis.* In *MGH: SRM* 4, 337–51. Hannover: Impensis bibliopolii Hahniani, 1902.

———, ed. *Vita sanctae Balthildis.* In *MGH: SRM* 2, new ed., 475–508. Hannover: Impensis bibliopolii Hahniani, 1956.

———, ed. *Vita sanctae Geretrudis.* In *MGH: SRM* 2, new ed., 447–64. Hannover: Impensis bibliopolii Hahniani, 1956.

————, ed. *Vita Vedastis episcopi Atrebatensis duplex.* In *MGH: SRM* 3, 399–427. Hannover: Impensis bibliopolii Hahniani, 1896.

————, ed. *Vita Wandregiseli abbatis Fontanellensis.* In *MGH: SRM* 5, 1–24. Hannover: Impensis bibliopolii Hahniani, 1910.

Labbé, Philippe, ed. *Vita (liber prima) S. Austregisilli Bituricensis archiep. Vita (liber prima).* In *Novae bibliothecae manuscriptorum librorum* 2, 354–59. Paris: Apud Sebastianum Cramoisy, 1657.

————, ed. *Vita sanctae Eustadiolae abbatissae.* In *Novae bibliothecae manuscriptorum librorum* 2, 376–79. Paris: Apud Sebastianum Cramoisy, 1657.

Le Blant, Edmond, ed. *Inscriptions chrétiennes de la Gaule antérieures au VIIIᵉ siècle* 1 and 2. Paris: A l'Imprimerie impériale, 1856 and 1865.

————, ed. *Nouveau recueil des inscriptions chrétiennes de la Gaule antérieures au VIIIᵉ siècle.* Paris: Imprimerie nationale, 1892.

Lehmann, Karl, ed. *Leges Alamannorum.* In *MGH: Leges* 3, 1–182. Hannover: Impensis bibliopolii Hahniani, 1888.

Levison, Wilhelm. "Das Testament des Diakons Adalgisel-Grimo vom Jahre 634." In *Aus rheinischer und fränkischer Frühzeit: Ausgewählte Aufsätze von Wilhelm Levison,* 118–38. Düsseldorf: Verlag L. Schwann, 1948.

————, ed. *Visio Baronti monachi Longoretensis.* In *MGH: SRM* 5, 368–94. Hannover: Impensis bibliopolii Hahniani, 1910.

————, ed. *Vita Hugberti episcopi Traiectensis.* In *MGH: SRM* 6, 471–96. Hannover: Impensis bibliopolii Hahniani, 1913.

Lowe, E. A., ed. *The Bobbio Missal: A Gallican Mass-Book (Ms.Paris.Lat. 13246)* 2. London: Harrison & Sons, 1920.

Migne, Jacques-Paul, ed. *Hincmarus archiepiscopus Rhemensis, Capitula synodica.* In *PL* 125, 2d ser., 774–803. Paris: Apud editorem in via dicta d'Amboise, 1852.

————, ed. *S. Aurelius Augustinus, Fragmenta sermonum 190.* In *PL* 39, 2100–101. Paris: Apud editorem in via dicta d'Amboise, 1847.

————, ed. *Sancti Aurelius Augustinus, Sermonum classes quatuor.* In *PL* 38, 1440–42. Paris: Apud editorem in via dicta d'Amboise, 1845.

————, ed. *S. Ferreolus Ucetiensis episcopus, Regula ad monachos.* In *PL* 66, 959–76. Paris: Apud editorem in via dicta d'Amboise, 1847.

Mohlberg, Leo Cunibert, ed. *Missale Gallicanum vetus (Cod.Vat.Palat. lat. 493),* Rerum ecclesiasticarum documenta, series maior, fontes 3. Rome: Casa Editrice Herder, 1958.

————, ed. *Missale Gothicum: Das gallikanische Sakramentar (Cod. Vatican. Regin. lat. 317) des VII.–VIII. Jahrhunderts*. Codices liturgici e Vaticanis praesertim delecti phototypice expressi 1. Augsburg: Dr. Benno Filser Verlag, 1929.

Mohlberg, Leo Cunibert, Leo Eizenhöfer, and Petrus Siffrin, eds. *Liber sacramentorum romanae aeclesiae ordinis annis circuli (Cod. Vat.Reg.lat 316/Paris B.N. 7193, 41/56) (Sacramentarium Gelasianum)*. Rerum ecclesiasticarum documenta, series maior, fontes 4. 3d ed. Rome: Casa Editrice Herder, 1981.

Mommsen, Theodor, ed. *Cassiodorus senator, Variae. MGH: Auctores antiquissimi* 12. Berlin: Apud Weidmannos, 1894.

Mommsen, Theodor, and Paul M. Meyer, eds. *Codex Theodosianus libri XVI cum Constitutionibus Simmondianis et Leges novellae ad Theodosianum pertinentes* 1 and 2. Berlin: Apud Weidmannos, 1905.

Morin, Germain, ed. *S. Caesarius, Ad sanctimoniales epistolae*. In *Sanctus Caesarius Arelatensis, Opera omnia* 2, 134–44. Brugge: Jos. van der Meersch, 1942.

————, ed. *S. Caesarius Arelatensis episcopus, Regula sanctarum virginum aliaque opuscula ad sanctimoniales directa*. In *Florilegium Patristicum* 34. Bonn: Sumptibus Petri Hanstein, 1933.

————, ed. *Sanctus Caesarius Arelatensis, Sermones. CCSL* 103, rev. ed. Turnhout: Typographi Brepols editores Pontificii, 1953.

Munier, C., ed. *Concilia Galliae A.314–A.506. CCSL* 148. Turnhout: Typographi Brepols editores Pontificii, 1963.

Mutzenbecher, Almut, ed. *Maximus episcopus Taurinensis, Sermones. CCSL* 23. Turnhout: Typographi Brepols editores Pontificii, 1962.

————, ed. *Sanctus Aurelius Augustinus, De octo dulcitii quaestionibus. CCSL* 44A. Turnhout: Typographi Brepols editores Pontificii, 1975.

Pardessus, Jean-Marie, ed. *Testamentum Aredii, abbatis Attanensis, et Pelagiae matris eius (Ann 573)*. In *Diplomata: Chartae, epistolae, leges aliaque instrumenta ad res Gallo-Francicas spectantia*, repr., 1,180, 136–41. Aalen: Scientia Verlag, 1969.

————, ed. *Testamentum Wideradi abbatis (Ann 721)*. In *Diplomata: Chartae, epistolae, leges aliaque instrumenta ad res Gallo-Francicas spectantia*, repr., 2,514, 323–27. Aalen: Scientia Verlag, 1969.

Petschenig, M., ed. *De baptismo libri VII*. In *Sanctus Aurelius Augustinus, Scripta contra Donatistas* 1. In *CSEL* 51, 143–375. Vienna: F. Tempsky, 1908.

Poncelet, Albert. "La plus ancienne vie de S. Riquier." *AB* 22 (1903): 173–94.

Prévot, Françoise, ed. *RICG* 8. Paris: CNRS Éditions, 1997.

Riché, Pierre, ed. *Dhuoda, Manuel pour mon fils.* Translated by Bernard de Vregille and Claude Mondesert. *SC* 225. Paris: Éditions du CERF, 1975.

Sohm, Rudolf, ed. *Lex Francorum Chamavorum.* In *MGH: Leges* 5, 269–76. Hannover: Impensis bibliopolii Hahniani, 1875–89.

Tangl, Michael, ed. *Die Briefe des heiligen Bonifatius und Lullus. MGH: Epistolae selectae* 1. Berlin: Weidmannsche Verlagsbuchhandlung, 1955.

Thorpe, Lewis, trans. *Gregory of Tours, History of the Franks.* London: Penguin Books, 1974.

Translatio corporis beatissimae Baltechildis reginae. Paris BN MS Latin 18296, fols. 17v–20v.

Verheijen, Lucas, ed. *Sanctus Augustinus, Confessionum libri XIII. CCSL* 27. Turnhout: Typographi Brepols editores Pontificii, 1981.

von Richthofen, Karl Friedrich, ed. *Lex Thuringorum.* In *MGH: Leges* 5, 103–44. Hannover: Impensis bibliopolii Hahniani, 1875–89.

Wasserschleben, Hermann, ed. *Die irische Kanonensammlung.* 2d ed. Leipzig: Verlag von Bernhard Tauchnitz, 1885.

Wuilleumier, Pierre, ed. *Inscriptions latines des Trois Gaules (France).* 17th supplement to *Gallia.* Paris: CNRS, 1963.

Zeumer, Karl, ed. *Leges Visigothorum. MGH: Leges* 1. Hannover: Impensis bibliopolii Hahniani, 1902.

Secondary Sources

Alföldy, Géza. "Die Inschrift der Bronzekanne aus dem fränkischen Fürstengrab von Krefeld-Gellep." *Bonner Jahrbücher* 166 (1966): 446–51.

Ament, Hermann. *Fränkische Adelsgräber von Flonheim in Rheinhessen.* Germanische Denkmäler der Völkerwanderungszeit, ser. B, vol. 5. Berlin: Gebrüder Mann Verlag, 1970.

Amory, Patrick. "The Meaning and Purpose of Ethnic Terminology in the Burgundian Laws." *EME* 2 (1993): 1–28.

Angenendt, Arnold. "Theologie und Liturgie der mittelalterlichen Toten-Memoria." In *Memoria: Der geschichtliche Zeugniswert des liturgischen Gedenkens im*

Mittelalter, MMS 48, edited by Karl Schmid and Joachim Wollasch, 79–199. Munich: Wilhelm Fink Verlag, 1984.

Appadurai, Arjun. "Introduction: Commodities and the Politics of Value." In *The Social Life of Things: Commodities in Cultural Perspective*, edited by Arjun Appadurai, 3–63. Cambridge: Cambridge University Press, 1986.

Atsma, Hartmut. "Die christliche Inschriften Galliens als Quelle für Klöster und Klösterbewohner bis zum Ende des 6. Jahrhunderts." *Francia* 4 (1976): 1–57.

————. "Les monastères urbains du Nord de la Gaule." *Revue d'histoire de l'église de France* 62 (1975): 163–87.

Auber, Abbé. *L'anneau de Sainte Radegonde et ses reliques à Poitiers*. Arras: Rousseau-Leroy, 1864.

Aubrun, Michel. "Caractères et portée religieuse et sociale des 'visiones' en Occident du VIᵉ au XIᵉ siècle." *CCM* 23 (1980): 109–30.

Barral I Altet, Xavier, Noël Duval, and Jean-Claude Papinot. "Poitiers: Chapelle funéraire dite 'Hypogée des Dunes.'" In *Les premiers monuments chrétiens de la France* 2, 302–9. Paris: Picard, 1996.

Barraud, Cécile, Daniel de Coppet, André Iteanu, and Raymond Jamous. *Of Relations and the Dead: Four Societies Viewed from the Angle of Their Exchanges*. Translated by Stephen J. Suffern. Oxford: Berg Publishers, 1994.

Barth, Fredrik. Introduction to *Ethnic Groups and Boundaries: The Social Organization of Culture Difference*, 9–38. Boston: Little, Brown & Co., 1969.

Bataille, Georges. "The Notion of Expenditure." In *Visions of Excess: Selected Writings, 1927–1939*, Theory and History of Literature 14, edited and translated by Allan Stoekl, 116–23. Minneapolis: University of Minnesota Press, 1985.

Behrends, Okko. "Grabraub und Grabfrevel in römischen Recht." In *Zum Grabfrevel*, 85–106.

Behrens, Gustav. "Der Bertichildis-Grabstein von Kempten bei Bingen." *Germania* 21 (1937): 113–17.

Benz, Ernst. *Die Vision: Erfahrungsformen und Bilderwelt*. Stuttgart: Ernst Klett Verlag, 1969.

Binford, Lewis R. "Mortuary Practices: Their Study and Potential." In *Approaches to the Social Dimensions of Mortuary Practices*, Memoirs of the Society for American Archaeology 25, edited by James A. Brown, 6–29. Washington, D.C.: Society for American Archaeology, 1971.

Bischoff, Bernhard. *Latin Paleography: Antiquity and the Middle Ages.* Translated by Dáibhí Ó Cróinín and David Ganz. Cambridge: Cambridge University Press, 1990.

Boddington, Andy. "Models of Burial, Settlement, and Worship: The Final Phase Reviewed." In *Anglo-Saxon Cemeteries: A Reappraisal: Proceedings of a Conference Held at Liverpool Museum, 1986,* edited by Edmund Southworth, 177–99. Phoenix Mill, Gloucestershire: Alan Sutton Publishing, 1990.

Boube, Jean. "Martres-Tolosane: Église et cimetière paléochrétiens." In *Les premiers monuments chrétiens de la France* 2, 170–76. Paris: Picard, 1996.

Bouillart, Jacques. *Histoire de l'abbaye royal de Saint Germain des Prez.* Paris: Grégoire Dupuis, 1724.

Boyer, Raymond. "Le sarcophage à sa découverte." In *Premiers temps chrétiens en Gaule méridionale: Antiquité tardive et haut moyen âge IIIème–VIIIème siècles,* exhibition catalogue, 82. Lyons: Association lyonnaise de sauvetage des sites archéologiques médiévaux, 1986.

Boyer, Raymond, et al. *Vie et mort à Marseille à la fin de l'antiquité: Inhumations habillées des Ve et VIe siècles et sarcophage reliquaire trouvés à l'abbaye de Saint-Victor.* Marseilles: Imprimerie municipale, 1987.

Brenk, Beat. "Marginalien zum sog. Sarkophag des Agilberts in Jouarre." *CA* 14 (1964): 95–107.

Brown, Peter. *The Cult of Saints: Its Rise and Function in Latin Christianity.* Chicago: University of Chicago Press, 1981.

———. "Eastern and Western Christendom in Late Antiquity: A Parting of the Ways." In *Society and the Holy in Late Antiquity,* 166–95. Berkeley and Los Angeles: University of California Press, 1982.

———. *The Rise of Western Christendom: Triumph and Diversity, AD 200–1200.* Oxford: Blackwell Publishers, 1996.

Brunner, Heinrich. *Deutsche Rechtsgeschichte* 1. 2d ed. Leipzig: Verlag von Duncker & Humblot, 1906.

———. "Der Todtentheil in germanischen Rechten." *Zeitschrift der Savigny-Stiftung für Rechtsgeschichte,* germanistische Abteilung 19 (1898): 107–39.

Budny, Mildred, and Dominic Tweddle. "The Early Medieval Textiles at Maaseik, Belgium." *Antiquaries Journal* 65 (1985): 353–89.

Bullough, Donald A. "Burial, Community, and Belief in the Early Medieval West." In *Ideal and Reality in Frankish and Anglo-Saxon Society: Studies Presented to*

J. M. Wallace-Hadrill, edited by Patrick Wormald, 177–201. Oxford: Basil Blackwell, 1983.

Bynum, Caroline Walker. *The Resurrection of the Body in Western Christianity, 200–1336.* New York: Columbia University Press, 1995.

Calkins, Robert G. *A Medieval Treasury: An Exhibition of Medieval Art from the Third to the Sixteenth Century.* Ithaca: Andrew Dickson White Museum of Art, Cornell University, 1968.

Callewaert, Camillus. "De cereis funalibus." In *Sacris erudiri: Fragmenta liturgica collecta a monachis Sancti Petri de Aldenburgo in Steenbrugge ne pereant,* 725–26. Steenbrugge: Abbatia S. Petri de Aldenburgo, 1940.

————. "De officio defunctorum." In *Sacris erudiri: Fragmenta liturgica collecta a monachis Sancti Petri de Aldenburgo in Steenbrugge ne pereant,* 169–77. Steenbrugge: Abbatia S. Petri de Aldenburgo, 1940.

Cameron, Averil. "How Did the Merovingians Wear Their Hair?" *Revue belge de philologie et d'histoire* 43 (1965): 1203–16.

Cannon, Aubrey. "The Historical Dimension in Mortuary Expressions of Status and Sentiment." *Current Anthropology* 30 (1989): 437–58.

Cantino Wataghin, Gisella. "The Ideology of Urban Burials." In *The Idea and Ideal of the Town Between Late Antiquity and the Early Middle Ages,* TRW 4, edited by Gian Pietro Brogiolo and Bryan Ward-Perkins, 147–63. Leiden: E. J. Brill, 1999.

Chartier, Roger. "Intellectual History and the History of *Mentalités:* A Dual Re-evaluation." In *Cultural History: Between Practices and Representations,* translated by Lydia G. Cochrane, 19–52. Cambridge: Polity Press, 1988.

Chavasse, Antoine. *Étude sur l'onction des infirmes dans l'Église latine du IIIe au XIe siècle* 1. Doctoral thesis. Lyons: La Faculté de Théologie de Lyon, 1942.

————. *Le sacramentaire gélasien (Vaticanus Reginensis 316).* Bibliothèque de théologie, ser. 4, vol. 1. Paris: Desclée et Co., 1958.

Christ, Yvan. *Les cryptes mérovingiennes de l'abbaye de Jouarre.* Paris: Éditions d'histoire et d'art, 1966.

Christlein, Rainer. "Der soziologische Hintergrund der Goldblattkreuze nördlich der Alpen." In *Die Goldblattkreuze des frühen Mittelalters,* Veröffentlichungen des Alemannischen Instituts Freiburg i. Br. 37, edited by Wolfgang Hübener, 73–83. Bühl: Verlag Konkordia, 1975.

Claude, Dietrich. *Topographie und Verfassung der Städte Bourges und Poitiers bis in das 11. Jahrhundert.* Lübeck: Matthiesen Verlag, 1960.

Cleary, Simon Esmonde. "Town and Country in Roman Britain?" In *Death in Towns: Urban Responses to the Dying and the Dead, 100–1600,* edited by Steven Bassett, 28–42. London: Leicester University Press, 1992.

Colardelle, Michel. *Sépulture et traditions funéraires du Vᵉ au XIIIᵉ siècle après J.-C. dans les campagnes des Alpes françaises du nord (Drôme, Isère, Savoie, Haute-Savoie).* Grenoble: Publication de la Société alpine de documentation et de recherche en archéologie historique, 1983.

———, ed. *Des burgondes à Bayard: Mille ans de moyen âge.* Grenoble: Imprimerie Dardelet, 1981.

Coon, Lynda L. *Sacred Fictions: Holy Women and Hagiography in Late Antiquity.* Philadelphia: University of Pennsylvania Press, 1997.

Coquet, Jean. *Pour une nouvelle date de la crypte Saint-Paul de Jouarre.* Ligugé: Abbaye Saint-Martin, 1970.

Cumont, Franz. *Lux Perpetua.* Paris: Librairie Orientaliste Paul Geuthner, 1949.

Dasnoy, André. "Le reliquaire mérovingien d'Andenne." *Annales de la Société archéologique de Namur* 49 (1958): 41–60.

Davidson, Hilda Ellis. *The Lost Beliefs of Northern Europe.* London: Routledge, 1993.

Davies, J. G. "Factors Leading to the Emergence of Belief in the Resurrection of the Flesh." *JTS* n.s. 23 (1972): 448–55.

de la Croix, Camille. *La découverte du Martyrium de Poitiers.* Société centrale des architectes, Conférences 2ᵉᵐᵉ série, vol. 1,4. Paris: Imprimerie Chaix, 1885.

———. *Monographie de l'Hypogée-Martyrium de Poitiers.* Paris: Librairie de Firmin Didot, 1883.

Delarue, T., and E. Thirion. "Amay (Liège): Le sarcophage de Chrodoara." In *L'archéologie en Wallonie: Découvertes récentes des cercles d'archéologie,* 133–34. Nivelles: Fédération des archéologues de Wallonie, 1980.

Delehaye, Gilbert-Robert. "Les sarcophages mérovingiens en plâtre de Villemomble: Fabrication, décor." *CA* 35 (1987): 41–49.

de Nie, Giselle. *Views from a Many-Towered Window: Studies of Imagination in the Work of Gregory of Tours.* Studies in Classical Antiquity 7. Amsterdam: Rodopi, 1987.

Deschamps, Paul. "Étude sur la paléographie des inscriptions lapidaires de la fin de l'époque mérovingienne aux dernières années du XII° siècle." *BM* 88 (1929): 5–86.

Dierkens, Alain. "A propos des cimetières mérovingiens de Franchimont (Belgique, Province de Namur)." In *Actes du 105° congrès national des Sociétés savantes, Caen 1980: La Normandie: Études archéologiques*, section archéologie et histoire de l'art, 297–312. Paris: Comité des travaux historiques et scientifiques, 1983.

———. "A propos du sarcophage de Sancta Chrodoara découvert en 1977 à Amay." *Art et Fact: Revue des historiens de l'art, des archéologues, des musicologues et des orientalistes de l'Université de Liège* 15 (1996): 30–32.

———. "Un aspect de la christianisation de la Gaule du Nord à l'époque mérovingienne: La 'Vita Hadelini' et les découvertes archéologiques d'Anthée et de Franchimont." *Francia* 8 (1980): 613–28.

———. "Interprétation critique des symboles chrétiens sur les objets d'époque mérovingienne." In *L'art des invasions en Hongrie et en Wallonie: Actes du colloque tenu au Musée royal de Mariemont du 9 au 11 avril 1979*, Monographie du Musée royal de Mariemont 6, 109–24. Morlanwelz: Musée royal de Mariemont, 1991.

———. "Superstitions, christianisme et paganisme à la fin de l'époque mérovingienne: A propos de l'*Indiculus superstitionum et paganiarum*." In *Magie, sorcellerie, parapsychologie*, Laïcité série recherches 5, edited by Hervé Hasquin, 9–26. Brussels: Éditions de l'Université de Bruxelles, 1984.

———. "La tombe privilégiée (IV°–VIII° siècles) d'après les trouvailles de la Belgique actuelle." In *L'inhumation privilégiée*, 47–56.

Dinzelbacher, Peter. *Vision und Visionsliteratur im Mittelalter*. Monographie zur Geschichte des Mittelalters 23. Stuttgart: Anton Hiersemann, 1981.

Dolbeau, François. "Nouveaux sermons de saint Augustin pour la conversion des païens et des donatistes (II)." *Revue des études augustiniennes* 37 (1991): 261–306.

Dubois, Jacques. "La malle de voyage de l'évêque Germain de Paris (†576)." *Bulletin de la Société nationale des antiquaires de France* (1983): 238–49.

———. "Utilisation religieuse du tissu." In *Tissu et vêtement: 5000 ans de savoir-faire, 26 avril–30 novembre 1986*, 144–52. Guiry-en-Vezin: Musée archéologique départemental du Val-d'Oise, 1986.

Durand-Lefebvre, M. "Les sarcophages mérovingiens de Paris." *CA* 6 (1952): 168–75.

Duru, Raymond, Paul-Albert Février, and Noël Duval. "Bordeaux: Saint-Seurin: Nécropoles et édifices cultuels (?)." In *Les premiers monuments chrétiens de la France 2*, 37–46. Paris: Picard, 1996.

Duval, Yvette. *Auprès des saints corps et âme: L'inhumation "ad sanctos" dans la chrétienté d'Orient et d'Occident du IIIe au VIIe siècle.* Paris: Études augustiniennes, 1988.

———. "Sanctorum sepulcris sociari." In *Les fonctions des saints dans le monde occidental (IIIe–XIIIe siècle): Actes du colloque organisé par l'École française de Rome, 27–29 octobre 1988,* Collection de l'École française de Rome 149, 333–51. Palais Farnèse: École française de Rome, 1991.

Duval, Yvette, and Jean-Charles Picard, eds. *L'inhumation privilégiée du IVe au VIIIe siècle en Occident: Actes du colloque tenu à Créteil les 16–18 mars 1984.* Paris: De Boccard, 1986.

Düwel, Klaus. "Epigraphische Zeugnisse für die Macht der Schrift im östlichen Frankenreich." In *Die Franken: Wegbereiter Europas* 1, 540–52. Mainz: Verlag Philipp von Zabern, 1996.

Eck, Werner. "Aussagefähigkeit epigraphischer Statistik und die Bestattung von Sklaven im kaiserzeitlichen Rom." In *Alte Geschichte und Wissenschaftsgeschichte: Festschrift für Karl Christ zum 65. Geburtstag,* edited by Peter Kneissl and Volker Losemann, 130–39. Darmstadt: Wissenschaftliche Buchgesellschaft, 1988.

———. "Römische Grabinschriften: Aussageabsicht und Aussagefähigkeit im funerären Kontext." In *Römische Gräberstraßen: Selbstdarstellung-Status-Standard: Kolloquium in München von 28. bis 30. Oktober 1985,* Bayerische Akademie der Wissenschaften, philosophisch-historische Klasse, Abhandlungen, n.s. 96, edited by Henner von Hesberg and Paul Zanker, 61–83. Munich: Verlag der Bayerische Akademie der Wissenschaften, 1987.

Effros, Bonnie. "Appearance and Ideology: Creating Distinctions Between Merovingian Clerics and Lay Persons." In *Encountering Medieval Dress and Textiles: Objects, Texts, and Images,* edited by Janet Snyder and Désirée Koslin. New York: Palgrave, forthcoming.

———. "Beyond Cemetery Walls: Early Medieval Funerary Topography and Christian Salvation." *EME* 6 (1997): 1–23.

———. *Creating Community with Food and Drink in Merovingian Gaul.* New York: Palgrave, forthcoming.

———. "*De partibus Saxoniae* and the Regulation of Mortuary Custom: A Carolingian Campaign of Christianization or the Suppression of Saxon Identity?" *Revue belge de philologie et d'histoire* 75 (1997): 269–87.

———. "Images of Sanctity: Contrasting Descriptions of Radegund of Poitiers by Venantius Fortunatus and Gregory of Tours." *UCLA Historical Journal* 10 (1990): 38–58.

———. *Merovingian Mortuary Archaeology and the Making of the Early Middle Ages.* Berkeley and Los Angeles: University of California Press, forthcoming.

———. "Monuments and Memory: Repossessing Ancient Remains in Early Medieval Gaul." In *Topographies of Power in the Early Middle Ages*, TRW 6, edited by Mayke de Jong and Frans Theuws, 93–118. Leiden: E. J. Brill, 2001.

———. "Symbolic Expressions of Sanctity: Gertrude of Nivelles in the Context of Merovingian Mortuary Custom." *Viator* 27 (1996): 1–10.

Elbern, Victor H. "Neue Aspekte frühmittelalterlicher Skulptur in Gallien." In *Kolloquium über spätantike und frühmittelalterliche Skulptur* 2, 13–24. Mainz: Verlag Philipp von Zabern, 1970.

Erlande-Brandenburg, Alain. *Le roi est mort: Étude sur les funérailles, les sépultures et les tombeaux des rois de France jusqu'à la fin du XIIIᵉ siècle.* Bibliothèque de la Société française d'archéologie 7. Geneva: Droz, 1975.

Études mérovingiennes: Actes des journées de Poitiers 1ᵉʳ–3 mai 1952. Paris: Éditions A. et J. Picard, 1953.

Everett, Nick. "Liutprandic Letters in Lombard Epigraphy." In *Roman, Runes, and Ogham: Medieval Inscriptions in the Insular World and on the Continent*, edited by Katherine Forsyth, John Higgitt, and D. Parsons. Stamford, Lincolnshire: Shaun Tyas, forthcoming.

Evison, Vera I. "The Frankish Glass Vessels." In *From Attila to Charlemagne: Arts of the Early Medieval Period in The Metropolitan Museum of Art*, edited by Katharine R. Brown, Dafydd Kidd, and Charles T. Little, 268–81. New York: The Metropolitan Museum of Art, 2000.

Ewig, Eugen. "La prière pour le roi et le royaume dans les privilèges épiscopaux de l'époque mérovingienne." In *Mélanges offerts à Jean Dauvillier*, 255–67. Toulouse: Université des sciences sociales, 1979.

———. "Résidence et capitale pendant le haut moyen âge." *Revue historique* 230 (1963): 25–72.

Fehring, Günther P. *The Archaeology of Medieval Germany: An Introduction.* Translated by Ross Samson. London: Routledge, 1991.

Ferdière, Alain, and Françoise Prévot. "Centre: Cher, Eure-et-Loir, Indre, Indre-et-Loire, Loir-et-Cher, Loiret." In *Les premiers monuments chrétiens de la France* 2, 78–86. Paris: Picard, 1996.

Février, Paul-Albert. "Saint-Maximin: Mausolée antique." In *Les premiers monuments chrétiens de la France* 1, 175–80. Paris: Picard, 1995.

Fixot, Michel. "Les inhumations privilégiées en Provence." In *L'inhumation privilégiée*, 117–31.

Fleury, Michel. "L'origine du décor des sarcophages de plâtre mérovingiens de la région parisienne." In *Problèmes de chronologie relative et absolue concernant les cimetières mérovingiens d'entre Loire et Rhin: Actes du IIe colloque archéologique de la IVe section de l'École pratique des hautes études (Paris, 1973)*, edited by Michel Fleury and Patrick Périn, 111–30. Paris: Librairie Honoré Champion, 1978.

Fleury, Michel, and Albert France-Lanord. "La tombe d'Aregonde." *Les dossiers d'archéologie* 32 (1979): 27–42.

Flint, Valerie I. J. *The Rise of Magic in Early Medieval Europe.* Princeton: Princeton University Press, 1991.

Foltz, Ernst. "Technische Beobachtungen an Goldblattkreuzen." In *Die Goldblattkreuze des frühen Mittelalters*, Veröffentlichungen des Alemannischen Instituts Freiburg i. Br. 37, edited by Wolfgang Hübener, 11–19. Bühl: Verlag Konkordia, 1975.

Folz, Robert. "Tradition hagiographique et culte de saint Dagobert, roi des Francs." *Le moyen âge* 69 (1963): 17–35.

————. "Vie posthume et culte de saint Sigisbert roi de Austrasie." In *Festschrift Percy Ernst Schramm zu seinem siebzigsten Geburtstag von Schülern und Freunden zugeeignet* 1, 7–26. Wiesbaden: Franz Steiner Verlag, 1964.

Fontaine, Jacques. "Le culte des saints et ses implications sociologiques: Réflexions sur un récent essai de Peter Brown." *AB* 100 (1982): 17–41.

Fossard, Denise. "Les anciennes églises suburbaines de Paris IVe–Xe siècles: Le cimetière Saint-Marcel." *Paris et Île-de-France: Mémoires* 11 (1960): 136–57.

————. "Répartition des sarcophages mérovingiens à décor en France." In *Études mérovingiennes*, 117–26.

Fossard, Denise, May Vieillard-Troïekouroff, and Élisabeth Chatel, eds. *Recueil général des monuments sculptés en France pendant le haut moyen âge (IVe–X[e]* siècles) 1. Mémoires de la Section d'archéologie 2. Paris: Bibliothèque nationale, 1978.

Fouracre, Paul. "The Work of Audoenus of Rouen and Eligius of Noyon in Extending Episcopal Influence from the Town to the Country in Seventh-Century Neustria." In *The Church in Town and Countryside: Papers Read at the Seventeenth Summer Meeting and Eighteenth Winter Meeting of the Ecclesiastical History Society*, edited by Derek Baker, 77–91. Oxford: Basil Blackwell, 1979.

France-Lanord, Albert. "La plaque-boucle reliquaire mérovingienne de Saint-Quentin: Étude analytique." *Comptes rendus de l'Académie des inscriptions et belles-lettres* (1956): 263–67.

Frantzen, Allen J. *The Literature of Penance in Anglo-Saxon England*. New Brunswick, N.J.: Rutgers University Press, 1983.

Fremersdorf, Fritz. *Das fränkische Reihengräberfeld Köln-Müngersdorf* 1. Germanische Denkmäler der Völkerwanderungszeit 6. Berlin: Walter de Gruyter, 1955.

Gaillard, Georges. "La représentation des évangélistes à l'Hypogée des Dunes." In *Études mérovingiennes*, 135–36.

Garnsey, Peter. "Child Rearing in Ancient Italy." In *The Family in Italy from Antiquity to the Present*, edited by David I. Kertzer and Richard P. Saller, 48–65. New Haven: Yale University Press, 1991.

Gauthier, Nancy. *L'évangélisation des pays de la Moselle: La province romaine de Première Belgique entre antiquité et moyen-âge (IIIe–VIIIe siècles)*. Paris: Éditions E. de Boccard, 1980.

Geary, Patrick J. "Ethnic Identity as a Situational Construct in the Early Middle Ages." *Mitteilungen der Anthropologischen Gesellschaft in Wien* 113 (1983): 15–26.

————. *Living with the Dead in the Middle Ages*. Ithaca: Cornell University Press, 1994.

Genrich, Albert J. "Grabbeigaben und germanisches Recht." *Die Kunde* n.s. 22 (1971): 189–226.

George, Judith W. *Venantius Fortunatus: A Latin Poet in Merovingian Gaul*. Oxford: Clarendon Press, 1992.

Gerberding, Richard A. *The Rise of the Carolingians and the "Liber historiae Francorum."* Oxford: Clarendon Press, 1987.

Gerchow, Jan. *Die Gedenküberlieferung der Angelsachsen*. Arbeiten zur Frühmittelalterforschung 20. Berlin: Walter de Gruyter, 1988.

Gladigow, Burkhard. *"Naturae deus humanae mortalis:* Zur sozialen Konstruktion des Todes in römischer Zeit." In *Leben und Tod in den Religionen: Symbol und Wirklichkeit,* edited by Gunther Stephenson, 119–33. Darmstadt: Wissenschaftliche Buchgesellschaft, 1980.

Goez, Werner. "Die Einstellung zum Tode im Mittelalter." In *Der Grenzbereich zwischen Leben und Tod,* 111–53. Göttingen: Vandenhoeck & Ruprecht, 1976.

Goldstein, Lynne. "One-Dimensional Archaeology and Multi-Dimensional People: Spatial Organisation and Mortuary Analysis." In *The Archaeology of Death,* edited by Robert Chapman, Ian Kinnes, and Klavs Randsborg, 53–69. Cambridge: Cambridge University Press, 1981.

Goody, Jack. "Against 'Ritual': Loosely Structured Thoughts on a Loosely Defined Topic." In *Secular Ritual,* edited by Sally F. Moore and Barbara G. Myerhoff, 25–35. Assen: Van Gorcum, 1977.

Gougaud, Louis. "Étude sur les 'Ordines commendationis animae.'" *Ephemerides liturgicae* 49 (1935): 3–27.

Graus, František. "Sozialgeschichtliche Aspekte der Hagiographie der Merowinger- und Karolingerzeit: Die Viten der Heiligen des südalemannischen Raumes und die sogenannten Adelsheiligen." In *Mönchtum, Episkopat und Adel zur Gründungszeit des Klosters Reichenau,* Vorträge und Forschungen 20, edited by Arno Borst, 131–76. Sigmaringen: Jan Thorbecke Verlag, 1974.

———. *Volk, Herrscher und Heiliger im Reich der Merowinger: Studien zur Hagiographie der Merowingerzeit.* Prague: Nakladatelství ceskoslovenské akademie ved, 1965.

Gray, Nicolette. "The Paleography of Latin Inscriptions in the Eighth, Ninth, and Tenth Centuries in Italy." *Papers of the British School at Rome* 16 (1948): 38–167.

Gurevich, Aaron J. "Au moyen âge: Conscience individuelle et image de l'Au-delà." *Annales ESC* 37 (1982): 255–75.

———. *Medieval Popular Culture: Problems of Belief and Perception.* Cambridge Studies in Oral and Literate Culture 14. Translated by Janos M. Bak and Paul A. Hollingsworth. Cambridge: Cambridge University Press, 1988.

Gussone, Nikolaus. "Cérémonial d'*adventus* et translation des reliques: Victrice de Rouen—*De laude sanctorum.*" In *Actes du colloque international d'archéologie: Centenaire de l'abbé Cochet,* 287–99. Rouen: Musée départemental des antiquités de Seine-Maritime, 1978.

Haberey, Waldemar. "Grabstein aus Niederdollendorf." In *Aus rheinischer Kunst und Kultur: Auswahlkatalog des Rheinischen Landesmuseums Bonn 1963* 9,68, 115. Düsseldorf: Rheinland-Verlag, 1963.

————. "Grabstein eines Priesters." In *Aus rheinischer Kunst und Kultur: Auswahlkatalog des Rheinischen Landesmuseums Bonn 1963* 9,69, 115–16. Düsseldorf: Rheinland-Verlag, 1963.

Halsall, Guy. "Burial, Ritual, and Merovingian Society." In *The Community, the Family, and the Saint: Patterns of Power in Early Medieval Europe*, edited by Joyce Hill and Mary Swan, 325–38. Turnhout: Brepols, 1998.

————. "Female Status and Power in Early Merovingian Central Austrasia: The Burial Evidence." *EME* 5 (1996): 1–24.

————. *Settlement and Social Organization: The Merovingian Region of Metz.* Cambridge: Cambridge University Press, 1995.

————. "Social Change Around A.D. 600: An Austrasian Perspective." In *The Age of Sutton Hoo: The Seventh Century in North-Western Europe*, edited by Martin Carver, 265–78. Woodbridge: Boydell Press, 1992.

————. "Towns, Societies, and Ideas: The Not-So-Strange Case of Late Roman and Early Merovingian Metz." In *Towns in Transition: Urban Evolution in Late Antiquity and the Early Middle Ages*, edited by Neil Christie and Simon T. Loseby, 235–61. Aldershot: Scolar Press, 1996.

Hamlin, Ann. "Early Irish Stone Carving: Content and Context." In *The Early Church in Western Britain and Ireland: Studies Presented to C. A. Ralegh Radford*, BAR British Series 102, edited by Susan M. Pearce, 283–96. Oxford: BAR, 1982.

Handley, Mark A. "Beyond Hagiography: Epigraphic Commemoration and Saints' Cults in Late Antique Trier." In *Revisiting Late Roman Gaul*, edited by Ralph Mathisen and Danuta Shanzer, 187–200. London: Ashgate, 2001.

————. "The Early Medieval Inscriptions of Britain, Gaul, and Spain: Studies in Function and Culture." Doctoral dissertation, University of Cambridge, 1998.

————. "Inscribing Time and Identity in the Kingdom of Burgundy." In *Ethnicity and Culture in Late Antiquity*, edited by Stephen Mitchell and Geoffrey Greatrex, 83–102. London: Duckworth & the Classical Press of Wales, 2000.

————. "The Origins of Christian Commemoration in Late Antique Britain." *EME* 10 (2001): 177–99.

————. "'This Stone Shall Be a Witness' (Joshua 24.27): Jews, Christians, and Inscriptions in Early Medieval Gaul." In *Christian-Jewish Relations Through the Centuries*, Journal for the Study of the New Testament, suppl. ser. 192, Roehampton Papers 6, edited by Stanley E. Porter and Brook W. R. Pearson, 239–54. Sheffield: Sheffield Academic Press, 2000.

Härke, Heinrich. "Die anglo-amerikanische Diskussion zur Gräberanalyse." *AK* 19 (1989): 185–94.

————. "Early Saxon Weapon Burials: Frequencies, Distributions, and Weapon Combinations." In *Weapons and Warfare in Anglo-Saxon England*, Oxford University Committee for Archaeology 21, edited by Sonia Chadwick Hawkes, 49–61. Oxford: Oxford University Committee for Archaeology, 1989.

————. "The Nature of Burial Data." In *Burial and Society: The Chronological and Social Analysis of Archaeological Burial Data*, 19–27. Århus: Århus University Press, 1997.

————. "'Warrior Graves'? The Background of the Anglo-Saxon Weapon Burial Rite." *Past and Present* 126 (1990): 22–43.

Harmening, Dieter. *Superstitio: Überlieferungs- und theoriegeschichtliche Untersuchungen zur kirchlich-theologischen Aberglaubensliteratur des Mittelalters*. Berlin: Erich Schmidt Verlag, 1979.

Harries, Jill. "Death and the Dead in the Late Roman Empire." In *Death in Towns: Urban Responses to the Dying and the Dead, 100–1600*, edited by Steven Bassett, 56–67. London: Leicester University Press, 1992.

Haskins, Charles Homer. *The Renaissance of the Twelfth Century*. Cambridge: Harvard University Press, 1927.

Hedeager, Lotte. "The Creation of Germanic Identity: A European Origin Myth." In *Frontières d'empire: Nature et signification des frontières romaines: Actes de la table ronde international de Nemours, 1992*, edited by Patrice Brun, Sander van der Leeuw, and Charles R. Whittaker, 121–31. Namur: A.P.R.A.I.F., 1993.

Heidrich, Ingrid. "Besitz und Besitzverfügung verheirateter und verwitweter freier Frauen im merowingischen Frankenreich." In *Weibliche Lebensgestaltung im frühen Mittelalter*, edited by Hans-Werner Goetz, 119–38. Cologne: Böhlau Verlag, 1991.

————. "Südgallische Inschriften des 5.–7. Jahrhunderts als historische Quellen." *RV* 32 (1968): 167–83.

————. "Von Plectrud zu Hildegard: Beobachtungen zum Besitzrecht adliger Frauen im Frankenreich und zur politischen Rolle der Frauen der frühen Karolinger." *RV* 52 (1988): 1–15.

Heinzelmann, Martin. *Bischofsherrschaft in Gallien: Zur Kontinuität römischer Führungsschichten von 4. bis zum 7. Jahrhundert: Soziale, prosopographische und bildungsgeschichtliche Aspekte.* Beihefte der Francia 5. Munich: Artemis Verlag, 1976.

————. "Neue Aspekte der biographischen und hagiographischen Literatur in der lateinischen Welt (1.–6. Jahrhundert)." *Francia* 1 (1973): 27–44.

————. *Translationsberichte und andere Quellen des Reliquienkultes.* Typologie des sources du moyen âge Occidental 33. Turnhout: Brepols, 1979.

Heitz, Carol. "L'Hypogée de Mellebaude à Poitiers." In *L'inhumation privilégiée,* 91–96.

Hen, Yitzhak. *Culture and Religion in Merovingian Gaul, A.D. 481–751.* Leiden: E. J. Brill, 1994.

————. "The Liturgy of St Willibrord." *Anglo-Saxon England* 26 (1997): 41–62.

————. "Priests and Books in the Merovingian Period." In *Priests in the Early Middle Ages,* edited by Rob Meens and Yitzhak Hen. Forthcoming.

Homeyer. "Der Dreißigste." In *Abhandlungen der Königlichen Akademie der Wissenschaften zu Berlin, 1864,* 87–120. Philologische und historische Abhandlungen. Berlin: Königliche Akademie der Wissenschaften, 1865.

Hubert, Jean. *L'art pré-roman.* Paris: Les éditions d'art et d'histoire, 1938.

————. *Les cryptes de Jouarre.* IVᵉ Congrès de l'art du haut moyen âge. Melun: Imprimerie de la préfecture de Seine-et-Marne, 1952.

Hulin, L. Carless. "The Diffusion of Religious Symbols Within Complex Societies." In *The Meanings of Things: Material Culture and Symbolic Expression,* One World Archaeology 6, edited by Ian Hodder, 90–98. London: Unwin Hyman, 1989.

Jacob, Jean-Paul, and Jean-Régis Mirbeau Gauvin. "Du don au mort à la rédemption: Évolution du dépôt funéraire du Bas-Empire à l'apparition du don *pro anima.*" *Revue d'histoire du droit* 48 (1980): 307–27.

James, Edward. *The Merovingian Archaeology of South-West Gaul* 1. BAR Supplementary Series 25(i). Oxford: BAR, 1977.

————. "A Sense of Wonder: Gregory of Tours, Medicine and Science." In *The Culture of Christendom: Essays in Medieval History in Commemoration of Denis*

L. T. Bethell, edited by Mark Anthony Meyer, 45–60. London: Hambledon Press, 1993.

Janes, Dominic. "Treasure Bequest: Death and Gift in the Early Middle Ages." In *The Community, the Family, and the Saint: Patterns of Power in Early Medieval Europe,* edited by Joyce Hill and Mary Swan, 363–77. Turnhout: Brepols, 1998.

Jankuhn, Herbert. "Axtkult." In *Reallexikon der germanischen Altertumskunde* 1, 2d ed., 562–66. Berlin: Walter de Gruyter, 1973.

Jankuhn, Herbert, Hermann Nehlsen, and Helmut Roth, eds. *Zum Grabfrevel in vor- und frühgeschichtlicher Zeit: Untersuchungen zu Grabraub und "Haugbrot" in Mittel- und Nordeuropa.* Abhandlungen der Akademie der Wissenschaften in Göttingen, philologisch-historische Klasse, 3d ser., no. 113. Göttingen: Vandenhoeck & Ruprecht, 1978.

Jarnut, Jörg. "Selbstverständnis von Personen und Personengruppen im Lichte früh-mittelalterlicher Personennamen." In *Personennamen und Identität: Namengebung und Namengebrauch als Anzeiger individueller Bestimmung und gruppenbezogener Zuordnung,* Grazer grundwissenschaftliche Forschungen 3, Schriftenreihe der Akademie Freisach 2, edited by Reinhard Härtel, 47–65. Graz: Akademische Druck- und Verlagsanstalt, 1997.

Jenn, Françoise. "Les plates-tombes inscrites de Saint-Outrille-du-Château à Bourges (Cher)." *CA* 34 (1986): 33–74.

Kajanto, Iiro. "The Hereafter in Ancient Christian Epigraphy." *Arctos* 12 (1978): 27–53.

———. "On the Idea of Eternity in Latin Epitaphs." *Arctos* 8 (1984): 59–69.

Kantorowicz, Ernst H. *Laudes regiae: A Study in Liturgical Acclamations and Medieval Ruler Worship.* University of California Publications in History 33. Berkeley and Los Angeles: University of California Press, 1946.

Knott, Betty I. "The Christian 'Special Language' in the Inscriptions." *Vigiliae christianae* 10 (1956): 65–79.

Koch, Ursula. "Beobachtungen zum frühen Christentum an den fränkischen Gräberfeldern von Bargen und Berghausen in Nordbaden." *AK* 4 (1974): 259–66.

Koch, Walter. "Insular Influences in Inscriptions on the Continent." In *Roman, Runes, and Ogham: Medieval Inscriptions in the Insular World and on the Continent,* edited by Katherine Forsyth, John Higgitt, and D. Parsons. Stamford, Lincolnshire: Shaun Tyas, forthcoming.

Koep, Leo. *Das himmlische Buch in Antike und Christentum: Eine religionsgeschichtliche Untersuchung zur altchristlichen Bildersprache*. Theophaneia 8. Bonn: Peter Hanstein Verlag, 1952.

Kopytoff, Igor. "The Cultural Biography of Things: Commoditization as Process." In *The Social Life of Things: Commodities in Cultural Perspective*, edited by Arjun Appadurai, 64–91. Cambridge: Cambridge University Press, 1986.

Kötting, Bernhard. "Die Tradition der Grabkirche." In *Memoria: Der geschichtliche Zeugniswert des liturgischen Gedenkens im Mittelalter*, MMS 48, edited by Karl Schmid and Joachim Wollasch, 69–78. Munich: Wilhelm Fink Verlag, 1984.

Krautheimer, Richard. "Mensa-Coemiterium-Martyrium." In *Studies in Early Christian, Medieval, and Renaissance Art*, 35–58. New York: New York University Press, 1969.

Krüger, Karl Heinrich. "Grabraub in erzählenden Quellen des frühen Mittelalters." In *Zum Grabfrevel*, 169–87.

———. *Königsgrabkirchen der Franken, Angelsachsen und Langobarden bis zur Mitte des 8. Jahrhunderts*. MMS 4. Munich: Wilhelm Fink Verlag, 1971.

Kuryluk, Ewa. *Veronica and Her Cloth: History, Symbolism, and Structure of a "True Image."* Oxford: Basil Blackwell, 1991.

Kyll, Nikolaus. *Tod, Grab, Begräbnisplatz, Totenfeier: Zur Geschichte ihres Brauchtums im Trierer Lande und in Luxemburg unter besonderer Berücksichtigung des Visitationshandbuches des Regino von Prüm (†915)*. Rheinisches Archiv 81. Bonn: Ludwig Röhrscheid, 1972.

Laporte, Jean-Pierre. "Pour une nouvelle datation du testament d'Ermenthrude." *Francia* 14 (1986): 574–77.

———. "Reliques du haut moyen âge à Chelles." *Revue d'histoire et d'art de la Brie et du pays de Meaux* 37 (1986): 45–58.

———. "Tissus médiévaux de Chelles et de Faremoutiers." In *Tissu et vêtement: 5000 ans de savoir-faire, 26 avril–30 novembre 1986*, 153–72. Guiry-en-Vezin: Musée archéologique départemental du Val-d'Oise, 1986.

Laporte, Jean-Pierre, and Raymond Boyer. *Trésors de Chelles: Sépultures et reliques de la reine Balthilde († vers 680) et de l'abbesse Bertille († vers 704)*. Catalogue de l'exposition organisée au Musée Alfred Bonno. Chelles: Société archéologique et historique, 1991.

Lauwers, M. "'Religion populaire,' culture folklorique, mentalités: Notes pour une anthropologie culturelle du moyen âge." *Revue d'histoire ecclésiastique* 82 (1987): 221–58.

Le Blant, Edmond. "Les bas-reliefs des sarcophages chrétiens et les liturgies funéraires." *RA* n.s. 38 (1879): 223–41, 276–92.

———. *L'épigraphie chrétienne en Gaule et dans l'Afrique romaine.* Paris: Ernest Leroux, Éditeur, 1890.

———. "Paléographie des inscriptions latines du IIIe siècle à la fin du VIIe." *RA* 3d ser. 29 (1896): 177–97, 345–55; 30 (1897): 30–40, 171–84; 31 (1897): 172–84.

———. *Les sarcophages chrétiens de la Gaule.* Collection de documents inédits sur l'histoire de France, troisième série archéologie. Paris: Imprimerie nationale, 1886.

Le Goff, Jacques. *La naissance du purgatoire.* Paris: Éditions Gallimard, 1981.

Leone, Mark P. "Time in American Archaeology." In *Social Archaeology: Beyond Subsistence and Dating,* edited by Charles L. Redman, Mary Jane Berman, et al., 25–36. New York: Academic Press, 1978.

Lestocquoy, Jean. "Épices, médecine et abbayes." In *Études mérovingiennes,* 179–86.

Levison, Wilhelm. "Bischof Germanus von Auxerre und die Quellen zu seiner Geschichte." *Neues Archiv* 29 (1904): 95–175.

———. "Die Politik in den Jenseitsvisionen des frühen Mittelalters." In *Aus rheinischer und fränkischer Frühzeit: Ausgewählte Aufsätze von Wilhelm Levison,* 229–46. Düsseldorf: Verlag L. Schwann, 1948.

Lionard, Pádraig. "Early Irish Grave Slabs." *Proceedings of the Royal Irish Academy* 61C (1961): 95–169.

Louis, René, and Gilbert-Robert Delehaye. "Le sarcophage mérovingien considéré sous ses aspects économiques et sociaux." In *Actes du 105e congrès national des Sociétés savantes, Caen 1980: La Normandie: Études archéologiques,* section d'archéologie et histoire de l'art, 275–95. Paris: Comité des travaux historiques et scientifiques, 1983.

Lowe, E. A. "The Vatican MS. of the Gelasian Sacramentary and Its Supplement at Paris." *JTS* 27 (1926): 357–73.

MacCormack, Sabine G. *Art and Ceremony in Late Antiquity.* Berkeley and Los Angeles: University of California Press, 1981.

MacMullen, Ramsay. "The Epigraphic Habit in the Roman Empire." *American Journal of Philology* 103 (1982): 233–46.

Mann, J. C. "Epigraphic Consciousness." *JRS* 75 (1985): 204–6.

Mann, Michael. *The Sources of Social Power* 1. Cambridge: Cambridge University Press, 1986.

Martin, Max. "Fibel und Fibeltracht: Späte Völkerwanderungszeit und Merowingerzeit auf dem Kontinent." In *Reallexikon der germanischen Altertumskunde* 8, 2d ed., 574–77. Berlin: Walter de Gruyter, 1994.

―――. "Gürtel und Bewaffnung des frühen Mittelalters." In *Frühe Baiern im Straubinger Land: Gaudemuseum Straubing*, edited by Max Martin and Johannes Prammer, 72–85. Straubing: Druckerei Bertsch, 1995.

―――. "Schmuck und Tracht des frühen Mittelalters." In *Frühe Baiern im Straubinger Land: Gaudemuseum Straubing*, edited by Max Martin and Johannes Prammer, 40–71. Straubing: Druckerei Bertsch, 1995.

Martiniani-Reber, Marielle. *Lyon, Musée historique des tissus: Soieries sassanides, coptes et byzantines $X^e–XI^e$ siècles.* Inventaire des collections publiques françaises 30. Paris: Éditions de la Réunion des musées nationaux, 1986.

Maurin, Louis. "Le cimetière mérovingien de Neuvicq-Montguyon (Charente-Maritime)." *Gallia* 29 (1971): 151–89.

McKitterick, Rosamond. *The Carolingians and the Written Word.* Cambridge: Cambridge University Press, 1989.

McLaughlin, Megan. *Consorting with Saints: Prayer for the Dead in Early Medieval France.* Ithaca: Cornell University Press, 1994.

McLynn, Neil B. *Ambrose of Milan: Church and Court in a Christian Capital.* Berkeley and Los Angeles: University of California Press, 1994.

Meaney, Audrey L. *Anglo-Saxon Amulets and Curing Stones.* BAR British Series 96. Oxford: BAR, 1981.

Meyer, Elizabeth Anne. "Explaining the Epigraphic Habit in the Roman Empire—The Evidence of Epitaphs." *JRS* 80 (1990): 74–96.

―――. "Literacy, Literate Practice, and the Law in the Roman Empire, A.D. 100–600." Ph.D. diss., Yale University, 1988.

Moore, Sally F., and Barbara G. Myerhoff. "Introduction: Secular Ritual: Forms and Meanings." In *Secular Ritual*, edited by Sally F. Moore and Barbara G. Myerhoff, 3–24. Assen: Van Gorcum, 1977.

Moreira, Isabel. *Dreams, Visions, and Spiritual Authority in Merovingian Gaul.* Ithaca: Cornell University Press, 2000.

Morin, Germain. "Problèmes relatifs à la règle de S. Césaire d'Arles pour les moniales." *Revue bénédictine* 44 (1932): 5–20.

Morris, Ian. *Death-Ritual and Social Structure in Classical Antiquity.* Cambridge: Cambridge University Press, 1992.

Morris, Richard. *The Church in British Archaeology*. CBA Research Report 47. London: CBA, 1983.

Münz. "Anathema und Verwünschungen auf altchristlichen Monumenten." *Annalen des Vereins für nassauische Alterthumskunde und Geschichtsforschung* 14 (1875): 169–81.

Muschiol, Gisela. *Famula Dei: Zur Liturgie im merowingischen Frauenklöstern*. Beiträge zur Geschichte des alten Mönchtums und des Benediktinertums 41. Münster: Aschendorff, 1994.

Nehlsen, Hermann. "Der Grabfrevel in den germanischen Rechtsaufzeichnungen: Zugleich ein Beitrag zur Diskussion um Todesstrafe und Friedlosigkeit bei den Germanen." In *Zum Grabfrevel*, 107–68.

Nelson, Janet L. "Queens as Jezebels: Brunhild and Balthild in Merovingian History." In *Politics and Ritual in Early Medieval Europe*, 1–48. London: Hambledon Press, 1986.

———. "Women at the Court of Charlemagne: A Case of Monstrous Regiment?" In *Medieval Queenship*, edited by John Carmi Parsons, 43–61, 203–6. New York: St. Martin's Press, 1993.

Nock, Arthur Darby. "Cremation and Burial in the Roman Empire." In *Essays on Religion and the Ancient World* 1, edited by Zeph Stewart, 277–307. Cambridge: Harvard University Press, 1972.

———. "Tomb Violations and Pontifical Law." In *Essays on Religion and the Ancient World* 2, edited by Zeph Stewart, 527–33. Cambridge: Harvard University Press, 1972.

Nonn, Ulrich. "Erminethrud—Eine vornehme neustrische Dame um 700." *Historisches Jahrbuch* 102 (1982): 135–43.

———. "Merowingische Testamente: Studien zum Fortleben einer römischen Urkundenform im Frankenreich." *Archiv für Diplomatik* 18 (1972): 1–129.

Ntedika, Joseph. *L'évocation de l'Au-delà dans la prière pour les morts: Étude de patristique et de liturgie latines (IVe–VIIIe siècle)*. Recherches africaines de théologie 2. Louvain: Éditions Nauwelaerts, 1971.

Oexle, Otto Gerhard. "Agilbert." In *Lexikon des Mittelalters* 1, 207. Munich: Artemis Verlag, 1980.

———. "Die Gegenwart der Toten." In *Death in the Middle Ages*, Mediaevalia Louvaniensia ser. 1, studia 9, edited by Hermann Braet and Werner Verbeke, 19–77. Louvain: Leuven University Press, 1983.

————. "Mahl und Spende im mittelalterlichen Totenkult." *FS* 18 (1984): 401–20.

————. "Memoria und Memorialüberlieferung im früheren Mittelalter." *FS* 10 (1976): 70–95.

Pader, Ellen-Jane. *Symbolism, Social Relations, and the Interpretation of Mortuary Remains.* BAR International Series 130. Oxford: BAR, 1982.

Papinot, Jean-Claude. *Notices sur les vestiges archéologiques de Civaux.* Poitiers: Société des amis du pays de Civaux, 1971.

Patterson, John R. "Patronage, *Collegia,* and Burial in Imperial Rome." In *Death in Towns: Urban Responses to the Dying and the Dead, 100–1600,* edited by Steven Bassett, 15–27. London: Leicester University Press, 1992.

Paxton, Frederick S. *Christianizing Death: The Creation of a Ritual Process in Early Medieval Europe.* Ithaca: Cornell University Press, 1990.

Périn, Patrick. "A propos des cryptes de Jouarre." *Document archeologia (Paris: Foyer d'art au moyen âge)* 3 (1973): 114–27.

————. "Die archäologischen Zeugnisse der fränkischen Expansion in Gallien." In *Die Franken: Wegbereiter Europas* 1, 227–32. Mainz: Philipp von Zabern, 1996.

————. "Aspects of Late Merovingian Costume in the Morgan Collection." In *From Attila to Charlemagne: Arts of the Early Medieval Period in The Metropolitan Museum of Art,* edited by Katharine R. Brown, Dafydd Kidd, and Charles T. Little, 242–67. New York: The Metropolitan Museum of Art, 2000.

————. "Le problème des sarcophages-cénotaphes du haut moyen âge: A propos de la nécropole de Quarré-les-Tombes, site d'une bataille légendaire." In *La chanson de geste et le mythe carolingien: Mélanges René Louis* 2, 823–35. Saint-Père-sous-Vézelay: Musée archéologique régional, 1982.

————. "Remarques sur la topographie funéraire en Gaule mérovingienne et à sa périphérie: Des nécropoles romaines tardives aux nécropoles du haut–moyen âge." *CA* 35 (1987): 9–30.

Périn, Patrick, and Alain Dierkens. *L'art mérovingien: Permanences et innovations.* Feuillets de la cathédrale de Liège 25–26. Liège: Trésor de la cathédrale de Liège, 1996.

Périn, Patrick, and Laure-Charlotte Feffer, eds. *La Neustrie: Les pays au nord de la Loire de Dagobert à Charles le Chauve (VIIe–IXe siècles).* Rouen: Musées et monuments départementaux de Seine-Maritime, 1985.

Périn, Patrick, and Michel Kazanski. "Männerkleidung und Bewaffnung im Wandel der Zeit." In *Die Franken: Wegbereiter Europas* 2, 707–11. Mainz: Verlag Philipp von Zabern, 1995.

Périn, Patrick, and Laurent Renou. "Les sarcophages mérovingiens de plâtre moulé trouvés à Paris: Technologie, ornementation, chronologie." *Bulletin de liaison: Association française d'archéologie mérovingienne* 5 (1981): 47–62.

Pietri, Charles. "Grabinschrift II (lateinisch)." In *Reallexikon für Antike und Christentum* 12, 514–90. Stuttgart: Anton Hiersemann, 1983.

Pietri, Luce. "Les sépultures privilégiées en Gaule d'après les sources littéraires." In *L'inhumation privilégiée*, 133–42.

Pigeon, M. E. A. "De l'embaumement des morts à l'époque mérovingienne." *Bulletin archéologique du Comité des travaux historiques et scientifiques* (1894): 138–45.

Pilet, Christian. *La nécropole de Frénouville: Étude d'une population de la fin du IIIe à la fin du VIIe siècle* 1. BAR International Series 83(i). Oxford: BAR, 1980.

Pirling, Renate. "Krefeld-Gellep im Frühmittelalter." In *Die Franken: Wegbereiter Europas* 1, 261–65. Mainz: Verlag Philipp von Zabern, 1996.

Pohl, Walter. "Telling the Difference: Signs of Ethnic Identity." In *Strategies of Distinction: The Construction of Ethnic Communities, 300–700*, TRW 2, edited by Walter Pohl and Helmut Reimitz, 17–69. Leiden: E. J. Brill, 1998.

Pomian, Krzysztof. *Collectors and Curiosities: Paris and Venice, 1500–1800*. Translated by Elizabeth Wiles-Portier. Cambridge: Polity Press, 1987.

——. "Collezione." In *Enciclopedia Einaudi* 3, 330–64. Turin: Giulio Einaudi Editore, 1978.

Prinz, Friedrich. *Frühes Mönchtum im Frankenreich: Kultur und Gesellschaft in Gallien, den Rheinlanden und Bayern am Beispiel der monastischen Entwicklung (4. bis 8. Jahrhundert)*, 2d ed. Darmstadt: Wissenschaftliche Buchgesellschaft, 1988.

——. "Heiligenkult und Adelsherrschaft im Spiegel merowingischer Hagiographie." *Historische Zeitschrift* 204 (1967): 529–44.

Prou, Maurice, and E. Chartraire. "Authentiques de reliques conservées au trésor de la cathédrale de Sens." *Mémoires de la Société nationale des antiquaires de France* 59 (1900): 129–72.

Ranke, Kurt. *Indogermanische Totenverehrung*, 1: *Der dreissigste und vierzigste Tag im Totenkult der Indogermanen*. Folklore Fellows Communications 140. Helsinki: Suomalainen Tiedeakatemia, 1951.

Rebillard, Éric. "La figure du catéchumène et le problème du délai du baptême dans la pastorale d'Augustine: A propos du *post-tractatum* Dolbeau 7: *De sepultura catechumenorum.*" In *Augustin prédicateur (395–411): Actes du colloque internationale de Chantilly (5–7 septembre 1996)*, Collection des études augustiniennes, série antiquité 159, edited by Goulven Madec, 285–92. Paris: Institut d'études augustiniennes, 1998.

———. "Les formes de l'assistance funéraire dans l'Empire romain et leur évolution dans l'antiquité tardive." *AnTard* 7 (1999): 269–82.

———. *"In hora mortis": Évolution de la pastorale chrétienne de la mort au IVe et Ve siècles dans l'Occident latin*. Bibliothèque des Écoles françaises d'Athènes et de Rome 283. Palais Farnèse: École française de Rome, 1994.

———. "KOIMHTHRION et COEMETERIUM: Tombe, tombe sainte, nécropole." *Mélanges de l'École française de Rome: Antiquité* 105 (1993): 975–1001.

Redlich, Clara. "Westgermanische Stammesbildungen." *Nachrichten aus Niedersachsens Urgeschichte* 36 (1967): 5–38.

Reinach, Salomon. "L'origine des prières pour les morts." *Revue des études juives* 41 (1900): 161–73.

Reinecke, Paul. "Reihengräber und Friedhöfe der Kirchen." *Germania* 9 (1925): 103–7.

Reusch, Wilhelm, ed. *Frühchristliche Zeugnisse im Einzugsgebiet von Rhein und Mosel*. Trier: Unitas-Buchhandlung, 1965.

Rietschel, Siegfried. "Heergewäte und Gerade." In *Reallexikon der germanischen Altertumskunde* 2, edited by Johannes Hoops, 467. Strasbourg: Verlag von Karl J. Trübner, 1913.

Ripoll López, Gisela, and Isabel Velázquez Soriano. "El epitafio de Trasemirus (Mandourle, Villesèque de Corbières, Aude)." *Espacio, tiempo y forma*, ser. I: *Prehistoria y arqueología* 3 (1990): 273–87.

Rollason, David. *Saints and Relics in Anglo-Saxon England*. Oxford: Basil Blackwell, 1989.

Roosens, Heli. "Reflets de christianisation dans les cimetières mérovingiens." *Les études classiques* 53 (1985): 111–35.

———. "Überlegungen zum Sarkophag von Amay." *AK* 8 (1978): 237–41.

Rops, Paul. "Les 'basilicae' des cimetières francs." *Annales de la Société archéologique de Namur* 19 (1890): 1–20.

Roth, Helmut. "Archäologische Beobachtungen zum Grabfrevel im Merowingerreich." In *Zum Grabfrevel*, 53–84.

————. "Bemerkungen zur Totenberaubung während der Merowingerzeit." *AK* 7 (1977): 287–90.

————. "Kunst der Merowingerzeit." In *Die Franken: Wegbereiter Europas* 2, 629–39. Mainz: Verlag Philipp von Zabern, 1996.

Ruffier, Olivier. "Notes sur les fouilles de Saint-Outrille-du-Château." *CA* 34 (1986): 40–45.

Salin, Édouard. *La civilisation mérovingienne d'après les sépultures, les textes et le laboratoire* 2 and 4. Paris: Éditions A. et J. Picard, 1952 and 1959.

Saller, Richard P., and Brent D. Shaw. "Tombstones and Roman Family Relations in the Principate: Civilians, Soldiers, and Slaves." *JRS* 74 (1984): 124–56.

Samson, Ross. "Social Structures from *Reihengräber:* Mirror or Mirage?" *Scottish Archaeological Review* 4 (1987): 116–26.

Sanders, Gabriel. "Les chrétiens face à l'épigraphie funéraire latine." In *Assimilation et résistance à la culture gréco-romaine dans le monde ancien: Travaux du vf^e congrès international d'études classiques (Madrid, septembre 1974)*, edited by D. M. Pippidi, 283–99. Bucharest: Editura Academiei, 1976.

————. "Les inscriptions latines païennes et chrétiennes: Symbiose ou métabolisme." *Revue de l'Université de Bruxelles* (1977): 44–64.

Sapin, Christian. "Architecture and Funerary Space in the Early Middle Ages." In *Spaces of the Living and the Dead: An Archaeological Dialogue*, American Early Medieval Studies 3, edited by Catherine E. Karkov, Kelly M. Wickham-Crowley, and Bailey K. Young, 39–60. Oxford: Oxbow Books, 1999.

Saxe, Arthur Alan. "Social Dimensions of Mortuary Practices." Ph.D. diss., University of Michigan, 1970.

Schleifring, Joachim H. "Antiker Grabraub: Ausgrabungsbefunde als Nachweis von Grabraub und Grabfrevel." *Das Rheinische Landesmuseum Bonn: Berichte aus der Arbeit des Museums* 3 (1991): 33–36.

Schmid, Karl, and Otto Gerhard Oexle. "Voraussetzungen und Wirkung des Gebetsbundes von Attigny." *Francia* 2 (1974): 71–122.

Schmid, Karl, and Joachim Wollasch. "Die Gemeinschaft der Lebenden und Verstorbenen in Zeugnissen des Mittelalters." *FS* 1 (1967): 365–405.

Schmitt, Jean-Claude. "'Religion populaire' et culture folklorique." *Annales ESC* 31 (1976): 941–53.

————. *Les revenants: Les vivants et les morts dans la société médiévale*. Paris: Éditions Gallimard, 1994.

Schubert, Gabriella. *Kleidung als Zeichen: Kopfbedeckungen im Donau-Balkan-Raum.* Wiesbaden: Harrassowitz Verlag, 1993.

Serralongue, Joël, and Cécile Treffort. "Inhumations secondaires et ossements erratiques de la nécropole de Combes, à Yvoire (Haute-Savoie): Analyse archéologique et questions historiques." *Pages d'archéologie médiévale en Rhône-Alpes* 2 (1995): 105–12.

Shaw, Brent D. "The Age of Roman Girls at Marriage: Some Reconsiderations." *JRS* 77 (1987): 30–46.

————. "The Cultural Meaning of Death: Age and Gender in the Roman Family." In *The Family in Italy from Antiquity to the Present*, edited by David I. Kertzer and Richard P. Saller, 66–90. New Haven: Yale University Press, 1991.

————. "Latin Funerary Epigraphy and Family Life in the Later Roman Empire." *Historia: Zeitschrift für alte Geschichte* 33 (1984): 457–97.

Sicard, Damien. *La liturgie de la mort dans l'Église latine des origines à la reforme carolingienne.* Liturgiewissenschaftliche Quellen und Forschungen 63. Münster: Aschendorffsche Verlagsbuchhandlung, 1978.

Siegmund, Frank. "Kleidung und Bewaffnung der Männer im östlichen Frankenreich." In *Die Franken: Wegbereiter Europas* 2, 691–706. Mainz: Verlag Philipp von Zabern, 1995.

Simmer, Alain. *Le cimetière mérovingien d'Audun-le-Tiche (Moselle).* Association française d'archéologie mérovingienne, Mémoire 2. Paris: Éditions Errance, 1988.

————. "La nécropole mérovingienne d'Audun-le-Tiche." *CA* 35 (1987): 31–40.

Solomonson, J. W. *Voluptatem spectandi non perdat sed mutet: Observations sur l'iconographie du martyr en Afrique romaine.* Amsterdam: North-Holland Publishing Company, 1979.

Spiegel, Gabrielle M. "In the Mirror's Eye: The Writing of Medieval History in America." In *Imagined Histories: American Historians Interpret the Past*, edited by Anthony Molho and Gordon S. Wood, 238–62. Princeton: Princeton University Press, 1998.

Sprandel, Rolf. "Dux und Comes in der Merowingerzeit." *Zeitschrift der Savigny-Stiftung für Rechtsgeschichte*, germanistische Abteilung 74 (1957): 41–84.

Spreckelmeyer, Goswin. "Zur rechtlichen Funktion frühmittelalterlicher Testamenta." In *Recht und Schrift im Mittelalter*, Vorträge und Forschungen 23, edited by Peter Classen, 91–113. Sigmaringen: Jan Thorbecke Verlag, 1977.

Steuer, Heiko. "Archaeology and History: Proposals on the Social Structure of the Merovingian Kingdom." In *The Birth of Europe: Archaeology and Social Development in the First Millennium A.D.*, Analecta romana instituti danici supplementum 16, edited by Klavs Randsborg, 100–122. Rome: L'Erma di Bretschneider, 1989.

―――. *Frühgeschichtliche Sozialstrukturen in Mitteleuropa: Eine Analyse der Auswertungsmethoden des archäologischen Quellenmaterials.* Abhandlungen der Akademie der Wissenschaften in Göttingen, philologisch-historische Klasse, 3d ser., no. 128. Göttingen: Vandenhoeck & Ruprecht, 1982.

―――. "Grabraub, archäologisches." In *Reallexikon der germanischen Altertumskunde* 12, ed. Johannes Hoops, 2d ed., 516–23. Berlin: Walter de Gruyter, 1998.

Stiennon, Jacques. "Le sarcophage de Sancta Chrodoara à Saint-Georges d'Amay: Essai d'interprétation d'une découverte exceptionnelle." *Bulletin du Cercle archéologique Hesbaye-Condroz* 15 (1977–78): 73–88.

Ström, Folke. *On the Sacral Origins of the Germanic Death Penalties.* Kungl. Vitterhets Historie och Antikvitets Akademiens Handlingar, Del. 52. Stockholm: Wahlström & Widstrand, 1942.

Tainter, Joseph A. "Mortuary Practices and the Study of Prehistoric Social Systems." In *Advances in Archaeological Method and Theory* 1, edited by Michael B. Schiffer, 105–41. New York: Academic Press, 1978.

Theuws, Frans, and Monica Alkemade. "A Kind of Mirror for Men: Sword Depositions in Late Antique Northern Gaul." In *Rituals of Power from Late Antiquity to the Early Middle Ages*, TRW 8, edited by Frans Theuws and Janet L. Nelson, 401–76. Leiden: E. J. Brill, 2000.

Thirion, E. "Le sarcophage de Sancta Chrodoara dans l'église Saint-Georges d'Amay." *Bulletin du Cercle archéologique Hesbaye-Condroz* 15 (1977–78): 33–71.

Thiry, Claude. *La plainte funèbre.* Typologie des sources du moyen âge Occidental 30. Turnhout: Brepols, 1978.

Toynbee, J. M. C. *Death and Burial in the Roman World.* Baltimore: Johns Hopkins University Press, 1971.

Treffort, Cécile. "Du *cimiterium christianorum* au paroissial: Évolution des espaces funéraires en Gaule du VIᵉ au Xᵉ siècle." In *Archéologie du cimetière chrétien: Actes du 2ᵉ colloque ARCHEA (Orléans, 29 septembre–1ᵉʳ octobre 1994)* (11th supplement of the *Revue archéologique du Centre de la France*), edited by Henri Galinié and Elisabeth Zadora-Rio, 55–63. Tours: FÉRACF, 1996.

―――. *L'église carolingienne et la mort: Christianisme, rites funéraires et pratiques commémoratives.* Collection d'histoire et d'archéologie médiévales 3. Lyons: Presses universitaires de Lyon, 1996.

Les trésors des églises de France. 2d ed. Paris: Caisse nationale des monuments historiques, 1965.

Vallet, Françoise. "Weibliche Mode im Westteil des merowingischen Königreiches." In *Die Franken: Wegbereiter Europas* 2, 684–90. Mainz: Verlag Philipp von Zabern, 1995.

Van Dam, Raymond. *Leadership and Community in Late Antique Gaul.* Berkeley and Los Angeles: University of California Press, 1985.

van Doorselaer, André. *Les nécropoles d'époque romaine en Gaule septentrionale.* Dissertationes archaeologicae Gandenses 10. Translated by Marcel Amand. Brugge: De Tempel, 1967.

Van Es, W. A. "Grabsitten und Christianisierung in den Niederlanden." *Probleme der Küstenforschung im südlichen Nordseegebiet* 9 (1970): 77–90.

van Uytfanghe, Marc. "L'hagiographie et son public à l'époque mérovingienne." In *Studia patristica* 16,2, Texte und Untersuchungen zur Geschichte der altchristlichen Literatur 129, 54–62. Berlin: Akademie-Verlag, 1985.

―――. "Latin mérovingien, latin carolingien et *rustica romana lingua:* Continuité ou discontinuité?" *Revue de l'Université de Bruxelles* (1977): 65–88.

Vieillard-Troïekouroff, May. "Le sarcophage décoré d'une châsse gravée, provenant de Saint-Samson-de-la-Roque, au Musée de Saint-Germain-en-Laye." In *Actes du 105ᵉ congrès national des Sociétés savantes, Caen 1980: La Normandie. Études archéologiques,* section archéologie et histoire de l'art, 267–73. Paris: Comité des travaux historiques et scientifiques, 1983.

―――. "Trois sarcophages mérovingiens découverts à Saint-Étienne de Nevers en janvier 1974." *BM* 138 (1980): 221–27.

Vierck, Hayo. "La 'chemise de Sainte-Bathilde' à Chelles et l'influence byzantine sur l'art de cour mérovingien au VIIᵉ siècle." In *Actes du colloque international d'archéologie: Centenaire de l'abbé Cochet,* 521–70. Rouen: Le Musée départemental des antiquités de Seine-Maritime, 1978.

———. "Folienkreuze als Votivgaben." In *Die Goldblattkreuʒe des frühen Mittelalters,* Veröffentlichungen des Alemannischen Instituts Freiburg i. Br. 37, edited by Wolfgang Hübener, 125–43. Bühl: Verlag Konkordia, 1975.

———. "Trachtenkunde und Trachtgeschichte in der Sachsen-Forschung, ihre Quellen, Ziele und Methoden." In *Sachsen und Angelsachsen: Ausstellung des Helmsmuseums, Hamburgisches Museum für Vor- und Frühgeschichte 18. November 1978 bis 28. Februar 1979,* 231–43. Hamburg, 1978.

———. "Werke des Eligius." In *Studien ʒur vor- und frühgeschichtlichen Archäologie: Festschrift für Joachim Werner ʒum 65. Geburtstag* 2, Münchner Beiträge zur Vor- und Frühgeschichte, suppl. vol. 1/II, edited by Georg Kossack and Günther Ulbert, 309–80. Munich: Verlag C. H. Beck, 1974.

———. "Zur seegermanische Männertracht." In *Sachsen und Angelsachsen: Ausstellung des Helmsmuseums, Hamburgisches Museum für Vor- und Frühgeschichte 18. November 1978 bis 28. Februar 1979,* 263–70. Hamburg, 1978.

Viollet-le-Duc, E. "L'église impériale de Saint-Denis." *RA* n.s. 2,3 (1861): 301–10, 345–53.

Vogel, Cyril. "Deux conséquences de l'eschatologie grégorienne: La multiplication des messes privées et les moines-prêtres." In *Grégoire le Grand: Chantilly, Centre culturel Les Fontaines, 15–19 septembre 1982,* edited by Jacques Fontaine, Robert Gillet, and Stan Pellistrandi, 267–76. Colloques internationaux du CNRS. Paris: Éditions du CNRS, 1986.

———. *La discipline pénitentielle en Gaule des origines à la fin du VIIᵉ siècle.* Doctoral thesis, Strasbourg, 1950. Paris: Letouzey et Ané, 1952.

———. "La discipline pénitentielle en Gaule des origines au IXᵉ siècle: Le dossier hagiographique." *RSR* 30 (1956): 1–26, 157–86.

———. "Une mutation cultuelle inexpliquée: Le passage de l'eucharistie communautaire à la messe privée." *RSR* 54 (1980): 231–50.

von Unruh, Georg Christoph. "Wargus, Friedlosigkeit und magisch-kultische Vorstellungen bei den Germanen." *Zeitschrift der Savigny-Stiftung für Rechtsgeschichte,* germanistische Abteilung 74 (1957): 2–34.

Wallach, Luitpold. "The Epitaph of Alcuin: A Model of Carolingian Epigraphy." *Speculum* 30 (1955): 367–73.

Weidemann, Margarete. *Kulturgeschichte der Merowingerʒeit nach den Werken Gregor von Tours.* Römisch-Germanisches Zentralmuseum Monographien 3,2. Mainz: Verlag der Römisch-Germanischen Zentralmuseums, 1982.

Weiner, Annette B. *Inalienable Possessions: The Paradox of Keeping-While-Giving.* Berkeley and Los Angeles: University of California Press, 1992.

Wemple, Suzanne Fonay. *Women in Frankish Society: Marriage and the Cloister, 500–900.* Philadelphia: University of Pennsylvania Press, 1985.

Werner, Joachim. "Die Gräber aus der Krypta-Grabung 1961/1962." In *Die Ausgrabungen in St. Ulrich und Afra in Augsburg 1961–1968* 1, 141–89. Munich: C. H. Beck'sche Verlagsbuchhandlung, 1977.

Wiessner, Polly. "Style and the Changing Relations Between the Individual and Society." In *The Meaning of Things: Material Culture and Symbolic Expression,* One World Archaeology 6, edited by Ian Hodder, 56–63. London: Unwin Hyman, 1989.

Williams, Daniel H. *Ambrose of Milan and the End of the Nicene-Arian Conflicts.* Oxford: Oxford University Press, 1995.

Wood, Ian. "The Code in Merovingian Gaul." In *The Theodosian Code,* edited by Jill Harries and Ian Wood, 161–77. Ithaca: Cornell University Press, 1993.

————. "Sépultures ecclésiastiques et sénatoriales dans la vallée du Rhône (400–600)." *Médiévales* 31 (1996): 13–27.

————. *The Merovingian Kingdoms, 450–751.* London: Longman, 1994.

Young, Bailey K. "Exemple aristocratique et mode funéraire dans la Gaule mérovingienne." *Annales ESC* 41 (1986): 379–407.

————. "Merovingian Funeral Rites and the Evolution of Christianity: A Study in the Historical Interpretation of Archaeological Material." Ph.D. diss., University of Pennsylvania, 1975.

————. "Paganisme, christianisation et rites funéraires mérovingiens." *AM* 7 (1977): 5–81.

————. *Quatre cimetières mérovingiens de l'Est de la France: Lavoye, Dieue-sur-Meuse, Mezières-Manchester et Mazerny.* BAR International Series 208. Oxford: BAR, 1984.

Zeller, Gudula. "Tracht der Frauen." In *Die Franken: Wegbereiter Europas* 2, 672–83. Mainz: Verlag Philipp von Zabern, 1995.

INDEX

CPSIA information can be obtained
at www.ICGtesting.com
Printed in the USA
LVOW07s0317271216
518785LV00001B/48/P

9 780271 027818